"The Creed calls the Church [...]
The author presents a centur[...]
preconciliar theologians, Vatican II, John Paul II—and on the question, sinful Church or Church of sinners? This careful study clarifies and illumines a century of complex reflection, a century that might be called, in theology, the century of ecclesiology, with Vatican I in the background and *Lumen Gentium* on the distant horizon. The author's conclusion is the right one: the matter is not concluded. A book recommended enthusiastically."

> — Joseph T. Lienhard, SJ
> Fordham University

"Exhaustively researched and written in a clear and comprehensive style, *A Holy Yet Sinful Church* captures an important feature of John Paul's efforts to move the Church forward in the twenty-first century. Informative and challenging, this monograph brings to light an important focus for contemporary Catholicism."

> — Richard Gribble, CSC
> Stonehill College

"In an ecclesial era of searching for ways forward for a new evangelization while constantly being confronted with our own failures to model the faith, new demands for a profound theology of the Church have confronted us. Sr. Jeanmarie Gribaudo has provided just such a careful examination of the variety of influences that shaped the Church's self-understanding after Vatican II, which allows us to profess once again a new faith in a Church that is at once sinful and holy, mediating salvific grace for a people as much in need of it as ever."

> — Christopher Collins, SJ
> Director of the Catholic Studies Program
> Saint Louis University

"In *A Holy Yet Sinful Church*, Sr. Jeanmarie Gribaudo offers a scholarly yet accessible account of the claim that the Church has always been understood as both holy and sinful. Exemplifying how historical scholarship can temper and broaden theological perspective, Gribaudo focuses in particular on the appearance of these themes in preconciliar thought as well as Vatican II's *Lumen Gentium*, as these prepared the ground for Pope John Paul II's remarkable litany of repentance for the Church's faults in March 2000. Her work offers a timely lesson about the nature of the Church as both holy and sinful, which, taken to heart, is a lesson for the communal dimension of theological anthropology as well."

> — Nancy Dallavalle
> Fairfield University
> Vice President for Mission and Identity
> Associate Professor of Religious Studies

"Gribaudo has provided a foundational genealogy of current teaching on ecclesial holiness and sinfulness in the documents of Vatican II and in the words and actions of John Paul II. This work is rooted in a careful, insightful analysis of the origins of that teaching in preconciliar *ressourcement* theologians such as Mersch and de Lubac, and midcentury thinkers such as Congar and Rahner. Gribaudo then collects and analyzes ecclesial holiness and sinfulness in *Lumen Gentium* and in the papacy of John Paul II. No other work has gathered and analyzed such a wide variety of twentieth-century sources on this topic in such a comprehensive, observant way. Gribaudo's book is valuable both as a historical study of the development of ecclesiology in this period and as an unsurpassed point of departure for all future systematic thought on the holiness and sinfulness of the Church."

> — Brian P. Flanagan
> Assistant Professor of Theology
> Marymount University

# A Holy Yet Sinful Church

Three Twentieth-Century Moments
in a Developing Theology

*Jeanmarie Gribaudo, CSJ*

**LITURGICAL PRESS**
Collegeville, Minnesota

www.litpress.org

Joe —
No words can express my gratitude to you for your friendship & support. Your faith & love fo all things Augustine are part of the fabric of your being. I hope Augustine would be happy with this book — I'll know when I get your review!

From a grateful heart,
Jeanmarie

Excerpts from the English translation of *The Roman Missal* © 2010, International Commission on English in the Liturgy Corporation. All rights reserved.

Excerpts from *Communion Ecclesiology* by Dennis Doyle. Copyright © 2000 by Dennis M. Doyle. Reprinted with permission of Orbis Books, Maryknoll, New York.

Excerpts from Hans Urs von Balthasar, "*Casta Meretrix*," in *Explorations in Theology: Spouse of the Word*, trans. John Saward (1991); Henri de Lubac, *Catholicism: Christ and the Common Destiny of Man*, trans. Lancelot C. Sheppard and Elizabeth Englund (1988); Henri de Lubac, *The Splendor of the Church*, trans. Michael Mason (1986); and Charles Journet, *The Theology of the Church*, trans. Victor Szczurek (2004). Reprinted by permission of Ignatius Press.

Unless otherwise indicated, excerpts from documents of the Second Vatican Council are from *Vatican Council II: Constitutions, Decrees, Declarations; The Basic Sixteen Documents*, edited by Austin Flannery, OP, © 1996. Used with permission of Liturgical Press, Collegeville, Minnesota.

Unless otherwise indicated, Scripture texts in this work are taken from the *New American Bible with Revised New Testament and Revised Psalms*, © 1991, 1986, 1970 Confraternity of Christian Doctrine, Washington, DC, and are used by permission of the copyright owner. All rights reserved. No part of the *New American Bible* may be reproduced in any form without permission in writing from the copyright owner.

1    2    3    4    5    6    7    8    9

Library of Congress Cataloging-in-Publication Data

Gribaudo, Jeanmarie.
    A holy yet sinful church : three twentieth-century moments in a
developing theology / by Jeanmarie Gribaudo, CSJ.
        pages  cm
    Includes bibliographical references.
    ISBN 978-0-8146-4771-4 — ISBN 978-0-8146-4796-7 (ebook)
    1. Church—History of doctrines—20th century.    2. Catholic
Church—Doctrines.    3. Nouvelle théologie (Catholic theology)    I. Title.

BX1746.G75    2015
262'.02—dc23                                                    2014027643

# Contents

# Introduction

On November 10, 1994, Pope John Paul II issued the apostolic letter *Tertio Millennio Adveniente*, in which he laid the groundwork for the acknowledgment that sin and error exist in the Church and have been a part of the Church's history. In this letter, the pope made an unprecedented public statement which called for the Church to seek pardon for the detrimental effect such sin and error have had on its credible living of the Gospel.

John Paul II's groundbreaking decision to seek forgiveness for the sins of the Church can be seen as the end result of an evolution in theology that began after the First World War and came to fruition at the time of the Second Vatican Council. In this study, I will examine how these new theological insights that came to the fore during the Second Vatican Council were not only reflective of *ressourcement* theology, that is, a theology that returned to the early sources of Christianity, particularly Scripture and the writings of the early fathers, but also opened up new vistas in understanding the holiness and sinfulness of the Church. Though these new vistas were not universally applauded by the Curia, they did set the course for John Paul II's celebration of the millennium by asking for pardon for the deeds done by the sons and daughters of the Church, which on historical reflection have been judged to be sinful in nature.

In *Tertio Millennio Adveniente* (TMA) the pope acknowledges the tension inherent in his decision to prepare for the "joy" of a Jubilee Year by asking for forgiveness of the sins of the Church:

> Nevertheless, the joy of every Jubilee is above all a *joy based upon the forgiveness of sins, the joy of conversion*. . . . Hence it is appropriate that, as the Second Millennium of Christianity draws to a close, the Church should become more fully conscious of the

sinfulness of her children, recalling all those times in history when they departed from the spirit of Christ and his Gospel and, instead of offering to the world the witness of a life inspired by the values of faith, indulged in ways of thinking and acting which were truly *forms of counter-witness and scandal.* (32, 33)[1]

John Paul II recognizes that the true joy of the millennial jubilee must be found in seizing the opportunity to call the entire Church to purification. This call, he noted, does not detract from the Church's innate holiness but makes it more credible:

> Although she is holy because of her incorporation into Christ, the Church does not tire of doing penance: before God and man *she always acknowledges as her own her sinful sons and daughters.* As *Lumen Gentium* affirms: "The Church, embracing sinners to her bosom, is at the same time holy and always in need of being purified, and incessantly pursues the path of penance and renewal." The Holy Door of the Jubilee of the Year 2000 should be symbolically wider than those of previous Jubilees, because humanity, upon reaching this goal, will leave behind not just a century but a millennium. It is fitting that the Church should make this passage with a clear awareness of what has happened to her during the last ten centuries. She cannot cross the threshold of the new millennium without encouraging her children to purify themselves through repentance, of past errors and instances of infidelity, inconsistency, and slowness to act. Acknowledging the weaknesses of the past is an act of honesty and courage which helps us to strengthen our faith, which alerts us to face today's temptations and challenges and prepares us to meet them. (TMA 33)[2]

John Paul II's desire to acknowledge the holy Church as sinful and in need of repentance was the subject of much discussion and controversy as the Jubilee Year approached. Questions about exactly how the Church can be simultaneously sinful and holy abounded. This study demonstrates

---

[1] John Paul II, Apostolic Letter *Tertio Millennio Adveniente* (November 10, 1994), http://w2.vatican.va/content/john-paul-ii/en/apost_letters/1994/documents/hf_jp-ii_apl_19941110_tertio-millennio-adveniente.html.

[2] Ibid., citing *Lumen Gentium* 8.

the critical importance of defining terms in order to explicitly state what definition of the "Church" is operative when one states that the Church is sinful. If one is defining the Church as the people of God or the hierarchy or laity or religious, one can unambiguously state that the Church is sinful. If one is defining the Church as the Mystical Body of Christ or the Bride of Christ, one must acknowledge that insofar as the Church is connected to Christ, it is holy; insofar as the Church is composed of humans who can and do sin, the Church can be described as sinful.

In chapter 1, I will trace the renewal of the Church's self-understanding of being both holy and sinful using key works written by six *ressourcement* theologians during the period from 1910 to 1960. These theologians from France, Germany, Belgium, and Switzerland were among those concerned that the neoscholastic manuals, which had become the standard manner of theological education,[3] were not addressing the needs and concerns of the Church in the modern era. These manuals followed a three-point approach to teaching, which began by explaining the Church's teaching on a subject, demonstrated the truth of this teaching through the use of Scripture and tradition, and then applied them to concrete issues. The problem with the theology that emanated from these manuals was that it was defensive and apologetic and failed to engage the new developments in historical and critical hermeneutics. The theologians explored in this book chose to turn to the Bible and the works of the early Church Fathers (the patristic sources) to find ways to overcome the rupture between theology and life that the defensiveness of the neoscholastic manuals was unintentionally causing.

This method of doing theology, known as *ressourcement*,[4] was part of a larger, four-pronged movement known as *nouvelle théologie*, which was begun by the Dominicans in Le Saulchoir, France. Jürgen Mettepenningen points out that the Dominicans' lead role in this was no surprise, as the first phase of *nouvelle théologie* called for a *ressourcement* of Thomistic theology, which had itself been replaced by neoscholasticism. The neoscholastic

---

[3] Francis Schüssler Fiorenza and John P. Galvin, *Systematic Theology: Roman Catholic Perspectives* (Minneapolis, MN: Augsburg Fortress Publishers, 2000), 30.

[4] For a detailed account of the *ressourcement* movement, see Gabriel Flynn and Paul D. Murray, eds., *Ressourcement: A Movement for Renewal in Twentieth-Century Catholic Theology* (New York: Oxford University Press, 2012).

method attempted to apply the Thomistic categories to the scientific and political discoveries that were made at the turn of the nineteenth century. This "new" scholasticism was seen by some as a reduction of the real St. Thomas and necessitated a retrieval of Thomas's true theological vision.

The second part of this four-pronged movement was led by the Jesuits. The Jesuits built on the foundation laid by the Dominicans' desire to retrieve the real Thomas and sought to retrieve the biblical and patristic sources as a way of using the rich tradition of the Church to address contemporary thought. The third phase of this movement was from roughly 1950 up to the eve of the Second Vatican Council and was characterized by the internationalization of the *nouvelle théologie* as theologians began to use this method in conjunction with spirituality and anthropology.[5] The fourth was the Second Vatican Council itself, which as Mettepenningen observes, "ultimately appropriated the central features of the ambitions of the *nouvelle théologie*."[6]

In 1942, Msgr. Pietro Parente, in an article in *Osservatore Romano*, first employed the term *nouvelle théologie* to describe the theological movement then taking place in France. His use of this term was intended as a condemnation of the work coming from Le Saulchoir "with its (exaggerated) interest in the subject, experience, religious sentiment, and the notion of development."[7] As Mettepenningen points out, however, just twenty years later, retrieval of the real Thomas and the patristic sources, both aspects of *nouvelle théologie*, would prove to be an important foundation for the deliberations of the Second Vatican Council. The argument that I will make in this study is that the retrieval of the patristic understanding of the holiness and sinfulness of the Church in the early twentieth century prepared the way for the fathers of the Second Vatican Council to acknowledge by way of the use of myriad images that the Church can be described as both sinful and holy at the same time. Subsequently, Vatican II and Hans Urs von Balthasar provided the foundation for the millennial program of John Paul II. The pope's millennial statement seeking pardon

---

[5] Jürgen Mettepenningen, *Nouvelle Theologie—New Theology: Inheritor of Modernism, Precursor of Vatican II* (Edinburgh: T. & T. Clark International, 2010), 36.

[6] Ibid.

[7] Ibid., 33.

exemplifies in practice the development occurring in the understanding of the Church's holiness and sinfulness.

In this study, the pertinent preconciliar works of Henri de Lubac (1896–1991), Hans Urs von Balthasar (1905–1988), and Yves Congar (1904–1995) will be explored because they break open an understanding of how the indefectibly holy Church can simultaneously be called sinful. Various works of Emile Mersch (1890–1940), Karl Rahner (1904–1984), and Charles Journet (1891–1975) will also be examined. Although these three theologians are not usually considered part of the *ressourcement* movement, they are included in this new analysis because their contributions helped advance the *ressourcement* movement: by preparing for it, as Mersch did; by offering a counterpoint to it, as Journet did; or by wedding this development in theology to the field of theological anthropology in order to address the concerns of the modern person, as Rahner did.

The writings of these twentieth-century theologians, some clearly immersed in *ressourcement* and others contributing to and/or grappling with it in other ways, had a significant influence on the preparation for and the deliberations related to the publication of Vatican II's documents. I argue in this study that the public acknowledgment of the presence of sin in the Church because of the actions performed by its members, leaders and laity, would not have been possible without the groundwork these preconciliar theologians laid and on which Vatican II built. In order to better understand how this change occurred, one must consider the historical situation in which the Church existed at the end of the nineteenth century.

## The Crisis of Modernism

On December 2, 1864, the Catholic Church's unwillingness to engage with modernity reached a crescendo with Pope Pius IX's *Syllabus of Errors*. John O'Malley characterizes this document:

> On December 2, 1864, Pius IX issued one of the most famous papal documents of modern times, the *Syllabus of Errors*. In the *Syllabus* he condemned eighty errors of modern times. Condemned were rationalism, religious indifferentism, atheism, socialism, communism, Protestant Bible societies, secret societies, divorce, separation of church and state, the idea that the church ought not have temporal

power, and many other aberrations. The final condemnation of the *Syllabus* brought it to a resounding and famous conclusion: "That the Roman Pontiff can and should reconcile himself and make peace with progress, with Liberalism, and with modern culture."[8]

The *Syllabus* was greeted with derision by the world; it was seen as the Catholic Church's refusal to come to terms with modern culture and with the innovative theological methods being proposed by liberal Protestant theologians that linked the effects of history with the development of religious thought.[9] One such school of thought emanated from the theological and historical studies of Albrecht Ritschl (1822–1889). Ritschl's major tenet was that religious faith is based on value judgments. Hence, the Ritschlian school

> turned aside from classical metaphysics or the investigation of the "universal foundations of all being," in large part because it failed to make the crucial differentiation between the realm of nature and that of the spiritual life, the life of persons. Consequently, they rejected the speculative theology of the rationalists and their "proofs" of the existence of God.[10]

Ritschl agreed with the German theologian and philosopher Friedrich Schleiermacher (1768–1834) that religion is a matter of experience; however, he did not embrace Schleiermacher's definition of religion that concentrated on the "Christian consciousness" of the individual because, in Ritschl's view, it was dangerously close to subjectivism. For Ritschl the historian, the proper object of theology is not the individual's consciousness but the historical reality of the Gospel as given in the New Testament. Christian doctrine is to be formed solely by reference to the Gospel norm, i.e., the historical Jesus Christ.[11]

The historical aspect of doing theology was paramount for Ritschl, as is evidenced by the work of his student Adolf von Harnack (1851–1930),

---

[8] John O'Malley, *A History of the Popes: From Peter to the Present* (Lanham, MD: Sheed & Ward, 2009), 245.

[9] James C. Livingston, *Modern Christian Thought*, 2nd ed. (Minneapolis MN: Fortress Press, 2006), 270.

[10] Ibid., 271.

[11] Ibid., 272–73.

who "carried forward Ritschl's concern to ground Christian theology in history."[12] As James C. Livingston summarizes, Ritschl's influence on von Harnack is seen particularly in Harnack's belief that:

> Christianity could only be understood as an historical movement and by the methods of historical interpretation. He called upon Christians to take upon themselves the historical responsibility of appropriating critically their religious heritage and making it their own. To be worthy of study, history, for Harnack must have a living relationship to the present.[13]

Harnack's rigorous historical orientation, when applied to the development of dogma, became extremely problematic for the Catholic Church. Although "Harnack did not consider the development of dogma an obviously bad thing, understood historically, it becomes clear that dogma became embodied in an authoritarian, ecclesiastical institution that made and continues to make claims and demands that are very foreign to the primitive gospel."[14]

These new theological methods proposed by liberal Protestant theologians in the course of the nineteenth century were considered an attack on the deposit of faith and on the teaching authority of the Church. Because of this, Church leaders from Pius IX's reign forward not only condemned them but also tried to find ways to ensure that Catholic theology would not be contaminated by these new methods. One such solution was proposed in 1879, when Pope Leo XIII (1810–1903) wrote the encyclical *Aeterni Patris* in which he "conferred a privileged status on the writings of Thomas Aquinas."[15]

> We exhort you, venerable brethren, in all earnestness to restore the golden wisdom of St. Thomas, and to spread it far and wide for the defense and beauty of the Catholic faith, for the good of society, and for the advantage of all the sciences. The wisdom of St. Thomas, We

[12] Ibid., 281.

[13] Ibid., 287.

[14] Ibid.

[15] Alister E. McGrath, *Historical Theology: An Introduction to the History of Christian Thought* (Malden, MA: Wiley-Blackwell, 1998), 239.

> say; for if anything is taken up with too great subtlety by the Scho-
> lastic doctors, or too carelessly stated—if there be anything that ill
> agrees with the discoveries of a later age, or, in a word, improbable
> in whatever way—it does not enter Our mind to propose that for
> imitation to Our age. Let carefully selected teachers endeavor to
> implant the doctrine of Thomas Aquinas in the minds of students,
> and set forth clearly his solidity and excellence over others.[16]

By reviving the use of real Thomistic philosophy and not some adaptation of it, Pope Leo XIII set the stage for the development of measures to control how theology was taught so that the Church and its teaching would not be infected by these new methods of research, which included a commitment to the historical and critical methods for studying the Bible and other early sources of Christianity. Gerald McCool describes the important task that Pope Leo XIII hoped to accomplish: "an analysis of *Aeterni Patris* reveals quite clearly Leo XIII's commitment to the neo-Thomist ideal of scholastic philosophy as the necessary means to equip the Church's ministers for their apostolate in the modern world."[17] Leo XIII thought that neoscholasticism could give a philosophical foundation to theology with arguments about the existence of God and the credibility of revelation and provide an apologetic basis for the truth of the Catholic Church. Because Thomas Aquinas had used medieval scholasticism as a means to answer the issues raised about the faith at that historical time, it seemed reasonable to return to scholasticism in order to provide an apologetic argument so that the Church could defend herself and her teaching against these modern approaches. By returning to the "real" scholasticism in order to apply it to modern issues plaguing the Church and by making it normative, Pope Leo XIII was trying to use "scholasticism's power in its respect for the objective truth of revelation and for the public and authoritative teaching of the universal Church."[18]

---

[16] Leo XIII, Encyclical Letter *Aeterni Partris* (August 4, 1879), http://w2.vatican.va/content/leo-xiii/en/encyclicals/documents/hf_l-xiii_enc_04081879_aeterni-patris.html.

[17] Gerald A. McCool, *Catholic Theology in the Nineteenth Century: The Quest for a Unitary Method* (New York: Fordham University Press, 1977), 228–29.

[18] Ibid., 233.

Toward the end of the nineteenth century, the modern approaches that Leo XIII had referenced in *Aeterni Patris* as integrating Christian thought with the spirit of the Enlightenment were taking root, particularly in France, with the writings of Alfred Loisy (1857–1940), and in England with the writings of George Tyrrell (1861–1909). On July 3, 1907, Pope Pius X condemned these errors that he saw as threatening the way theology was being done in the Catholic Church by issuing *Lamentabili Sane*, a syllabus condemning sixty-five errors of the modernists. Soon afterward, on September 8, 1907, Pius X proposed his solution to the problems these new theological methods were creating, in his encyclical *Pascendi dominici gregis*. John O'Malley summarizes its contents with these words:

> The pope presented a synthesis of the teachings of the Modernists in which he described the heresy as resting on two false principles: the rejection of metaphysical reason, which led to skepticism regarding rational proofs for God's existence, and (2) rejection of the supernatural, which led to the idea that Christian doctrine derived solely from religious experience. He especially rejected the idea that "dogma is not only able but ought to evolve and be changed, for at the head of what the Modernists teach is their doctrine of evolution." Modernism was not so much a heresy as "the synthesis of all heresies."[19]

In this encyclical, Pius X not only criticized the new theological methods but also joined others in using the term "Modernists"[20] to speak of them disparagingly. Pius maintained that "every Modernist sustains and comprises within himself many personalities; he is a philosopher, a believer, a theologian, a historian, a critic, an apologist, a reformer. These roles must be clearly distinguished from one another by all who would accurately know their system and thoroughly comprehend the principles and the consequences of their doctrines."[21] Because of the apparent comprehensiveness of Modernism, Pius X believed that it needed to be condemned

---

[19] O'Malley, *A History of the Popes*, 267.

[20] Pius X, Encyclical Letter *Pascendi Dominici Gregis* (August 9, 1907), http://w2 .vatican.va/content/pius-x/en/encyclicals/documents/hf_p-x_enc_19070908 _pascendi-dominici-gregis.html.

[21] Ibid.

in order to safeguard the deposit of faith. Thereby, Pius X unwittingly gave these modern approaches an identity as a "movement."

Charles Talar, writing over a century after the promulgation of *Pascendi dominici gregis*, describes the encyclical of Pius X as raising concerns and issues about Modernism that created an identity for it and presented it as a movement that necessitated its condemnation by the Church in these words:

> Modernism was presented as a coherent doctrinal system. Its philosophical roots were exposed, and the extent of its inroads into multiple areas of Catholic intellectual and practical life were alarmingly portrayed. The Vatican definition of Modernism did not go uncontested at the time and must be seen as part of the historical dynamic of positioning the movement, rather than as a definitive statement of Modernism's substance and the motivation of its partisans. While not neglecting perspectives offered by *Pascendi*, current scholarship views Modernism as a collection of loosely organized tendencies, reflecting great diversity among and within their regional expressions. Scholars today thus use a more inductive approach, taking account of writings by their innovators and their critics, in preference to the deductive, neo-scholastic procedure followed in the encyclical.[22]

In the early part of the twentieth century, there was a preference for the "deductive, neo-scholastic procedure" over the current preference for a "more inductive approach." It is helpful to understand these two trends in Roman Catholic theology as they demonstrate different points of departure from which Pius and the Modernist theologians were embarking. Pius's approach was defensive and apologetic regarding any new methods of doing theology that included attending to new social, political, scientific, and philosophical techniques. The Modernist theologians, on the other hand, saw the importance of theology being engaged with these new methods so as to make faith more accessible to the current milieu of Christians.

---

[22] Charles Talar, "Modernism," in *New Catholic Encyclopedia: Supplement 2010*, 3rd ed., 2 vols. (Detroit, MI/Washington, DC: Gale Cengage Learning in Association with The Catholic University of America).

In addition to the leaders of the Catholic Church at that time preferring the deductive, neoscholastic approach over a more inductive one, there was also a different ecclesiological standpoint from which these Church leaders were operating. Jürgen Mettepenningen describes the ecclesiology of the Church in the late nineteenth and early twentieth century in this way:

> At the level of ecclesiology, the focus prior to the 1920s was almost exclusively as institution with a great deal of attention afforded the pope, the authority of the magisterium, and the organizational structure of the Church and the rights and obligations attached thereto.[23]

With such a focus on the rules and regulations, an important aspect of the holiness of the members of the Church was their being obedient to rules and fulfilling their obligations to the institution. Therefore, members of the Church were often considered merely rule followers and not full, active participants in the life of the Church.

While the teaching authority of the Church continued to express its strong preference for the manuals of neoscholasticism as the premier means to handle the problems created by modern exegesis and modern historical method, some theologians began to turn to Scripture and the writings of the Fathers of the Church to search for answers to the concerns raised by Modernism. In an ironic turn of events, by using the same methods as the so-called Modernists—exegesis and historical method—these theologians recovered the tradition of the Church found in Scripture and the patristic sources. Their recovery of the early Fathers became known as *ressourcement*, and its openness to dialogue with the contemporary world was a part of the overall movement of *nouvelle théologie*. The *ressourcement* approach offered an alternative way to address the theological concerns of the contemporary world.

Though it was a slow process, *ressourcement* theology finally gained some acceptance. Acceptance from the council fathers at Vatican II was important because it allowed the Church to begin to embrace a "creative hermeneutical exercise in which the 'sources' of Christian faith were

---

[23] Mettepenningen, *Nouvelle Theologie—New Theology*, 27.

're-interrogated' with new questions, the burning questions of a century in travail."[24] Being able to bring the Christian faith to bear on the problems and issues of the world during the era of 1910 to 1950 was of critical import. The social and political turmoil of those years included the Great Depression and two world wars and had a significant impact on the lives of the faithful. The theologians using the *ressourcement* method were trying to discover ways in which Scripture and tradition could help address the urgent questions emerging in the twentieth century. They wanted to find a way for faith to impact the daily lives of the faithful and on the world. *Ressourcement* and the *nouvelle théologie* not only provided a way to respond more adequately to the Modernist crisis of the early twentieth century but also opened the way for a new self-understanding for the Church that would prove invaluable for the work of the fathers of Vatican II in the mid-twentieth century and for the millennial writings of John Paul II.

In order to evaluate the impact of this "creative hermeneutical exercise" on the life of the Church during and after Vatican II, chapter 1 begins with an overview of how ecclesiology was taught at the beginning of the twentieth century by examining the treatment of the Church in A. D. Tanquerey's *A Manual of Dogmatic Theology*.[25] I then discuss the works of six twentieth-century theologians whose theology spanned 1910 to 1960 to see to what extent their works helped to establish this way of doing theology that focused on a revival of scriptural and patristic writings. I pay particular attention to the way in which these theologians used the methods of *ressourcement* in their writing on the holiness and sinfulness of the Church.

In chapter 2, through a close reading of key sections of *Lumen Gentium* and the process and structure of the drafts that led to the final document, I will examine the extent to which the theologians discussed in chapter 1 influenced the council fathers' understanding of the holiness and sinfulness of the Church.

---

[24] Marcellino D'Ambrosio, "Ressourcement Theology, Aggiornamento, and the Hermeneutics of Tradition," *Communio* 18 (December 1, 1991): 550.

[25] Adolphe Tanquerey, *A Manual of Dogmatic Theology* (1st ed. 1913), trans. John J. Burns (New York: Desclee Co., 1959).

Finally, chapter 3 will explore how the Vatican fathers' understanding of holiness and sinfulness as expressed in *Lumen Gentium* became an integral component of the millennial program of John Paul II. I argue that *Lumen Gentium* provided the foundation for the statement seeking forgiveness for the sins of the sons and daughters of the Church that the pope made in March, 2000.

A brief conclusion notes the need in the twenty-first century for revisiting *Lumen Gentium* to find ways, as John Paul II did in his millennial program, for the Church to acknowledge that sin and error exist in the Church, not as an aberration, but as a reality and an occasion for grace and growth in holiness. As the twenty-first century continues to unfold, there is an ever more urgent need for the Church to find the language to admit sinfulness and error and yet continue to profess indefectible holiness.

# CHAPTER ONE

# The Treatment of the Church's Holiness and Sinfulness in Key Works of Preconciliar Theologians

## Introduction

### "A Look Back to See How Far We Have Come"

A significant change took place in the way theology was approached from the early twentieth century to the close of Vatican II. To understand it, one must begin by considering the way in which theologians at the beginning of the twentieth century, operating under the edict in Pope Leo XIII's encyclical *Aeterni Patris*, did theology. This decree, which stated that the doctrine of St. Thomas was to be the foundation of all theology, was the reason why the neoscholastic manual method had become the approved mode of studying theology for the Catholic Church. In order to understand the significance of how this changed the way theology was approached, we will begin by considering A. D. Tanquerey's *Manual of Dogmatic Theology*, first published in 1913,[1] as an example of the old method. We will then proceed to consider the life and work of six theologians who were influential in changing the way theology was done prior to Vatican II.

Tanquerey expands the classic three points of neoscholasticism (thesis, proof, application) by dividing the proof into three categories, that is, *biblical* or *historical*, which explicates and proves each dogma from the sources

---

[1] Adolphe Tanquerey, *A Manual of Dogmatic Theology* (1st ed. 1913), trans. John J. Burns (New York: Desclee Co., 1959). First published in 1913, this book had three reprints. The 1959 version is a reprint.

of revelation, Scripture and tradition; *scholastic*, which scientifically and philosophically reconciles dogmas of faith with reason and combines them into one collection of doctrine; and *mixed*, which harmoniously joins the biblical/historical method and the scholastic method.[2] After defining these categories, Tanquerey explains that these proofs are part of a bigger picture, that of apologetics.[3] Apologetics, he writes, "is the science of the motives of credibility and of credentity of the entire divine revelation which was preached by Christ and which has been set forth through the Catholic Church."[4] Any Catholic theologian at that time was obliged to work within the three-step method of neoscholasticism when teaching theology. To understand how this method worked, one need only examine the "Tract on the Church of Christ" in Tanquerey's manual.

Tanquerey begins the tract from the broad concept of Church and asks of the Protestants, Greek schismatics, and Catholics, which group is true in the mind of God? He then demonstrates through theses and proofs that "we should believe that Christ who wanted His Gospel preached to every creature, chose as a religious authority a living and infallible magisterium."[5] The next step Tanquerey takes is to prove through historical facts, i.e., the gospels and the early history of the Church, that the Church is infallible in its popes and magisterium. At the end of this chapter, he concludes from historical evidence that Christ established the Church as a hierarchical society which was to be ruled by an infallible college of bishops and as a monarchical society whose supreme authority is the infallible Roman Pontiff, thereby, rendering the Church ruled by the Roman Pontiff the true Church of Christ.[6] He then employs the same method to prove that the four marks of the Church were divinely established. At the end of this proof, he concludes that there is no salvation outside the Catholic Church.

Though in his use of the neoscholastic method Tanquerey did use Scripture and the history of the early Church to prove the various theses

---

[2] Ibid., 1.

[3] For further information on the nature of apologetics, consult Avery Dulles, *A History of Apologetics* (San Francisco: Ignatius Press, 2005).

[4] Tanquerey, *A Manual of Dogmatic Theology*, 3.

[5] Ibid., 103.

[6] Ibid., 131.

set forth, it is evident that he paid little attention to the historical context out of which these reasons or proofs emanated. Rather, the neoscholastic method employed deductive reasoning in its application of Scripture and tradition to prove various theological truths. In contrast, the *ressource-ment* method employed inductive reasoning and relied on Scripture and tradition to show how various theological truths developed. Although the extent to which the theologians to be discussed in this chapter used the *ressourcement* method varied, their premise was the same. They saw a need to find ways to make theology more accessible to the modern world and, the *ressourcement* method, returning to the sources, offered an answer. Theologians who used this method became advocates of a greater open-ness to dialogue with the world on the contemporary issues of theology and found within the writings of the early Fathers and Scripture ways to foster that openness.

In this chapter, I will provide a brief biographical sketch of each theo-logian to be considered so that the context of that particular author's life can be taken into account. Knowing the historical context allows for an understanding of how the education and training of the theologian influ-enced his writing about the Church, its nature, and its mission.

Understanding historical context is an important component in the study of ecclesiology. In *The Christian Community in History*, Roger Haight suggests that "ecclesiology cannot be done apart from the history of the church and the world in which it has existed along the way." Therefore, in his work, he "tries consistently to insert the church at any given time into its context in order implicitly to draw out the influence of the age on the particular forms of the church."[7] Haight's premise, rooted in history, is applicable both to those who write about ecclesiology as well as to those who engage in the task of developing how one lives ecclesiologically.

Toward that end, we proceed now to consider how Emile Mersch, Henri de Lubac, Hans Urs von Balthasar, Yves Congar, Karl Rahner, and Charles Journet brought Scripture and the writings of the Fathers to bear on the Church of the twentieth century from a historical perspective. I have chosen to place the first three theologians whose works I will explore

[7] Roger Haight, *The Christian Community in History*, vol. 1, *Historical Ecclesiology* (New York: Continuum, 2004), 2.

in the category of "christological foundations" as their works retrieve from Scripture and the writings of the Fathers an understanding of how the Church is centered on Christ and how the Church can be described as his Mystical Body. Since these theologians focus on Christ, their writings can be categorized as christological in nature. The last three theologians that I will discuss will be placed in the category of "pneumatological foundations." Since their work focuses more on the role of the Spirit, they demonstrate the importance of retrieving from Scripture and the writings of the Fathers the significance of that role in the ongoing life of the Church.

## Emile Mersch: Recapturing the Mystical Body

### *Life and Career*

Emile Mersch, SJ, was born in Belgium on July 30, 1890. He entered the Society of Jesus in 1907.[8] He began his Jesuit novitiate at Arolon in September 1907; he studied the classics at Tronchiennes from 1909 to 1910 and philosophy at Louvain from 1910 to 1913. At the beginning of his theological studies in Brussels, which lasted from 1914 to 1918, the Germans captured the capital of Belgium. It is in this atmosphere of living in an occupied country that Mersch wrote and presented a paper to the Academy of Theologians of Louvain on the Mystical Body of Christ as the central idea of all the Christian dogmas. His view that the Mystical Body of Christ was central to all Christian dogma was revolutionary because in the early twentieth century, the understanding of the Church as institution had a premier place in theological thought. Mersch's paper was the precursor to his two major works on the subject of the Mystical Body, *The Whole Christ*, published in 1938, and *The Theology of the Mystical Body*, published posthumously in 1946. Of Mersch's theology, Jim Arraj comments, "we will not find in Mersch any of the fearfulness and timidity

---

[8] On page 13 of Jim Arraj's *Mind Aflame: The Theological Vision of One of the World's Great Theologians; Emile Mersch* (Chiloquin: Inner Growth Books, 1994), Arraj states that "the most accessible and complete sources of Emile Mersch's life and writings are to be found in the first French edition (1) of his *Theology of the Mystical Body*, and in a doctoral dissertation by Gregory Malanowski, 'The Christocentrism of Emile Mersch and Its Implications for a Theology of the Church' (2)."

that sometimes afflicts Christians when they face the prospect of truly thinking about their faith. Far from thinking being in opposition to faith, it demands it, and Mersch makes his own the statement of Augustine, 'If faith is not charged with thought it is nothing.'"[9]

One cannot underestimate the effect that the historical milieu had on Mersch's choice to think and write about the Mystical Body of Christ. Mersch lived during the entire span of the First World War and the beginning of the Second World War. Clearly he knew the meaning of unrest and the uncertainty of life. He lived in an occupied country that was plagued by constant bombings. He saw firsthand the suffering, death, and deprivation caused by a world at war. It is no wonder that he found a surcease for the pain and suffering around him in the unity of humanity as incorporated into the Mystical Body of Christ as portrayed in Scripture and the patristic sources. During these years, Mersch's main labor was writing on this topic and forming a theological synthesis on the Mystical Body. During the Second World War, however, as the Germans approached France, he also "was charged by his superiors with the responsibility of leading a group of aged and infirm Jesuit priests to some haven of safety."[10] In performing this task, Mersch was killed by a bomb on May 23, 1940.

Although the Mystical Body of Christ was not a new idea for theology, as St. Paul writes about it in his letters to his various communities, it had not been given much theological attention during the late nineteenth and early twentieth centuries. Mettepenningen observes that "the focus prior to the 1920's was almost exclusively on the Church as institution, with a great deal of attention afforded the pope (cf. Vatican I), the authority of the magisterium (cf. the Modernist crisis), and the organizational structure of the Church and the rights and obligations attached thereto (cf. the *Codex Iuris Canonici* of 1917)."[11] Arraj further notes that "the scholastics, because of their attempts at rigorous exposition, preferred certain aspects of the mystical body, but at their hands other aspects regressed from the

---

[9] Arraj, *Mind Aflame*, 22–23.

[10] Emile Mersch, *The Theology of the Mystical Body*, trans. Cyril Vollert (St. Louis: Herder, 1951), x.

[11] Jurgen Mettepenningen, *Nouvelle Theologie—New Theology: Inheritor of Modernism, Precursor of Vatican II* (Edinburgh: T. & T. Clark International, 2010), 27.

vigor by which they had been treated by the Fathers, and their remarks on this subject were often lost in the vastness of their summas."[12] Mersch's research and writing on the Church as the Mystical Body of Christ not only helped its resurgence and made a significant contribution to it but also paved the way for a new way of doing theology with a focus on historical and biblical underpinnings of theology.

Because the theology of the Mystical Body of Christ can be used to understand the Church's sinfulness in light of its holiness, Mersch's work in this area is important. Describing the expansiveness of the history covered in Mersch's first work, *The Whole Christ*, Gregory Malankowski writes that "it seems to be the first study of the tradition of Mystical Body theology to deal not only with the Scriptures, but also with a broad, albeit selective, range of Greek and Latin Church Fathers, as well as Scholastic theologians and modern developments."[13]

Mersch's research on the Mystical Body of Christ and its historical and scriptural foundations was "seminal and opened new dimensions for theological work; it was born from his apostolic desire to expound Christian truths in an attractive and synthetic manner for a world athirst for unity and completion. The capital idea of his theology is that Christianity is Jesus Christ continued and completed in his mystical Body, the Church."[14] Mersch's work, grounded in a desire to take the Christian truths and make them "attractive" to the modern world, did not employ the defensive and apologetic method of neoscholasticism. Rather, he took a pastoral approach, reaching out to a world athirst and bringing the good news of Christianity to it. Mersch has not been considered a *ressourcement* theologian because he died in 1940, prior to the rise of the *nouvelle théologie* whose groundwork had just begun to be laid by the Dominicans around 1935 in Le Saulchoir, France. Mersch's work, however, gathered the historical and scriptural foundations of the Mystical Body of Christ and was an important beginning from which new vistas in ecclesiology could be opened.

---

[12] Arraj, *Mind Aflame*, 16.

[13] Gregory E. Malanowski, "The Christocentrism of Emile Mersch and Its Implications for a Theology of Church," STD dissertation, Catholic University of America, 1988, p. 62.

[14] John Auricchio, *The Future of Theology* (New York: Alba House, 1970), 215–16.

Gary Badock suggests that Mersch's "fresh theological perspective" arose from placing the incarnation at the center of his theological reflection on the Church as the Body of Christ and from his wide-ranging analysis of patristic and medieval sources as a way to renew the theology of his day.[15] Mersch retrieved the scriptural and patristic sources that emphasize the roots of ecclesiology as connected to the doctrine of Christ's human nature and point to Christ as center of the Church.

The "capital idea" of Mersch's theology is that "Jesus Christ is continued and completed in his mystical body, the Church."[16] In this idea lies the seed for understanding how the Church can define itself as holy while being composed of sinners. If the Church is the continuation of Christ, it is thereby made holy through Christ; at the same time, it is Christ's holiness that makes it possible to acknowledge that the Church is composed of human beings who can and do sin.

In *The Whole Christ*, Mersch lays out the scriptural and patristic foundations for the doctrine of the Catholic Church known as the Mystical Body of Christ. The idea of the Mystical Body enables him to demonstrate how humanity has participated and can continue to participate in the ongoing life of Christ through the Church. Mersch begins by explaining that there are four aspects of the mystery inherent in the doctrine of the Mystical Body of Christ. The first aspect is "that Christ is the head, we are the members; He is the Vine, we are the branches; He is Life in its source, and we are animated by that life; He is Unity, and we many are one in Him who is One. Between Him and ourselves all is common."[17]

Humanity is made holy by its union with the Head, that is, with Christ. Mersch clarifies that this relationship is not just one way: indeed, the members receive holiness from Christ because Christ willingly takes on the sinfulness of the members. By his Blood and by his Cross, sin has been destroyed and the consequences of sin—sufferings, humiliations, and death—become a source of life. In him and him alone is the

---

[15] Gary D. Badcock, *The House Where God Lives: Renewing the Doctrine of the Church for Today* (Grand Rapids, MI: Eerdmans, 2009), 86.

[16] Auricchio, *The Future of Theology*, 215–16.

[17] Emile Mersch, *The Whole Christ: The Historical Development of the Doctrine of the Mystical Body in Scripture and Tradition*, trans. John R. Kelly (Milwaukee, WI: Bruce, 1938), 4.

restoration and the ennobling of man.[18] The sins of the members, once united to Christ, the Head, are transformed. Christ takes sin and death upon himself and transforms them out of love for the members into love and eternal life. This transformation is given to humanity through the Church's sacrament of baptism which unites us with God, making men and women adopted sons and daughters. This transformation is a divinization of humanity. Once all humanity is united with God, it is also united in a new way with all other human beings. Finally, this union of humanity with God and with each other "imposes an obligation, we must live for God and for our brethren, since we are to live with them in Christ."[19] With this transformation into adopted sons and daughters of God comes the obligation to care for all humanity. When humanity falls short of this obligation, sin and disunity occur. Thus the holiness and unity of the body of Christ are affected.

Although Mersch's work is mainly focused on the divinity of the Mystical Body of Christ and on the transformation of humanity by participation in it, he also is careful to acknowledge the role of each person's free will to accept or reject the transformation being offered. Free will and choice are critical for the Mystical Body of Christ to become fully what the Lord intended it. So, although Mersch does not stress the sin that is present in and affects the holiness of the Church, the body of Christ, he certainly recognizes its existence in the Church.[20]

Mersch points out that Jesus' life as recounted in the gospels is shared with us after his death and resurrection through the working of the Holy Spirit in the life of his Mystical Body, the Church. Jesus did not leave the world "in defeat, because in reality He did not leave at all. What the Church has accomplished, He has accomplished, but He has done so in her."[21] As Gregory Malanowski observes, Christ's life being continued in the life of the Church is "a fundamental insight derived from Paul's conversion experience on the road to Damascus."[22]

---

[18] Ibid.

[19] Ibid., 5.

[20] Ibid., 369.

[21] Ibid., 51.

[22] Malanowski, *The Christocentrism of Emile Mersch*, 109.

When Mersch recounts Luke's story of the conversion of Saul in Acts 9:3-6, he notes that Jesus identifies his very self as the newly formed Church. This identification is a critical component in Saul's conversion. As Mersch makes clear:

> Thus far, Christ had revealed Himself in His brethren. It is I, He says, who am persecuted when they are persecuted. Now, however, he effaces Himself, and where He was, the Church appears to speak in His name. It is she who will tell Paul, not what she thinks and what she wills, but who that Christ is who has just appeared, and what she is in Him.[23]

From the moment of his conversion onward, Paul's understanding of the inseparability of Christ and the Church is embedded in his preaching. Mersch explicates this dynamic by noting that the doctrine of our incorporation in Christ is at the heart of Paul's teaching and that it is used in the explanation of many points of Christian doctrine as well as for the inculcation of moral precepts.[24] For Paul, everything is Christ, nothing exists without Christ; indeed, "to live is Christ" (Phil 1:21).

Because Paul sees the close association of Christ with the Church, he is troubled when he learns of divisions and factions in the various communities he has founded, warning them that "to attack the unity of the Church is to dismember Christ Himself"[25] (1 Cor 1:10-13). The holiness of the Church for Paul is evidenced by his constant references to the inherent unity of the Church and Christ (1 Cor 1:10-13; 12:12; Col 1:15-20; Gal 3:25-29; Eph 1:20-23; 5:21-32). The Church is the body of Christ in the world. In and through the Church, humanity becomes part of Christ; in and through the Church, human beings become Christ's very body. Christ's life continues through the members of his body, the Church.

Mersch considers Paul's conversion and subsequent preaching significant for the development of the doctrine of the Church as the Mystical Body of Christ.[26] For Paul, each member of the body of Christ must strive

---

[23] Mersch, *The Whole Christ*, 83.
[24] Ibid., 89.
[25] Ibid., 138.
[26] Ibid., 139–40.

to be worthy of such a calling. Sin, evil, and division must be eradicated. Paul does not doubt the holiness of the Church where he acknowledges the presence of sin among its members, since he sees each person as open to grace so that he or she can be made one with Christ, can become one body in Christ (1 Cor 12:12). Paul makes it very clear that Christ continues to live in the life of the Church and, therefore, the unity and holiness of the Church are nonnegotiable (Col 1:15-19).

Although Mersch's research on the Mystical Body of Christ includes the works of both the Greek and Latin Fathers, for the purposes of this study, the writings of the Latin Fathers will be more helpful as they are more analytical in nature and grapple with how to hold in tension the holiness and sinfulness of the Church. Mersch explains that the Latin Fathers employ this "analytical method" as a means of addressing the "problem of Christian life and action, the problem of grace and free will. For its solution they go to the source of grace and of Christian life; they go to Christ, who, by incorporating men in Himself, unites them with God and endows them with supernatural activity."[27] According to Mersch, this analytical method could be summed up "with the bald assertion that the doctrine of the West is practical."[28] What he meant by that was that the Latin theology of the Mystical Body had its grounding in the interaction of grace and free will in the everyday lives of Christians.

Mersch takes two examples from history to illustrate the practical application of theology to serious pastoral problems: the way in which Cyprian and Augustine deal with serious problems of disunity in their local churches.[29] The decisions that Cyprian and Augustine made in these situations would prove to have a lasting effect on how the Church universal understood its nature and mission, its holiness and its sinfulness.

In the middle of the third century, Cyprian (c. 200–258), bishop of Carthage, was presented with the problem of division between the local bishop and the faithful. Cyprian had fled Carthage during the Decian persecution. When he returned, he began to receive back into the Church those who had apostatized (the lapsed) during this time of persecution.

[27] Ibid., 369.
[28] Ibid., 368.
[29] Ibid., 382–85.

Among those who had remained faithful during this persecution were some priests and other confessors of the faith who denounced Cyprian's decision that only the bishop could allow the lapsed back into the Church. When faced with the threat of schism on this issue in Rome, Cyprian wrote his treatise "On the Unity of the Catholic Church" for a council of North African bishops. In it he reminded the bishops and the faithful about the importance of unity in the Church, particularly of unity between the bishop and his flock. As Mersch points out, "Cyprian declared that the unity of the Church and of the Mystical Body is attained through the bishops."[30] This teaching for the time being helped to address in Carthage the problem of schism brought about by receiving the lapsed back into the Church.

Not long thereafter, however, another controversy arose between Cyprian and Stephen (Stephen was bishop of Rome from c. 254–257) regarding the validity of baptisms of those in schism. Cyprian won the day in Carthage and there was no schism there. But there was schism in Rome, led by Novatian.[31] As that movement rapidly lost ground, some of those baptized by Novatian and his clergy wanted to enter the "catholic" church—hence the issue of whether they were really baptized or not. Francine Cardman explains,

> Cyprian affirmed traditional North African practice that baptism outside the unity of the church was not efficacious, so that converts from schism or heresy were to be baptized—not again, but for the first time. Stephen, bishop of Rome, asserted his church's tradition of recognizing the validity of schismatic, or heretical, baptism and receiving such converts into the church as penitents.[32]

Though both disagreed on how to handle this issue, they remained in communion and the matter ended with their deaths in the renewed persecution of Christians in 258. This dispute is important because the

---

[30] Ibid., 381.

[31] Henry Chadwick, *The Early Church*, The Penguin History of the Church, rev. ed. (New York: Penguin, 1993), 118–19.

[32] Francine Cardman, "Cyprian of Carthage," in *The Encyclopedia of Christianity*, vol. 1, A–D, ed. Erwin Fahlbusch, Geoffrey W. Bromiley, David B. Barrett, and Jan Milic Lochman (Grand Rapids, MI, and Leiden: Eerdmans and Brill, 1999).

Donatists (305) will try to use Cyprian's words to support their dispute with Augustine (354–430), bishop of Hippo, about the purity of the Church.

The Donatists, by referencing Cyprian, insisted that ordinations performed by bishops who had compromised by some cooperation with Roman officials during the persecution were invalid and that only the Donatists themselves were the true Catholic Church as they had the only true ministry, baptism, and Eucharist. Augustine, who still had to deal with them in Hippo in the early 400s, spoke forcefully about the need for unity in the Church. Schism for Augustine was unacceptable. Schism destroys the unity of Christ and the Church, the Head and the Body. This type of dismemberment could not be tolerated. Augustine argued:

> This unity is as vast as the world, that it is one as Christ is one, broad enough and human enough to include a multitude of sinners, yet so divine and so pure that it can remain undefiled within them and can sanctify them in itself. And the reason he gives is always the same: it is the unity of Christ, the unity and the life of Christ communicated to men.[33]

For Augustine, the Mystical Body of Christ, the Church, "can remain undefiled" while claiming among its members "a multitude of sinners." Augustine argues that the Church, Christ's body, contains both the wheat and the chaff. It is not until judgment day that the winnowing occurs. Augustine saw membership in the Church as dynamic. The members of the Body of Christ are a people on the way, a people in need of sanctification that can only come through the unity of Christ communicated to them. Augustine also makes it clear that the hierarchy can be found among this multitude of sinners. They too are people on the way. Their sanctity comes in and through their unity with Christ. The holiness of the Church is not contingent on the holiness of its ministers. The holiness of the Church comes from its unity with its Head, Christ. This unity with Christ that makes the Church holy is incomplete on earth but will be absolute at the end of time. Therefore, Augustine urged the Donatists to follow Cyprian's practice of unity but not his theology in regard to baptism by schismatics.

---

[33] Mersch, *The Whole Christ*, 392.

Augustine's teaching on the need for unity within the Church and his acknowledging that sin can exist among the members of the Church are of critical import as he deals with the theology of Pelagius regarding original sin, grace, and free will. Mersch notes that

> Pelagianism is Christianity minus two mysteries, both of which are in great part mysteries of solidarity. Gone is the mystery of human helplessness and of the divine assistance that is ever necessary for us, members who can do nothing without the Head. Gone is the mystery of our fall, and of the sin that we all bear who have sinned in Adam. Gone, in a word, is the mystery of solidarity in sin and in death, and the corresponding mystery of solidarity in good and in life.[34]

In Mersch's view, Pelagius, who believed that humanity is not completely helpless in the face of sin and, therefore, did not need to rely on the grace of God to live a good life, brings heresy into the Mystical Body of Christ, the Church. For Pelagius, one relies on one's own strength and not that of the solidarity of the community to live a life of holiness. Mersch contends that the result of Pelagianism is that humanity no longer needs the gratuitous grace of God that was given in the life, death, and resurrection of Jesus. Pelagius was capitalizing on the inherent goodness of all that God created by insisting that the concepts of original sin and concupiscence are incompatible with such goodness. Additionally, Pelagius was strongly arguing for free will and human responsibility. Pelagius believed that because of the example of Christ, each human being can either rise or fall on his or her own. Pelagianism, as Augustine argued, is very individualistic.[35] The Mystical Body of Christ, as Mersch insists, is about being in "solidarity," not being solitary.[36]

Mersch writes that the Mystical Body of Christ is built on unity: of Body and Head, of members and Christ. Because Christ is principal and Head of all Christian life, this life can have nothing in common with the sins of the faithful or of their bishops.[37] Since, however, the Church

[34] Ibid., 400.
[35] Ibid.
[36] Ibid., 401.
[37] Ibid., 403.

claims the holiness of Christ while also acknowledging the sinfulness of its members, the Church can, as Augustine noted, lay claim to being both holy and sinful simultaneously.[38] Augustine writes, "Human frailty will not destroy this holiness; little by little our infirmities will be consumed by it. Nor on the other hand will this holiness in Christ destroy our own poor individuality."[39] Because of this unity, little by little each person receives the grace necessary to overcome his or her sin and weakness so as to become incorporated more fully into Christ.[40] Augustine saw incorporation into Christ becoming a reality in the way those who are in Christ treat all their brothers and sisters, including those who are not yet in Christ. For Augustine, indeed, "for all Christians, there is only Christ. The love of God for us, our love for Him, the love of each for all and of all for each; in short, the very plenitude of charity: not one of these is outside the fullness of Christ."[41]

For Mersch, the "fullness of Christ" is made visible in the life of the Church. The Church is the way par excellence that humanity can participate in the ongoing life of Christ as "the Church is the continuation of Christ, for it is His mystical body."[42] Since the Church is composed of people who can and do sin, Mersch builds on the foundation laid in *The Whole Christ* and raises the question of the holiness of the Church in his second book, *The Theology of the Mystical Body*. Mersch explains that holiness was conferred on the Church through the life, death, and resurrection of Jesus Christ. Because Christ died for all, each person, no matter how sinful, can repent, receive forgiveness for his or her sins through the sacramental life of the Church, and thereby participate in the holiness of the Church. All are called to repentance, forgiveness, and holiness. Yet all members of the Church, priests as well as laity, struggle with the ongoing conversion needed to live a life of holiness. Mersch points out that God assists the Church on earth to fight against the sin in its leaders as well as in its members. He further observes that in the Church's prayer, liturgy, and psalms, the officiating priest who speaks in the name of the Church

---

[38] Ibid., 407.

[39] Ibid., 428–29.

[40] Ibid., 420.

[41] Ibid., 440, citing Augustine *In Epistolam Ioannis*, 10.3.

[42] Mersch, *The Theology of the Mystical Body*, 479.

unceasingly avows his guilt; and in her teaching, the Church affirms with all her might that sinners are indeed her members, and her priests and pontiffs, though laden with faults, are nevertheless priests and pontiffs.[43]

Mersch's response to the question about the holiness of the Church is comprehensive. First, like Augustine and Paul, he concurs that both sin and holiness are present in the Church. Then, because he is keenly aware that he must find ways to balance free will and grace in his answer, he emphasizes that it is only in and through the grace of God that all of the members of the Church, priests and laity, can be raised from their sins and participate in the life of holiness to which God calls them. Mersch expands his understanding of holiness as being "universally human and truly catholic" and begins to see ways that all humanity, just by being human, can participate in God's holiness. Gregory Malanowski observes that Mersch's thinking embodies a "less juridical, more vital view of the Church"[44] in which this life-giving union with Christ is the basis of the Church. Mersch's insight opens up the possibility not only for the Church to have a relationship with other Christian denominations and non-Christian religions but also for all Church members to take responsibility for their own faith commitment. Thereby, Malankowski argues, Mersch's emphasis on the sacramentality and humanness of the Church portrays the Church not as triumphalistic but as on a progressive path of renewal and growth.[45]

Mersch's extensive research on the biblical and patristic sources for the doctrine of the Mystical Body of Christ contribute to making theology more accessible and understandable to people in the days prior to the convocation of Vatican II. Through his research, he demonstrated a new way of doing theology by going back to Scripture and the patristic sources to gain a view of the Church in that light. By retrieving the doctrine of the Mystical Body of Christ, he showed ways rooted in historical and biblical sources of seeing the Church through different lenses. Through this method, Mersch presented the Church as a dynamic, living organism in which each Christian has his or her own personal grace, and these individual graces remain united in their common source, which is Christ. In the supernatural order there is but one living organism in Christ. This

---

[43] Ibid., 511–12.

[44] Malanowski, *The Christocentrism of Emile Mersch*, 190.

[45] Ibid., 190–91.

organism grows and develops through the ages and it extends itself to all peoples over the entire face of the earth; yet all of this, all this life, all the good that is wrought in heaven by the saints and by men here on earth, in the whole universe and throughout all time—all this is one Christ, Head and members, *unus Christus amans seipsum*.[46] As Mersch describes it, the Church does not and should not remain stagnant, as the Church is a living organism. The Church's doctrine of the Mystical Body of Christ has developed throughout its history, as Mersch demonstrated through his retrieval of the scriptural and patristic sources of this doctrine. Because the Church is a living organism, it is always on the way. On that journey, the Spirit has the task of ensuring the Church's holiness while simultaneously calling its members who are sinners back to the grace and holiness the Church offers.

## Conclusion

Mersch's contributions to the development of the Church's self-understanding as being both holy and sinful lies in his retrieval of the scriptural and patristic foundations of the Mystical Body of Christ. These foundations speak of both the human and divine aspects of the mystery of this Mystical Body of Christ. Speaking of the continuation of Christ in the Church and the ongoing incarnation sets the stage for the Church to better understand itself as existing in history. Perhaps, if Mersch had not been tragically killed during the war, he would have been able to explore more fully how his way of approaching theology moved beyond the neoscholastic understanding of Church with its emphasis on institution and authority and opened up an understanding of the Church and all its members, hierarchy and faithful, as participants in the Body of Christ.

This significant contribution of Mersch in laying the foundation for the work of the *ressourcement* theologians of the twentieth century cannot be overstated. Mersch basically puts in place the necessary groundwork for the Church to come to terms with its historicity and the existence of holiness and sin in the Church from its beginning. Although Mersch was only able to lay out the pieces of the puzzle—not to put the puzzle together—we

---

[46] Mersch, *The Whole Christ*, 573, citing Augustine in *Homilies on 1 John*, 10.3.

will see that Henri de Lubac picks up where Mersch left off.[47] De Lubac will find ways through the use of paradox to apply Mersch's retrieval of the scriptural and patristic understandings of the Church as the Mystical Body of Christ to the Church and its mission in the twentieth century.

## Henri de Lubac and Paradox

### Life and Career

Henri de Lubac, SJ, was born in Cambrai, France, on February 20, 1896, and entered the Society of Jesus in 1913.[48] De Lubac's novitiate was done in England because French law enacted an anticlerical movement in 1901 that exiled the Jesuits and other religious orders. In 1915, de Lubac was drafted into the French army and was severely wounded in the First World War. He was unable to resume his studies until 1920. His war service time, however, became the impetus for his first major work, *Catholicism*, which "was intended to bring out the singular unitive power of Catholic Christianity and its capacity to transcend all human divisions."[49]

De Lubac completed his theological training at Lyon-Fourvière, where he was ordained a priest on August 23, 1927. He was named professor of fundamental theology in the School of Catholic Theology at Lyon in 1929, and in 1935 he was asked to join the faculty of the theologate at Fourvière. In 1938, *Catholicism* was published. As Susan Wood observes, it "contains in seminal form the major themes of his theological career. Subtitled 'A Study of Dogma in Relation to the Corporate Destiny of Mankind,' it emphasizes the communal character of salvation and the solidarity of the human race in its common vocation."[50]

---

[47] Contemporaneous with Mersch's work was that of Pius XII who issued the encyclical *Mystici Corporis* in 1943. The contribution of Pius's encyclical to the discussion of the Church as the Mystical Body of Christ at Vatican II will be discussed more fully in chapter 2.

[48] A work that traces the life and writings of Henri de Lubac is Rudolf Voderholzer's *Meet Henri De Lubac*, trans. Michael J. Miller (San Francisco: Ignatius Press, 2007).

[49] Avery Dulles, "Henri de Lubac: In Appreciation," *America* 165, no. 8 (September 28, 1991): 180–82.

[50] Susan K. Wood, *Spiritual Exegesis and the Church in the Theology of Henri De Lubac* (Grand Rapids, MI: Eerdmans, 1998), 2–3.

In 1940 de Lubac and Jean Daniélou, SJ, began publishing a collection of patristic texts and translations, *Sources chrétiennes*. During the Nazi occupation of France, de Lubac became coeditor of a series of *Cahiers du Témoignage chrétien*. Both works were important representations of the growing desire for a fully fledged return to the sources of the faith.[51] Additionally, in these papers and in his lectures, de Lubac strove particularly to exhibit the incompatibility between Christianity and the anti-Semitism that the Nazis were seeking to promote among French Catholics. On several occasions his friends had to spirit him away into hiding to prevent him from being captured and executed by the Gestapo, as happened to his close friend and colleague Yves de Montcheuil, SJ.[52]

De Lubac's theological works were the cause of controversy not only in secular circles but also in Church circles. This controversy among his colleagues in the Church was evidenced in 1946 when he published his most controversial book, *Surnaturel*, which "maintains that the debate between the Baianists and the scholastics in the seventeenth century rested on misinterpretations both of Augustine and of Thomas Aquinas."[53] Both parties took offense at de Lubac's critique of their methodology and doctrine and sought a condemnation from Rome for this work. Shortly after that, in 1950 the Jesuit General, John Baptist Janssens removed de Lubac from his teaching position, for he was accused of promoting *nouvelle théologie*. "In 1953, during this time of exile in Paris, de Lubac published a popular work on the Church, *The Splendor of the Church*. The intention of this book was to atone for the offense given by his previous works."[54] In an amazing turn of events, not even a decade later, in 1960, Pope John XXIII invited de Lubac to be a consultant for the Preparatory Theological Commission of the Second Vatican Council. This invitation seemed to signal that any heretofore offense or suspicion of de Lubac's theology had dissipated.

For the purposes of this study, I have chosen to examine de Lubac's theology from the perspective of two of his works, *Catholicism* and *The*

---

[51] Mettepenningen, *Nouvelle Theologie—New Theology*, 96.
[52] Dulles, "Henri de Lubac."
[53] Ibid.
[54] Ibid., 181.

*Splendor of the Church*. *Catholicism* was chosen because in this first book he lays the groundwork for understanding his theological insights in subsequent works. *The Splendor of the Church* was chosen because it is concerned primarily with the nature and mission of the Church. In both works, de Lubac uses the *ressourcement* method of doing theology and the lens of paradox to enter into discussion of the theological issues under consideration.

In *Catholicism*, de Lubac begins to make his mark in theology by returning to the writings of the Fathers (*ressourcement*) and gleaning from them a comprehensive and expansive understanding of what the Catholic faith brought to the early centuries of the Church's existence. Using paradox as a technique in his writing, he finds ways to draw on keen patristic insights, such as the significance of the communal dimension of the faith, to address issues being raised by the modern world for the Church. De Lubac, thereby, offers ways for the pre–Vatican II Church not to succumb to Modernism but to provide solid, theological answers to the crises raised by it.

De Lubac also elucidates his fundamental thoughts about the way in which theology should be done. Most important, through his retrieval of the patristic sources, he uncovers the patristic understanding of the Church as a social institution as well as a historical entity. This understanding of the nature of the Church as a historical society provided a much-needed foundation for Church to engage the concerns that Modernism was raising. Additionally, de Lubac's reflections on the historicity of the Church opened up new ways to understand the nature of the Church as both human and divine, holy and sinful, in time and beyond time. Prior to this, the emphasis in ecclesiology was on the divinely instituted and hierarchical aspects of the Church. *Catholicism* is foundational for de Lubac's thought and for understanding his treatment of the holiness and sinfulness of the Church from the vantage point of its historical context, as he does in *Splendor of the Church*.

De Lubac had no intention of introducing a new way of doing theology. Rather, he was looking to the early Fathers for inspiration and insight. In writing about the aim of de Lubac's theological pursuits Avery Dulles states:

> For his part, de Lubac had no desire to innovate. He considered
> that the fullness was already given in Christ and that the riches of
> Scripture and tradition had only to be actualized for our own day.[55]

Dulles calls attention to the fact that de Lubac's desire was to find ways
to bring the beauty and expansiveness of the faith of the Church that the
writings of the Fathers of the Church and Scripture articulated into the
current historical milieu.

## Theologian of Paradox

De Lubac's "fundamental conviction was that in order for Christianity to be adaptable to a modern generation, it must first discover its essence through a return to the originating creative thought of its doctrines
and institutions. Such a theological program required a solid historical
foundation established upon the patristic and medieval giants, whose
chief value, in turn, lies in their witness to the apostolic tradition."[56] This
"theological program" was in itself paradoxical in that he was retrieving
history to address modernity. Susan Wood clarifies the paradox inherent
in de Lubac's theology when she writes that although "intellectual history
situates de Lubac within a movement known as the 'new theology,' he
himself disliked this title because it contradicted the very impetus of the
movement which was to renew theology by a return to its biblical and
patristic sources."[57] De Lubac's dislike for the label "new theology" could
come from his acknowledgment that his theological reflection on the
Church was not "new," but was deeply rooted in history. It was from that
historical perspective that he wrote:

> I am told that she is holy, yet I see her full of sinners. . . . Yes, a
> paradox is this Church of ours! I have played no cheap rhetorical
> trick. A paradox of a Church for paradoxical mankind and one that
> on occasion adapts only too much to the exigencies of the latter![58]

---

[55] Ibid., 182.

[56] Wood, *Spiritual Exegesis and the Church in the Theology of Henri De Lubac*, 5.

[57] Ibid., 6.

[58] Henri de Lubac, *The Church: Paradox and Mystery*, trans. James R. Dunne (New
York: Alba House, 1969 [French orig. 1967]), 2.

Through the lens of paradox rooted in history, de Lubac was able to see the Church as holy yet full of ambiguities because she is composed of sinners.

An important example of how de Lubac's theology has its foundation in writings retrieved from the patristic sources is demonstrated in *Catholicism*. He opens the work with this sentence from Leo the Great: "The supernatural dignity of one who has been baptized rests, we know, on the natural dignity of man, though it surpasses it in an infinite manner: *agnosce, christiane, dignitatem tuam—Deus qui humanae substantiae dignitatem mirabiliter condidisti*."[59] This quotation from Leo the Great reflects de Lubac's use of paradox. In the teachings of the Fathers, de Lubac retrieves a foundational aspect of the faith, that is, the bringing together of the natural and the supernatural. The faith is based on the life, death, and resurrection of Jesus, God becoming man or the supernatural being united with the natural. We share through baptism in this coming together in time of the supernatural with the natural. Our supernatural dignity cannot be separated from our natural dignity. Our natural dignity roots us in time, in history. Our supernatural dignity roots us in eternity. By explicating the paradox at work in this fact, de Lubac shows how the Church is the vehicle through which the paradoxes inherent in the faith are mediated.

De Lubac explicates what Pope Leo highlights, namely, that all humanity shares in the holiness that emanates from our supernatural dignity as well as the holiness that emanates from our natural dignity. After the fall, however, the potential for humanity to sin became a reality. Thereby, a tension was created: the natural dignity of humanity is holy because humans are made in the image and likeness of God; after the fall, however, humanity's inclination to sin is inevitable. Because what affects one member of human family affects all members, the result of the fall is that all humanity shares in original sin and its consequences.

Patristic theology "envisages salvation in its collective dimension as the salvation of humanity rather than in its individual dimension."[60] Throughout *Catholicism*, de Lubac demonstrates the significance of retrieving

---

[59] Henri de Lubac, *Catholicism: Christ and the Common Destiny of Man*, trans. Lancelot C. Sheppard and Elizabeth Englund (San Francisco: Ignatius Press, 1988), 25, citing Leo the Great, *Sermo 21* in Nat. Dom., 3: PL 54, 192C.

[60] Wood, *Spiritual Exegesis and the Church in the Theology of Henri De Lubac*, 8.

this patristic understanding of the collective, communal dimension of salvation for the modern age. Aidan Nichols describes how de Lubac accomplishes this when he writes of *Catholicism* that:

> De Lubac's own theological apologetics, *Catholicism* would in its evocation of the "social aspects of dogma," offers the Catholic faith as the answer to a very human problem, the unity and peace of mankind, achieved in God, certainly, and not in quasi-humanist abstraction from him.[61]

De Lubac's retrieval of patristic theology on humanity being made in the image and likeness of God proposes anew that Catholicism is not merely an individual enterprise but must be concerned and involved with all people because we share the same humanity made in God's image and likeness. De Lubac is trying to make the case that, without losing its integrity, the Catholic faith can and must be engaged with the world for the sake of all humanity.

Therefore Aidan Nichols is correct in saying that de Lubac's theology offers the Catholic faith to modern man as the answer to society's problems. That answer is found in the belief that humanity is united to God by being made in his image and thereby, can share in the life and salvation offered by the Triune God through the grace of Christ. These beliefs rooted deeply in the Catholic faith are what enable de Lubac to state that the "supernatural dignity" given in the sacrament of baptism in the Church "rests" on what all humanity holds in common, namely, our being made in the image and likeness of God. He concludes that "the unity of the Mystical Body of Christ, a supernatural unity, supposes a previous natural unity, the unity of the human race."[62]

For de Lubac, participation in this gift of supernatural life and salvation is made available to humanity through the Church, whose mission is to bring about the unity of all humanity.[63] As he has noted, however, this unity is hampered by the sins of individuals. Since one person's sin

---

[61] Aidan Nichols, *Catholic Thought Since the Enlightenment: A Survey*, 1st ed. (Pretoria: University of South Africa, 1998), 136.

[62] De Lubac, *Catholicism*, 25.

[63] Ibid., 49.

affects the whole community, bringing about this unity of humanity is no easy task. Drawing on the works of Origen and Maximus the Confessor, de Lubac shows that sin is never an individual matter. He notes that sin, like salvation, always has a collective dimension to it.

> all infidelity to the divine image that man bears in him, every breach with God, is at the same time a disruption of human unity. It cannot eliminate the natural unity of the human race—the image of God, tarnished though it may be, is indestructible—but it ruins that spiritual unity which, according to the Creator's plan, should be so much the closer in proportion as the supernatural union of man with God is the more completely effected. *Ubi peccata, ibi multitudo.*[64]

When one sins, it never causes a rupture between only oneself and God. Rather, sin causes both a "breach with God" and "a disruption of human unity."[65] Drawing from Maximus the Confessor, de Lubac observes that sin separates, "whereas God is working continually in the world to the effect that all should come together into unity."[66]

*Catholicism* elucidates the paradoxical nature of faith, namely, that there is a communal call to holiness for humanity and there is an acknowledgment of the communal dimension to the weakness and sinfulness of all humanity. This communal perspective opens the way to understanding that the holy or sinful actions of one member of the community have an effect on the entire body for good or ill.

Expanding on this insight, de Lubac notes that both Augustine and Maximus the Confessor considered evil as an "inner disruption that went hand in hand with the social disruption."[67] Although he is aware that theology since about the sixteenth century[68] dwelt more on the individual aspect of sin and redemption, de Lubac believes much can be gained by retrieving how the Fathers understood the collective, communal dimension of sin and redemption. He writes:

[64] Ibid., 33, citing Origen, *In Ezech.*, Hom. 9, n1.
[65] Ibid.
[66] Ibid., 33, citing Maximus the Confessor, *Quaestiones ad Thalassium*, q. 2, PG 90, 272.
[67] Ibid., 34.
[68] Ibid., 320–22.

> Let us abide by the outlook of the Fathers: the redemption being a
> work of restoration will appear to us by that very fact as the recovery
> of lost unity—the recovery of supernatural unity of man with God,
> but equally of men among themselves.[69]

For de Lubac, the Fathers' emphasis on redemption as a recovery of supernatural unity as well as a recovery of unity among men themselves is
at the heart of his own understanding of the completeness and comprehensiveness of Catholicism. Joseph Komonchak observes that de Lubac's
expansive understanding of Catholicism "frees Catholic theology from
its narrow confines so that it could engage the problems posed by the
modern world."[70]

### Sacrament, Mystery, Paradox

The mission of the Church is to be a means of grace in history to medi-
ate salvation. For de Lubac, this is done by bringing together, through the
lens of paradox, the mystery and sacramentality of the Church. Paradox,
mystery, and sacrament come together in the life, death, and resurrection
of Jesus Christ, the perfectly sinless one, who took upon himself our sin
to restore our unity to God. The holy one takes on sin; death becomes life.
All of us can participate in this mystery of the life, death, and resurrection
of Christ through the sacramental life of the Church. De Lubac elucidates
the role that paradox, mystery, and sacramentality play in understanding
the nature of the Church when he writes:

> We are now in a better position to understand what the Church
> is. For all the dogmas are bound up together. The Church which is
> "Jesus Christ spread abroad and communicated" completes—so far
> as it can be completed here below—the work of the spiritual reunion
> which was made necessary by sin; that work which was begun at
> the Incarnation and was carried on up to Calvary.[71]

---

[69] Ibid., 35.

[70] Dennis M. Doyle, *Communion Ecclesiology: Vision and Versions* (Maryknoll,
NY: Orbis Books, 2000), 60.

[71] De Lubac, *Catholicism*, 48.

Sinful humanity can only be reunited with God through the work of the Church, which is "Jesus Christ spread abroad and communicated." This is the great paradox of the faith of the Church. Avery Dulles further details the paradoxical nature of de Lubac's ecclesiology:

> The center is the mystery of Christ, which will be complete and plainly visible at the end of time. The universal outreach of the church rests on its inner plenitude as the body of Christ. Catholicity is thus intensive as well as extensive. The church, even though small, was already Catholic at Pentecost. Its task is to achieve, in fact, the universality that it has always had in principle. Embodying unity in diversity, Catholicism seeks to purify and elevate all that is good and human.[72]

If the Church's mission is "to purify and elevate all that is good and human," one can infer that the Church's mission is also concerned with transforming what is sinful in humanity into what is good and holy. Therefore, through its sacraments, the Church is always working with the weak and sinful as it walks through history in order to accomplish the mission given to her by the Lord.

Taking baptism as the example, de Lubac discusses the corporate nature of the sacraments. He writes that "the first effect of baptism, for example, is none other than this incorporation in the visible Church."[73] This incorporation is not just visible, that is, merely joining a social group, but also invisible, that is, being incorporated into the Mystical Body of Christ and receiving the status of adopted sons and daughters of God. The need for community as manifested in the sacramental life of the Church is an intrinsic part of salvation and of being united to Christ. De Lubac argues that the sacraments:

> should be understood as instruments of unity. As they make real, renew or strengthen man's union with Christ, by that very fact they make real, renew or strengthen his union with the Christian community. And this second aspect of the sacraments, the social aspect, is so intimately bound up with the first that it can often be

---

[72] Dulles, "Henri de Lubac: In Appreciation," 3.
[73] De Lubac, *Catholicism*, 83.

said, indeed in certain cases it must be said, that it is through his union with the community that the Christian is united to Christ.[74]

Through his study of the scriptural and patristic foundations of the Church, de Lubac realized the need to retrieve this communal aspect of the sacraments.

The communal aspect of the sacraments, which makes the Church more accessible to the world, underscores the social dimension of the Church. With this insight, De Lubac can now address the paradox of holiness and sinfulness and the way in which each member can and does have an effect on the whole body of the Church. De Lubac's discussion of the efficacy of the sacrament of penance illustrates this dynamic.

> The double functions of this sacrament as a disciplinary institution and as a means of inner purification are not merely associated in fact; they are united, if one may so put it, by the nature of things. The Church's primitive discipline portrayed this relationship in a more striking manner. The whole apparatus of public penance and pardon made it clear that the reconciliation of the sinner is in the first place a reconciliation with the Church, this latter constituting an efficacious sign of reconciliation with God.[75]

De Lubac sees in the "primitive" Church's practice of public penance—wherein the sinner was publicly reconciled with the community of the Church—an acceptance by the Church of sinners in her midst.[76] He further explicates the importance of confessing sin to a minister, a representative of the Church, when he writes that "it is precisely because there can be no return to the grace of God without a return to the communion of the Church that the intervention of a minister of that Church is normally required."[77] By sinning, an individual breaks from the communion of the Church. In order for this individual to return to communion, the sinner needs to be accepted back into the Church. The "intervention of

---

[74] Ibid., 82.
[75] Ibid., 87.
[76] Ibid., 88.
[77] Ibid.

the minister" who represents the Church is a critical component of being reconciled, for sin is never merely an individual, private affair.

Given De Lubac's retrieval of the Fathers' communal understanding of the sacrament of penance and given his drawing on *Sermo 2* of Isaac de Stella in the twelfth century who states, "Only the whole Christ, the head upon his Body, Christ with the Church, can remit sins,"[78] one can infer that de Lubac agrees with his predecessors on the fact that sin always has ramifications for the entire body of Christ, the whole Christ, head and body. De Lubac's retrieval of this understanding of the sacrament of reconciliation demonstrates how sinfulness affects the whole community. By being received back into the Church by the minister, there is a coming together of the holiness of the Church as represented by the minister and of the sinfulness of her members. This should not be taken to mean that the ministers cannot and do not sin, as they too are members of the community; it is just when the minister is acting *in persona Christi*, i.e., in sacramental/liturgical functions, that the minister represents Christ, the head and holiness of the Church.

## The Paradox of Holiness and Sinfulness

In *Catholicism*, de Lubac continues his discussion of the paradox of the holiness and sinfulness of the Church when he writes that the "Church which is not tarnished by our sins, is also not straitened by our artificial boundaries nor paralyzed by our prejudices. Her ambition is to gather the human family together, and she has nothing in common with our cheap pretentions."[79] The question is raised as to how in one part of this book de Lubac can write that the sin of the individual affects the whole, and later he writes that the Church is not tarnished by our sins. Here de Lubac is trying to hold the holiness of the Church and the sinfulness of the Church together in tension by showing that all humanity is united. He writes:

> The human race is one. By our fundamental nature and still more in virtue of our common destiny we are members of the same body. Now the life of the members comes from the life of the body . . .

[78] Ibid.
[79] Ibid., 293–94.

and salvation for this body, for humanity, consists in its receiving the form of Christ, and that is possible only through the Catholic Church.[80]

Dennis Doyle describes how the holiness of the Church and the sinfulness of its members intersect when he shows how de Lubac uses paradox to hold these opposites in tension in his theology:

> De Lubac found the Church to be full of paradox. As a Patristics scholar and theologian *par excellence* of *ressourcement*, he drew upon the Church Fathers to label the Church a *complexio oppositorum*: a complex of opposites held in tension. The de Lubac who envisioned the Church as the Bride of Christ could also, along with the patristic authors, see the Church as a harlot (*Catholicism* 26). The Church is both a spring and an autumn, an achievement and a hope (*Catholicism* 136). It is the wretched woman saved from prostitution and the bride of the Lamb.[81]

De Lubac clearly sees the Church as a "both/and." The Church is holy because she is intimately connected with Christ as the Bride of Christ and the Body of Christ; simultaneously, she is sinful because she is composed of human beings who can and do sin. The Church as it exists in history is subject to the pressures and concerns that each historical milieu presents. At the same time, it is invisible and includes the communion of saints who are sharing eternal life with Christ and are no longer subject to history and its constraints.[82]

The visible and invisible aspects of the Church are present each time a sacrament is celebrated. In baptism, the faith takes root in an individual who becomes a member of the visible community of faith. Then, through the subsequent reception of the other sacraments, the individual and the community nurture the gift of faith so that it can blossom into a gift for the whole human race. As de Lubac says:

> Although the Church rests on eternal foundations, it is in a continual state of rebuilding, and since the Fathers' time it has undergone

---

[80] Ibid., 222–23.

[81] Doyle, *Communion Ecclesiology*, 58–59, citing *Catholicism*.

[82] De Lubac, *Catholicism*, 132–33.

> many changes in style; and without in any way considering ourselves
> better than our Fathers, what we in turn have to build for our own
> use must be built in our own style, that is, one adapted to our own
> needs and problems.[83]

The beauty of the Church is found in its timelessness; it is ever ancient, ever new. Yet because the Church is a historical reality, it can and must go through "a continual state of rebuilding" and adapt to the needs and problems of the current era in which it is existing. Doing theology in a way that adapts to and addresses the current milieu is clearly a break from the neoscholastic method, which was a predictable, unchanging presentation of thesis, proof, and application.

## The Church and the World

In *The Splendor of the Church*, de Lubac builds on the fundamental theological program that he laid out in *Catholicism*. Building on Mersch's theological research, de Lubac specifically deals with what the Church as the Mystical Body of Christ can bring to the world. In the introduction to this work, de Lubac states that he wrote the book by meditating on certain aspects of the mystery of the Church as elucidated in the essential texts of tradition. For his ambition was simply to be its echo—that is all. He wanted to share with others the recurrent thrill that comes from recognizing that impressive and undivided voice in all its modulations and all its harmonics.[84] Again, we see de Lubac's desire to let the "voice" of that tradition be heard by the faithful of the twentieth century. He is careful, however, not to idealize the tradition or the mystery we call Church. Rather, he immediately tells his reader that, "My love is for the Holy City not only as it is ideally, but also as it appears in history, and particularly as it appears to us at present."[85] Maureen Sullivan, commenting on the aspect of *ressourcement* in de Lubac's theology, observes:

---

[83] Ibid., 321–22.

[84] Henri de Lubac, *The Splendor of the Church*, trans. Michael Mason (San Francisco: Ignatius Press, 1986), 9.

[85] Ibid., 9–10.

> De Lubac recognized that *ressourcement* was not simply a return to
> forms and customs of the past but a return in the sense that "the life
> which gave birth to the church must spring up ever more vigorously
> without endangering her own proper and unalterable nature."[86]

In his theology and particularly in this book, de Lubac is trying to
hold several paradoxes in tension, namely, how the Church as it appears
in history can be relevant in the present and how the visible Church in
history and the invisible Church wrapped in mystery and beyond history
operate in concert. As Susan Wood has observed:

> In de Lubac's theology, grace is concretely embodied in the world
> because revelation has, in Christ, taken a historical form. The
> Church, as a social institution, is a social embodiment of this grace
> because of its inherent relationship to Christ. The demonstration of
> this, however, rests, first, on the historical character of the revelation
> and the Church's relation to this history and second, on the Church's
> relationship to Christ.[87]

Wood's point is significant as we now turn to de Lubac's reflections on
the "splendor" of the Church, which is rooted in the historical reality
as well as the mystical reality of the eternal grace of Christ in which the
Church exists.

De Lubac points out that even though faith has no history, substantially
speaking—for the eternal is not subject to becoming—"the man of faith
and the world in which he dwells have one." And we cannot avoid the
problems of our own day. If we are to live in the Church, then we have
to become involved in the problems she faces now, and the assent of our
intelligence is owed to her doctrine as we find it set out today.[88] This
background is critically important because it again emphasizes that de
Lubac is not trying to invent something new in his theology or retreat
to a former age but to hold in tension the paradox of the timelessness of
the faith with the fact that humanity is bound in time. The Church is an

---

[86] Maureen Sullivan, *The Road to Vatican II: Key Changes in Theology* (New York: Paulist Press, 2007), 21.

[87] Wood, *Spiritual Exegesis and the Church in the Theology of Henri De Lubac*, 23–24.

[88] De Lubac, *Splendor of the Church*, 20–21.

integral part of this balance, as it is in and through the Church that these two aspects of time meet. It is in and through the Church that humanity finds an entry point to unite with the eternal. Furthermore, it is at this point of intersection of time with the eternal that we will see how the Church can lay claim to being both holy and sinful.

De Lubac attempts to explain how this interaction between time and the eternal works in the life of the Church when he writes:

> The Church is a mystery for all time out of man's grasp because, qualitatively, it is totally removed from all other objects of man's knowledge that might be mentioned. And yet, at the same time, it concerns us, touches us, acts in us, reveals us to ourselves.[89]

Thus, the Church is simultaneously ever other, ever beyond "man's grasp" and ever touching and acting in us. The Church is at once beyond time, yet in time.

De Lubac clearly sees the importance of time in understanding the mystery of the Church. His insights are significant, given the need at the turn of the twentieth century for the Church to acknowledge that it has a history and that this history changes and develops in time, all the while acknowledging that there is a privileged place in that history for Scripture and tradition as they are at once in and beyond time. The "splendor" of the Church is that it carries with it the past while it walks in both the present and the eternal. Because the Church is in history and made up of human beings who can and do sin, the Church can be seen as sinful. Simultaneously, because the Church is beyond history and divine in origin, the Church must always be seen as holy. Dennis Doyle explains that through the use of such paradoxes, de Lubac "was able to take things that others would see only in terms of opposition or of subordination and orchestrate them as a harmonious symphony."[90]

De Lubac wants always to keep in the fore that the Church "is above all an invitation to share in the divine life of the Trinity"[91] and, therefore, that it is in and through the Church that humanity can grow in holiness.

---

[89] De Lubac, *The Church: Paradox and Mystery*, 14.

[90] Doyle, *Communion Ecclesiology*, 63.

[91] De Lubac, *Splendor of the Church*, 174–75.

He points out that the Church "occupies a definite place"[92] in our faith as demonstrated by its location in the ancient creedal formulas right after the profession of belief in the Trinity, Father, Son, and Holy Spirit. Its placement implies that the Church emanates from the life of the Trinity.[93] De Lubac observes: "Today she appears in the Creed as the first of the Spirit's works, before the Communion of Saints, the remission of sins, the resurrection of the body, and life everlasting."[94] Here de Lubac calls attention to the important role that the Church plays in bringing humanity to faith, to participation in the holiness of those who have gone before, and to forgiveness that enables us to continue our quest for holiness when we have failed. As the first work of the Spirit, the Church has a divine aspect and can be described as unequivocally holy.

Because the Church is both in time and in eternity, de Lubac sees it as a Church on the way. He writes:

> The holy Church has two lives: one in time and the other in eternity.
> We should not separate them, as we should do were we to consider
> *Ecclesia deorsum* (the Church below) as a stranger to *Ecclesia sur-
> sum* (the Church above). We must always keep a firm hold on the
> continuity of the one Church in and through the diversity of her
> successive states, just as we see the unity of Christ in his life on earth,
> his death, and his glorious Resurrection.[95]

In making such a statement, de Lubac is not relying on his own thoughts. Within this brief quotation, he invokes Gregory the Great and St. Augustine to explain how the mystery of the Church walks "in time and in eternity." He further explicates how this dual aspect of time is operative in the life of the Church and its members:

> It is one and the same Church that is to see God face to face, bathed
> in his glory, and yet is our actual Church, living and progressing

---

[92] Ibid., 29.

[93] Ibid., 30

[94] Ibid., 30.

[95] Ibid., 79, citing Gregory the Great, *In Ezech.*, 2.10; Augustine, *Sermo* 181.7; Augustine, *De Civitate Dei*, 20.9.1; and Augustine, *Brevis Coll. Contra Donat.*, 10.20.

laboriously in our world, militant and on pilgrimage, humiliated daily in a hundred different ways.[96]

Again, he relies on the works of the Fathers, Gregory and Ambrose, to demonstrates how "the two aspects of the one Church"[97] make the tradition a living, active one by bringing elements of the past to bear on the present.

De Lubac is trying to hold in tension both the visible Church that exists in time and is subject to human frailty and the invisible Church that exists divine and is in the spiritual realm of eternity. Although there are two temporal aspects to the Church, de Lubac strives to show that the Church is still one community, embracing two realities, visible and invisible. Aware of how difficult it is to keep the visible and the invisible in a healthy balance, he notes that there have always been people who have made a distinction between the visible, temporal, hierarchical Church that exists among us and a sort of invisible Church—wholly "interior," wholly "spiritual," "the luminous community of God dispersed throughout the universe." In such a view, the title "Church of God" could only be applied to this vast *communio sanctorum*. It alone would be divine; the first Church, the "bodily" Church, would be a "human creation" and no more. She is, after all, always and inevitably limited and infected with impurities.[98] Again de Lubac emphasizes that the Church is neither a merely "human creation" nor is it solely composed of holy, saintly people. No, the Church is both human and divine as well as in service to both the holy and the sinful.

James Connolly sums up de Lubac's concern when he observes that "the constant problem and 'scandal' of the human element in the Church, according to de Lubac, have led many erroneously to distinguish the 'visible Church' and the 'Mystical Body of Christ.'"[99] Claiming that the Church is at once human and divine is a challenge. As Doyle explains, however, "one of the major strengths of de Lubac is that he is able to operate on the

---

[96] Ibid., 82, citing Gregory the Great, *In Ezech.* 2.1.5; Ambrose, *In Psalm.* 118, *Exposition, sermo* 15.35; and Song 1:3; Pseudo-Alciun, *Compendium in Cant.*

[97] Ibid., 84.

[98] Ibid., 84–85, citing Eckharthausen in his *The Cloud upon the Sanctuary*, and Luther, *Treatise on the Papacy.*

[99] James M. Connolly, *The Voices of France* (New York: Macmillan, 1961), 94.

level of ideal, mystical speech about the Church while at the same time acknowledging fully the level of dark abominations. For de Lubac, the Church is not only a bride; it is also a harlot." Doyle adds that "de Lubac is highly aware of how idealized speech about the Church has been used to mystify and to cover-up by clothing all too human decisions and failings in the guise of sacral legitimations."[100]

De Lubac unabashedly highlights the controversial yet critical issues in holding those realities in tension:

> There is something yet more "scandalous" and "foolish" about belief in a Church where the divine is not only united with the human but presents itself to us by way of the all-too-human, and that without any alternative. For, granted that the Church is really Christ perpetuated among us, Christ "spread abroad and passed on," still the Church's members, lay and clerical, are not the inheritors of the privilege that caused Christ to say so boldly: "Which of you shall convict me of sin?"[101]

Here he makes a link between the Church and its life in Christ. "We must keep a firm hold on the continuity of the one Church in and through the diversity of her successive states, just as we see the unity of Christ in his life on earth, his death, and his glorious Resurrection."[102]

If the Church is the connection with the ongoing life of Christ, then the Church can be said to be composed of visible and invisible aspects as well as transitory and eternal aspects because the Church is in time and Christ is eternal. For this reason, too, the Church can be described as being indefectibly holy. Grasping the meaning of the inseparability of Christ and the Church has implications for how one understands the holiness and the sinfulness of the Church. To make this point, De Lubac cites Pius XII's *Mystici Corpori Christi* in which the distinction is made between human weakness and tendency to sin that we all share and the juridical constitution of the Church which is not sinful. De Lubac does acknowledge, however, that "there are able pastors and incompetent ones, good pastors and bad.

---

[100] Doyle, *Communion Ecclesiology*, 64–65.
[101] De Lubac, *The Splendor of the Church*, 48–50.
[102] Ibid., 79.

Whether he be a member of the hierarchy or not, a zealous Catholic can still be no more than a mediocre Christian."[103] The Church's holiness is not contingent on the holiness of her leaders but rather on Christ who makes the Church holy. De Lubac is clearly aware of the presence of sin and evil in members of the Church, including those who have a responsibility for the flock. He also sees, however, that the human element of the Church is essential to the structure and life of the whole, just as the divine aspect is because Christ willed the Church to be divine in its foundation.[104]

De Lubac further explains the tension between the holiness and sinfulness of the Church by noting that everybody is in the process of being sanctified and in danger of shipwreck, and so prays "forgive us our trespasses." The idea that we are all in process emphasizes that the sanctity of the Church is not static, but dynamic. The sanctity of the Church is something for which all Christians must strive. De Lubac recalls that the early Christians understood that "being a Christian implied an obligation to sanctity."[105] By doing so, he is acknowledging that the Church Fathers

> were well aware that at one and the same time the Church is without sin in herself and never without sin in her members, and they echoed St. Ambrose's "The Church is wounded not in herself but in us," though they also added, like him: "Let us have a care, lest our sin should become the Church's wound," and in doing so make it clear the that "the-Church-in-our-persons" is still the Church.[106]

But sin does not have the final say. The Church's holiness is eschatological; it will only be perfected in eternity.

This mystery of a Church that can lay claim to being in time and beyond time, being sinful and yet indefectibly holy comes to a crescendo in the life of the Church each time the sacrament of baptism is celebrated. It is in and through becoming a member of the Church as well as in every Eucharistic Liturgy that a bridge is crossed between the temporal and the eternal, the sinful and the holy. De Lubac explains:

[103] Ibid., 89.
[104] Ibid., 101.
[105] Ibid., 116.
[106] Ibid., 116–17.

> The Church is a mystery; that is to say that she is also a sacrament. She is the "total *locus* of the Christian sacraments," and she is herself the great sacrament that contains and vitalizes all others. In this world, she is the sacrament of Christ, as Christ himself, in his humanity, is for us the sacrament of God. That which is sacramental—"the sensible bond between two worlds"—has a twofold characteristic.[107]

Later he sums up the purpose of the Church in these words: "Her whole end is to show us Christ, lead us to him and communicate his grace to us; to put it in a nutshell, she exists solely to put us into relation with him. She alone can do that, and it is a task she never completes." De Lubac makes it clear that the life and mission of the Church is concerned with nothing less than the salvation of the world. Hence, her mission exists as long as the world does.

For de Lubac, through the sacramental life of the Church, the visible and invisible worlds, time and eternity are united. De Lubac observes that "the Church is human and divine at once even in her visibility, 'without division and without confusion,' just like Christ himself, whose body she mystically is."[108] De Lubac also highlights the fact that since the Church is the Mystical Body of Christ, one cannot distinguish between which parts are human and which parts are divine. Dennis Doyle further explicates de Lubac's emphasis on the sacramentality of the Church:

> For de Lubac, the sacramental form of relationality is the one that ties together the Church as the Mystical Body of Christ with the Church as the historical People of God. It forms "the sensible bond between two worlds" (*Splendor* 147).[109]

Explicating the ecclesial sacramentality in de Lubac's theology, Susan Wood notes the following:

---

[107] Ibid., 202, citing "Du Sacrement de l'Église et de ses réalisations imparfaites," IK 22 (1949): 345–67; Council of Florence, *Decretum pro Jacobitis* (1441–1442); *Ambrosian Missal*, Preface for the First Sunday of Advent; and Joseph de Maistre, "Lettre à une dame russe," in *Oeuvres*, 8:74.

[108] De Lubac, *The Splendor of the Church*, 102.

[109] Doyle, *Communion Ecclesiology*, 65, citing *Splendor of the Church*.

> Crucial to his notion of sacramentality is that the sign makes Christ present. The referent of the sacramental symbol is therefore not immanent, but transcendent. De Lubac maintains the distinction between the human and the divine at the same time that he asserts their union. . . . The structure of paradox which governs so much of de Lubac's thought demands that Christ and Church, grace and nature, be distinct at the same time that they are united.[110]

Wood's observations echo the words with which de Lubac began his first theological treatise, *Catholicism*. For de Lubac, the Church is a living, active reality whose sacraments, beginning with baptism, sanctify the sinful. The Church can be said to be sinful insofar as her members throughout their lives sin and need to receive the grace of the sacraments to be purified. The sacramentality of the Church raises human nature through grace to a sharing in divine life. In this sacramentality, there is a union of the temporal with the eternal as well as the sinful with the holy.

## Conclusion

In evaluating De Lubac's work, the significance of his use of scriptural and patristic sources to demonstrate the significance of the work of *ressourcement* must first be acknowledged. In applying the scriptural and patristic writings to the nature and mission of the Church today, de Lubac can be seen as advancing Mersch's research on the Church as the Mystical Body.

De Lubac's unique theological contribution to the developing theology of the holiness and the sinfulness of the Church, however, is his use of paradox to describe the Church as mystery and able to hold both its human and divine elements in tension. De Lubac's use of paradox enabled him to see the union of opposites while always keeping their individual distinctions. His theological reflection on paradox led him to write about the mystery of the Church as embracing the visible and invisible aspects of the Church as well as the temporal and eternal aspects of the Church. All these paradoxes were then incorporated into his major contribution to the theology of the Church, his work on the sacramentality of the Church.

---

[110] Wood, *Spiritual Exegesis and the Church in the Theology of Henri de Lubac*, 107.

De Lubac is able to hold in tension the holiness of the Church while simultaneously always acknowledging that in and through its members, the Church can be sinful. Because his theology emphasizes the christo-centricity of the Church and therefore its historicity, he is able to offer an alternative to the neoscholastic manual method that emphasized the authoritarian and hierarchical aspects of the Church and did not consider the question of the sinfulness of the Church.

De Lubac's disciple, Hans Urs von Balthasar, however, employs a different tactic in working with this paradox of how the Church can claim indefectible holiness while being composed of members who sin. Von Balthasar isn't focused on ensuring the Church's indisputable holiness. Rather, his concern is with showing how God works in all things, even with and through human sinfulness. It is to von Balthasar's work in this area that we now turn.

## Hans Urs von Balthasar: Finding God in All Things
### *Life and Career*

Hans Urs von Balthasar was born in Lucerne, Switzerland, on August 12, 1905. After completing secondary school under the tutelage of the Benedictines and Jesuits, he pursued doctoral studies that consisted of nine university semesters alternating in Zurich, Berlin, and Vienna. He completed his dissertation on the theme of apocalyptic German literature in 1929.[111] Von Balthasar then entered the Society of Jesus in Germany as the Society was still banned in Switzerland. During his formation, he pursued theological studies at the Jesuit theologate at Lyon in France where he came under the influence of Henri de Lubac, with whom he began a lifelong friendship.[112] To say that von Balthasar did not relish his theological studies in the Society of Jesus is an understatement. Of them, he wrote that they were based on neoscholasticism's myopic obsession with late mediaeval philosophy and its insistence on the centrality of abstract and neutral rationality[113] and that his "entire period of study in the Society of Jesus was

---

[111] See John O'Donnell, *Hans Urs von Balthasar* (New York: Continuum International, 2000) for a study of his life and writings.

[112] Ibid.

[113] Kevin Mongrain, *The Systematic Thought of Hans Urs von Balthasar: An Irenaean Retrieval* (New York: Crossroad, 2002), 2.

a grim struggle with the dreariness of theology, with what men had made out of the glory of revelation."[114] Those years of study had a profound effect on von Balthasar, however; so much so that "after his seminary training he (Balthasar) became increasingly convinced of his vocation to defend the Catholic faith by challenging what he believed was neoscholasticism's narrow intellectualism."[115] In pursuing this goal of challenging neoscholasticism, von Balthasar encountered five major influences: Henri de Lubac, Erich Przywara, Karl Barth, Adrienne von Speyr, and the *Spiritual Exercises* of St. Ignatius of Loyola. Each one of them added a different facet to von Balthasar's own theological inquiry.

De Lubac introduced von Balthasar to "the so-called movement of the *nouvelle théologie* which sought to overcome the manual tradition of a dried and decadent scholasticism and to return to the rich patristic heritage of theology."[116] From von Balthasar's own admission of his dislike for neoscholasticism, one can readily understand his attraction to de Lubac's way of doing theology.

Erich Przywara (1889–1972), a Jesuit philosopher whom von Balthasar came to know during his tenure at Munich, made an impression with his dynamic interpretation of the analogy of being. As John O'Donnell summarizes Przywara,

> every creature is a dynamism toward God. As a creature it resembles the creator but in its dynamism toward the creator, the creature experiences an ever-greater *excessus* toward the Transcendent who recedes with every approach of the creature. Far from capturing God in human categories, the doctrine of analogy preserves the transcendence of God and reveals God to be the ever-greater one. Przywara thus places the doctrine of analogy within the framework of negative theology. His philosophy has the merit of reviving for Catholic theology the principle of analogy enunciated by the Fourth Lateran Council (1215), "For all the similarity between God and the creature, there exists an ever-greater dissimilarity." This principle, so important for Balthasar, became a cardinal point in his discussions

---

[114] Fergus Kerr, *Twentieth-Century Catholic Theologians* (Malden, MA: Wiley-Blackwell, 2007), 122.

[115] Mongrain, *The Systematic Thought of Hans Urs von Balthasar*, 2.

[116] O'Donnell, *Hans Urs von Balthasar*, 3.

with the great Protestant champion of neo-orthodoxy, Karl Barth (1886–1968).[117]

Von Balthasar embraced Przywara's understanding of the analogy of being. And so, von Balthasar differed greatly with another writer on the same topic who also had a profound influence on him, Karl Barth.

Unlike Przywara, O'Donnell observes, Barth did not believe there should be two sources of theology, one from philosophy and one from faith. Barth actually held the view that "the analogy of being represented the anti-Christ and the most serious obstacle to becoming a Catholic."[118] Von Balthasar, however, was greatly impressed by Karl Barth's christocentrism and sought to "integrate the analogy of being into the analogy of faith."[119] Von Balthasar's ability to find some point to embrace in Barth's theology is an example of how von Balthasar's theological reflection, based on finding God in all things, attempts to find how God is working in the minds of others, even those with whom he differs theologically.

Perhaps one of the greatest influences on von Balthasar's life began in 1940, when he met Adrienne von Speyr (1902–1967). This friendship with the Swiss convert started when he not only received her into the Church but also began to serve as her spiritual director. From Speyr, a Swiss medical doctor and mystic, von Balthasar gained the following insights which proved to be key for his theology:

> Christ's descent into hell as his solidarity with the abandoned, Jesus's Sonship as obedience to the point of powerless identification with the God-forsaken . . . the bodiliness of Christian existence, the naked standing before God and the Church in the sacramental act of confession as expressing the fundamental Christian attitude.[120]

These themes of humanity as standing powerless and in need of the forgiveness and the grace of God are foundational to von Balthasar's theology and are ways in which he sees how God works not only in humanity's call to holiness but also through humanity's fall into sinfulness. The sacra-

---

[117] Ibid., 4.
[118] Ibid.
[119] Ibid.
[120] Ibid., 5.

mental role of the Church in fostering humanity's turn from sinfulness to holiness is key for von Balthasar. Through the Church's role as mediator of this forgiveness, one can see how the sinfulness of the members can be transformed into holiness through the reception of the sacraments.

In his essay "*Casta Meretrix*" (1961), von Balthasar demonstrates that throughout both the Old and New Testaments, humanity needs to look for God in both the holy and the sinful that arises again and again. It is not that God is in the sin, but God's love and forgiveness are there, calling humanity back to God and holiness. God's love and forgiveness come in unexpected places, such as in the fragility, nakedness, and dependence exemplified in the life, death, and resurrection of his Son, Jesus. Both humanity and institutions, such as the Church, are often unaware that God can be found in such places. Von Balthasar's contention is that by embracing God in the fragility, nakedness, and dependence that sin elicits, one will paradoxically experience the holiness and glory of God. Truly, God is present in all things for von Balthasar.

Because of this, it can be said that the Ignatian spirituality of finding God in all things was the guiding force behind von Balthasar's entire theological program. This Ignatian principle provided von Balthasar with a method to "overcome traditional dichotomies between theology and spirituality, not by subordinating one to the other, but by calling in question both cherished convictions of academic theology and traditional expectations as well as some current trends in spirituality."[121] Through this principle, von Balthasar was able to find ways to connect academic theology, tradition, and spirituality. It is from the convergence of theology and spirituality that von Balthasar writes his theology.

### "Chaste Whore"

In the brief essay "*Casta Meretrix*" (1961), von Balthasar elucidates the scriptural and patristic foundations as well as the spiritual implications inherent in referring to the Church as the "Chaste Whore." He begins the essay with these words: "Ours is a purely historical undertaking. We

---

[121] Alister E. McGrath, *The Blackwell Encyclopedia of Modern Christian Thought* (Malden, MA: Wiley-Blackwell, 1995), 27.

intend, without prejudgment, by critical examination and in temperate language, to set out the most important themes." He ends his introductory remarks by stating that:

> Without endangering the immaculateness, holiness, and infallibility of the Church, one must look the other reality in the eye and not exclude it from consideration. Much would be gained if Christians learned more and more to realize at what price the holiness of the Church has been purchased.[122]

By examining the reality of the Church in history, von Balthasar is able to discover that spirituality is not only present in history but also a very important component of that history. That spirituality is reflected in how God relates to his people when they are faithful and when they sin. Through the lens of spirituality, von Balthasar discovers how God is at work in the "immaculateness, holiness, and infallibility of the Church" as well as in the great price at which "the holiness of the Church has been purchased."

Von Balthasar begins the discussion of the price paid for the holiness of the Church by returning to the roots of God's relationship with his people found in the Old Testament. In claiming that Christianity has its roots in the Old Testament, von Balthasar explains that he "agrees with Karl Barth when he says that there is only one People of God, consisting of Synagogue and Church."[123]

Von Balthasar discusses the long history of the marriage covenant theme in the Old Testament, which teaches Israel about God's justice and love. God's love is exclusive and committed as husband to wife. "Deserting Yahweh, Israel's God and Covenant Lord, is like adultery. Israel must expect from God the same treatment reserved for the adulteress and wife turned whore not only in the law but also in the logic of love and fidelity."[124] Rather, this relationship of God and his people has been fraught with betrayal, infidelity, and disobedience on the people's part. God addressed this adulterous behavior through the prophets. Von Balthasar notes that a new dimension

---

[122] Hans Urs von Balthasar, "*Casta Meretrix*," in *Explorations in Theology: Spouse of the Word*, trans. John Saward (San Francisco: Ignatius Press, 1991), 198.

[123] Mongrain, *The Systematic Thought of Hans Urs von Balthasar*, 87.

[124] Von Balthasar, *Explorations in Theology*, 198.

in Hosea is God's command to marry and have children with a harlot, thus calling attention to the fact that God's love for his people, Israel, is both relentless and unconditional.

Jeremiah also develops the themes of fidelity and infidelity, reminding Israel of Yahweh's devotion to her despite her harlotry. But God first abandons his former beloved to her enemies and to wild animals (Jer 12:7-9), having forbidden the prophet to intercede for her (11:14).[125] Yet Yahweh's rejection of Israel is a way of guiding her back to him. Von Balthasar points out that in Ezekiel, Israel first takes the Egyptians as her lovers and then, without giving up the Egyptians, takes the Assyrians as her lovers as well. "After the Egyptians and Assyrians, she makes love with the sons of Babel, sends messengers to them, and commits fornication with them, whose sexual power is like that of rutting asses and horses."[126]

Although on the surface it may seem that von Balthasar is merely recounting the history of Israel's unfaithfulness to the covenantal relationship with God, he is doing much more than that. By using the spiritual lens of finding God at work in all things, time and again, through the various prophets he is able to demonstrate that the history of Israel's relationship with God is not static and stagnant. Rather, it is embedded in a living, active relationship, and covenant of love with Yahweh. In addition to the biblical narrative of God and Israel, one can also see the influence of Erich Przywara's interpretation of the analogy of being affecting von Balthasar's theology. Przywara's understanding of the analogy of being was that every creature is a dynamism toward God. This dynamism toward God is operative when the Israelites, having realized that they have broken their covenant with Yahweh, desire to return to him and take the necessary steps to do so.

John O'Donnell asks how this central motif of the covenant can be worked out if "the more God places himself in self-gift to his people, the more humanity refuses his offer?"[127] Von Balthasar's answer to this question is found when he turns to the writings of the early Fathers and the New Testament.

Von Balthasar's view changes drastically when he begins this discussion. He begins by moving from the sinfulness caused by the Israelites' infidelity

[125] Ibid., 199–200.
[126] Ibid., 203.
[127] O'Donnell, *Hans Urs von Balthasar*, 99

to their covenant with God, to the infidelity and sinfulness of individuals, who because of their female gender bring more poignancy to the use of the word *meretrix*. Von Balthasar points out that the sinful women in the gospels always fascinated the Fathers of the Church as they represented ultimate forces and decisions that occur when humans meet God in human form. First, the sinless Mary, the Mother of God, is introduced as the initial caretaker of the Lord. "Then, her figure almost entirely disappears to emerge just once more (and then only in John) at the foot of the Cross (alongside Mary Magdalene the sinner)."[128] Between these two points, the birth and death of the Lord, there are several encounters between the Lord and sinful women, i.e., Luke 7, John 8, and John 12. The final encounter occurs when the "Magdalen, from whom seven demons were driven out, the woman splashed by the blood of the Cross is the first person to proclaim the Resurrection to the Church."[129] It is through the role of women, sinful and sinless, that Jesus is made available to humanity.

Furthermore, as Boersma comments, "For Balthasar, Christ was the narrow passage where God and creature met."[130] This narrow passage was opened because of the "yes" of a woman. Also, it is in this narrow passage that we find "divine fidelity in the face of sin."[131] Von Balthasar finds in the life, death, and resurrection of Jesus the answer to the question of "how can God remain faithful to himself and to his holiness when his people break the covenant of friendship?"[132] Von Balthasar highlights the fact that "Jesus is the fulfillment of the promises made to Israel. He is the New Covenant in person."[133] Hence, one sees the importance of the encounter that each woman referenced has with Christ, with "the New Covenant in person."

Each woman, except Mary, the Lord's mother, is a sinner. Each sinful woman, however, needs the sinless virginal woman to encounter the Lord. Without Mary's willingness to "to look after the beginnings and the Child himself," the sinful women would never have had the opportunity to meet

---

[128] Von Balthasar, *Explorations in Theology*, 205.

[129] Ibid., 205.

[130] Hans Boersma, *Nouvelle Théologie and Sacramental Ontology: A Return to Mystery* (Oxford: Oxford University Press, 2009), 134.

[131] O'Donnell, *Hans Urs von Balthasar*, 36.

[132] Ibid.

[133] Ibid.

the Lord in his human form.[134] At the foot of the cross, the holiness and purity represented by the person of the Blessed Virgin Mary is forever linked in the birth of the Church to the sinfulness and harlotry represented by Mary Magdalene.[135] Although the holiness of the Virgin Mary is not tainted by her encounter with the sinfulness of Mary Magdalene, their coming together at the foot of the cross is of critical importance for the Church. The christocentrism of this meeting should not be overlooked. Christ brings the holy one and the sinful one together at the foot of the cross. It is from the side of Christ on the cross that the Church is born. The holy and the sinful are present at this birth. For the holy one, Mary, the mother of Jesus, her mission has been accomplished. She gave birth and cared for Christ until the end of his earthly life. For Mary Magdalene, the sinful one, however, her mission has just begun. She will be the first person to proclaim the Resurrection to the Church.

Given von Balthasar's interpretation of Mary Magdalene as a sinner, her role as "the first person to proclaim the Resurrection to the Church" indicates that sinners are called to become members of the Church. Von Balthasar points out that one who is not pure can be part of something so pure—the Church, the Body of Christ, the Spouse of Christ—when he writes that all those who repent in the gospels experience liberation from sin brought by the light of the Lord. This same light:

> falls on the assertion that "Christ loved the Church and gave himself up for her, that he might sanctify her [consecrate her, *hagiazein*], having *cleansed* her by the washing of water with the word, that he might present the Church to *himself* in splendor, without spot or wrinkle or any such thing" (Eph 5:25-27).[136]

---

[134] It should be noted that all sinful humanity, male and female, have had the opportunity for a relationship with the Lord because of Mary's role as his mother.

[135] Although von Balthasar thought Mary Magdalene was the woman taken in adultery, all contemporary biblical scholars note the way in which what is actually written and named about Mary Magdalene is conflated with other texts to make her into a prostitute and adulteress.

[136] Von Balthasar, *Explorations in Theology*, 207. N.B. Of course, one realizes that von Balthasar's reading of Mary Magdalene as a prostitute is mistaken as was demonstrated by later biblical scholarship.

Repentant sinners are purified in and through the Church and its sacramental life. All that is necessary on the part of the sinner is to be open to grace and choose to sin no longer.

Von Balthasar is, however, very realistic. He juxtaposes the Lord's command in John 8:11, "Go and sin no more," with the First Letter of John 1:9: "But he is a liar if he maintains he has no sin." Given the reality that we all are sinners and have a tendency to sin, von Balthasar admonishes every Christian that "to live is to follow the way of the Cross in penance and conversion. That is how the Church sees herself before God in the liturgy, which is her surest *lex credendi*: 'Keep, we beseech thee, O Lord, thy Church in thine unfailing mercy, and since without thee human frailty cannot but fall, keep her ever by thy help from all harm and lead her to salvation.'"[137] For von Balthasar, the Church's mission is to call to holiness her members who sin. Because the Church's permanent home is not on this earth, the Church is constantly in need of the mercy and protection of the Lord who loves her and gave his life to save her.

For von Balthasar, this paradox of sin and holiness in the Church is further accentuated by "the clear and deliberate way in which St. Matthew selected the female figures in Christ's genealogy."[138] Von Balthasar points to the observation of Anselm of Laon (c. 1050–1117) on the genealogy of Christ that "these are named 'to show that Christ was to be born not only of the Jews, but of the Gentiles; not only of the righteous, but also of sinners.' One of the three Old Testament harlots is mentioned three times in the corpus of the New: Rahab."[139]

The early Fathers of the Church found the mention of the harlot Rahab (Josh 2:1-7) in the New Testament intriguing, as her story recalls many of the other stories of salvation embedded in the Old Testament. Her home is the place of refuge as the ark was in the time of the flood. The scarlet cord was the sign for her house to be passed over as was the blood of the lamb at the Passover. The meaning of "Rahab," however, does not stop with the Old Testament. As von Balthasar points out, Origen writes a detailed account of what her character means for the theology of the Church:

---

[137] Ibid., 210.
[138] Ibid., 211.
[139] Ibid.

> Rahab means breadth [*latitude*]. What is this breath if not the
> Church of Christ assembled out of sinners as well as harlots. . . .
> From a prostitute she [Rahab] becomes a prophetess . . . so you
> see how the woman who was once a whore, godless and impure, is
> now filled with the Holy Spirit. . . . She herself places a scarlet sign
> on her house, by which she escaped the destruction of her city. She
> chose none other than a scarlet sign, as a symbol of the Blood, for
> she knew that no one could be saved except in the Blood of Christ.[140]

The chosen people were sinners, and so too are those who follow Christ
in the Church.

How this understanding of the Church of Christ being assembled out
of sinners is worked out is crucial. Of this paradox, von Balthasar writes
that the Church's purity can be known only through the humans who form
her. These human beings are nature, not grace. When they unite to form
the Church, however, their nature is elevated beyond them. "Left to themselves, they can fall back again on themselves and become sinners. The
dialectic of existence in the Church lies within the undeniable reality of
these two poles: 'There is an infallibly pure Church! It is made up of fallible
human beings!'"[141] There is an inherent paradoxical dynamism at work.
Von Balthasar explicates this dynamism further when he notes that "the
Church has her grounding in Mary, but in her members she constantly
tends to lapse back into being Eve, or at best to strive upward from Eve to
Mary."[142] By using the seeming contradictions of describing the Church as
pure yet composed of sinners and of describing the Church as being sinless as Mary yet working with sinners such as Eve, von Balthasar is trying
to articulate the hope that sinners have in being called back to holiness.

> Furthermore, Balthasar observes that this struggle between holiness
> and sinfulness is internal as well as external: The seriousness of
> the issue dawns on us when we stop seeing the bride's infidelity as
> something largely outside her, in heresy, and realize that it exists
> inside her. All Christians are sinners, and if the Church does not sin

---

140 Ibid., 215.
141 Ibid., 238–39.
142 Ibid., 243.

as Church, she does sin, in all her members and through the mouths of all her members she must confess her guilt.[143]

Von Balthasar is not making judgments about the Church but merely stating the fact that sin must exist in the Church as she is composed of members who are sinners. Von Balthasar cites the writings of several of the Fathers of the Church to validate this position that, indeed, sin does exist within the Church.

> And *St. Bernard* says; "Were the bride to say that she had nothing black in her, she would be deceiving herself, and the truth would not be in her." "Once the Church has attained salvation," says *Eusebius*, "she remains in constant need of that same salvation." St. Augustine says, "We are the Holy Church. . . . Let us honor her, for she is the spouse of such a great Lord. What else can I say? Great and singular is the condescension of the Bridegroom. When he found her, she was a harlot. He made her a virgin. That she was a harlot we must not deny, lest we forget the mercy of him who set her free.[144]

Since all members of the Church, including her leaders, are human beings, they all can and do sin. Because of humanity's tendency to sin, there is always a need for conversion and transformation.

The role of the Holy Spirit in this transformation is critical. Of it, von Balthasar writes, "it is true that the Church 'has' the Holy Spirit, but that does not mean that the Church as a whole—and each of her members—does not have to pray constantly for the presence of the Spirit. It is true that the Church is immaculate (in the sense that she is the place where God sanctifies human beings with his grace), but that does not exclude but rather includes the Church's unceasing confession of sin."[145]

Von Balthasar's highlighting the genealogy of Christ brings together both the divine and human as well as the christological and pneumatological aspects of the Church. Von Balthasar sees how these various ways in which God works come together in a particular fashion in the sacrament of confession. In this sacrament, not only does the individual acknowledge

---

[143] Ibid., 244–45.
[144] Ibid., 245.
[145] Ibid., 261.

his or her sin but also the Church acknowledges that its members can and do sin. It is in and through this acknowledgment of the presence of sin in the lives of the members of the Church that the meaning of the two seemingly paradoxical words *casta meretrix* can be found. Sin, that is, the *meretrix*, is the place in the lives of human beings wherein they stand in need of grace. *Casta* is the purity that results from the reception of that grace. Since sin can be absolved in and through the power of the Holy Spirit at work in the Church, von Balthasar refers to the Church as the *casta meretrix*. The Church is the chaste whore. The Church is the place to which humanity comes laden with sin, receives forgiveness, and receives the grace to become chaste again. The Church is the place where the holy and the sinful meet. And, suggesting that the Church itself needs forgiveness, von Balthasar writes, "the Church as a whole says, 'Forgive us our trespasses!' She thus possesses spots and wrinkles. But through confession and cooperation with the grace therein received one's wrinkles can be smoothed out, the spots washed away. The Church stands in prayer in order, through confession, to be purified, and as long as men live on earth, that is how she stands."[146] For von Balthasar, the pilgrim Church, the Church on the way, stands ever holy though composed of members who sin. During this earthly pilgrimage, the indefectibly holy Church is called to work tirelessly to purify its members who sin and bring them back to a faithful relationship with the Lord. It is this work of purification of the members of the Church that allows von Balthasar to refer to the Church as a *casta meretrix*. Von Balthasar's understanding of the Church as a *casta meretrix* also demonstrates how the Ignatian principle of finding God in all things—things human, divine, holy, and sinful—is operative.

## Conclusion

The foundation of von Balthasar's work stems from finding God in all things. This focus on how one experiences, both individually and communally, the objective revelation of God in Christ Jesus can open up new ways to view theology and history.

The strength of von Balthasar's work is found in his use of this lens of spirituality as the foundation from which to view the history and theology of

---

[146] Ibid., 284.

the Church. This lens, which is based on the relationship between God and humanity, gives a dynamism to history and theology, dynamism that finds ways to bring together the holiness of God with the sinfulness of humanity. Thereby, theology in history takes on new importance because one can see a living, active God at work in the real circumstances of life. One can begin to find God in all things in the striving for holiness and in the falling from holiness—which is basic to the Ignatian principle that had such a tremendous influence on von Balthasar's theology.

Von Balthasar's theology, though christologically centered, is open to pneumatological influences perhaps because he is able to find ways to see God at work in all things, even in God's response to humanity's sinfulness. Perhaps von Balthasar's openness to pneumatology is because he is convinced of the need for the outpouring of the Spirit in order for humanity to turn away from sin and return to God.

I chose to end the "christological foundations" section of this study with von Balthasar because, although he acknowledges the significance of the role of the Spirit in the life of the Church, he places a stronger emphasis on the Word taking on flesh. Though von Balthasar's theology emanates from God in the person of Jesus Christ taking on human flesh, he always recognizes a need for the outpouring of the Spirit in order to sustain the life of Christ in the Church. Von Balthasar's work thus prepares the way for considering the "pneumatological foundations" of the holiness and sinfulness of the Church in the writings of Yves Congar, Karl Rahner, and Charles Journet. The works of Congar, Rahner, and Journet not only demonstrate how the Spirit has been at work in Scripture and tradition but also open up new ways of seeing the Spirit at work in Scripture and tradition as interpreted and lived in the Church of the current milieu. To these works we will now turn.

## Yves Congar

### Life and Career

Yves Congar was born on April 13, 1904, in the French town of Sedan, in the Ardennes. Although he wrote many works on ecclesiology, for the purpose of this study two of his works will be considered, *Divided Christendom* (1937) and *True and False Reform in the Church* (1950). I have chosen *Divided Christendom* because in it Congar handles what he considers to be the major sin of Christianity, the disunity and division that exists among Christian communities and churches. I selected *True and False Reform in the Church* because in that work, Congar carefully demonstrates how sin caused by disunity and divisions can be addressed through reform of the Church on many different levels from the membership to the leadership.

During Congar's childhood in Sedan, he had many experiences with people of different faiths and religious beliefs that helped him discover his "first and last theological love, ecumenism."[147] Of these experiences, Paul Lakeland comments:

> Congar tells us himself of spending time as a fourteen-year-old arguing with his Protestant friend about the sacrifice of the Mass, and he had many Protestant and Jewish friends in his early years in Sedan. But, he says, there was a "more mystical connection to Protestantism: Our parish Church, which was situated in a suburb of our little town of Sedan, had been deliberately set on fire by the Uhlans when they entered the Sedan on August 15, 1914. The [Lutheran] pastor, M. Cosson, offered our Curé a little Protestant chapel right next to my parents' garden and for the next six years this served as our parish Church." Here, thought Congar, was where his vocation to ecumenism was somehow kindled, and he "was often fired with a desire to make some return to the Protestants" for their generosity.[148]

Here also was planted the seed of Congar's theological career, which began when he wrote his first book, *Divided Christendom*.

Having survived the bombings and occupation of Sedan during the First World War, Congar decided in 1919 to begin his studies for the diocesan priesthood. While studying philosophy in Paris, Congar met the distinguished Dominican theologian Father Reginald Garrigou-Lagrange (1877–1964) whose influence led him to the Dominicans. In 1925, after his compulsory year of military service, he left diocesan priestly formation and

---

[147] See Paul Lakeland, *Yves Congar: Spiritual Writings* (Maryknoll, NY: Orbis Books, 2010) for Congar's life and writings; quotation at p. 15.

[148] Ibid., citing Congar, *Dialogue Between Christians: Catholic Contributions to Ecumenism* (Westminister, MD: Newman, 1966), 4.

entered the novitiate of the Dominicans in Amiens. When he finished his philosophical studies in Paris, he went on to theology studies at Le Saulchoir in Belgium, where the French Dominicans had established their seminary after having been expelled from France at the turn of the century.[149] As Aidan Nichols summarizes,

> At Le Saulchoir, Congar met his master, Marie-Dominique Chenu who communicated an enthusiasm (to Congar) for the infant Ecumenical Movement, now drawing Protestants and Orthodox together, notably at Lausanne Faith and Order Conference of 1927. . . . On the eve of his ordination to the priesthood on 25 July 1930, he prepared himself by meditating on Jesus' high-priestly prayer for the unity of his disciples in John 17, with the help of the commentaries of Thomas and the contemporary biblical scholar Marie-Joseph Lagrange. This he recognized in retrospect as the true launching of his ecumenical vocation.[150]

### Divided Christendom

These ecumenical influences on Congar's life coalesced in the publication of his first major work, *Divided Christendom*, which appeared in 1937 and marked the first public expression of a new theological orientation toward the ecumenical movement.[151] Clearly his theology was emanating from his life experiences—we will see that Congar's experiences will form a pattern of concentric circles out of which his theological thought will flow.

Jakob Laubach notes that, according to Congar, the great contribution Catholicism can make to the reunion of divided Christendom is the return, rightly understood, to the sources and to the deepest life of the Church.[152] *Divided Christendom*, steeped in *ressourcement*, was a landmark work in the field of ecumenism, although Congar later considered it as deficient.

---

[149] Ibid., 14.

[150] Aidan Nichols, *From Newman to Congar: The Idea of Doctrinal Development from the Victorians to the Second Vatican Council* (Edinburgh: T. & T. Clark, 1990), 249.

[151] Connolly, *The Voices of France*, 98.

[152] Jakob Laubach, "Yves Congar," in *Theologians of Our Time*, ed. Leonhard Reinisch (Notre Dame, IN: University of Notre Dame Press, 1964), 166–67.

Of it, Paul Lakeland writes: "it was undoubtedly an extraordinary accomplishment for a young man of thirty-three, though it led to all kinds of difficulties with the institutional authorities of the Roman Catholic Church. Congar's growing difficulty with the Church over his work for unity had, at its heart, an understanding of ecumenical theology that was threatening to a Church only just emerging from the Modernist crisis."[153]

In *Divided Christendom*, as well as in his January 18, 1935, opinion piece titled "Déficit de la théologie," published in the French Catholic newspaper *Sept*, one can see Congar's theological position beginning to take root. As Mettepenningen observes, "According to Congar, the gulf between theology on the one hand, and faith, society, and real life on the other could only be closed by emphasizing incarnation, history, and pastoral affinity. Such an approach implied the abandonment of closed scholasticism, the system that had shackled theology and separated it from reality and everyday life."[154] Congar's abandonment of scholasticism was not well received by a Church whose theological program had so emphasized it. Maureen Sullivan further notes that Congar's theology stressed a vision of the Church embedded in history that was thereby open to change. Of this she writes:

> Like so many theologians of *nouvelle theologie*, he understood the church as a mystery—divinely founded, but in the hands of humans. And just as humans grow and develop, so too the human organism called "church" must do the same, remaining always attentive to the presence of God's Spirit in its midst.[155]

Congar's "stress on an historically dynamic vision of church open to change"[156] was born out of an understanding that the tradition of the Church is a living, active tradition. Evidenced in his 1966 work *Tradition and Traditions*, Congar presents an exposé of the significance of tradition, that is, the handing on of faith from two similar but different vantage

---

[153] Lakeland, *Yves Congar*, 17.

[154] Mettepenningen, *Nouvelle Theologie—New Theology*, 47.

[155] Sullivan, *The Road to Vatican II*, 19.

[156] Ibid., 19, citing Dennis Doyle, "Different Schools of Reform Led to Vatican II," address given at the University of Dayton, October 31, 1997.

points. In the first part of this work, Congar writes about tradition from the standpoint of a Church that exists in history, with an emphasis on the human aspect of tradition; in the second part of the work, Congar delves into an understanding of tradition from a theological perspective, with an emphasis on how the divine is revealed in tradition. As Aidan Nichols observes, Congar saw the origin of the tradition in the Father's handing over the Son to betrayal at the hands of sinful men. This tradition is then handed on through the grace of the Holy Spirit by the entire Church, lay and clerical together.[157] Congar's appreciation of the role of the Holy Spirit in the mediation of the tradition of the Church through all of its members, lay and clerical, is important as it accentuates a dynamism in the life of the Church. James Connolly explains that Congar, like de Lubac, pulls these various strands together in his theological writing by envisioning the Church of Christ not in juridical terms but as God's continual dwelling with the faithful who are the Body of Christ animated and united by his Spirit.[158]

Congar's theology, then, emanates from his reflections on the Church in history, in the tradition, and in Scripture. Of his ecclesiology, Jakob Laubach observes:

> Nor does he ever stop reflecting on the Church. The right concept of Catholicity; the mystery of the Church as institution and as community; the church concept of his orthodox and Protestant brothers; the causes of the disastrous division; true and false Church reform; the layman's place in the Church; the problems of a living missionary Church in France: these are the issues around which his thinking moves as if in concentric circles.[159]

Laubach's image of concentric circles is a wonderful way to express Congar's understanding of the holiness and sinfulness of the Church. Congar's ecclesiology takes into account the fact that the Church exists in history. Because of that, as time unfolds there are issues and concerns with which the Church must deal. Sometimes the way in which the Church handles

---

[157] Nichols, *From Newman to Congar*, 253.

[158] Connolly, *The Voices of France*, 99–100, citing *Le Mystère du temple*, 281.

[159] Laubach, "Yves Congar," in Reinisch, 166–67.

these issues and concerns reflects the holiness of the Church and at other times, its sinfulness. The interaction of the human and divine aspects of the Church has a profound effect on Congar's ecclesiology, which is deeply rooted in pastoral concern for the unity of the Church. Congar realizes the necessity of addressing the sinfulness of the Church's disunity.

In *Divided Christendom*, Congar demonstrates the significant role that the members of the Church have in either fostering the unity and holiness of the Church or in causing the sinfulness and disunity of the Church. He begins *Divided Christendom* by insisting that humanity must cooperate with God, and that we as humans must allow ourselves to be his instruments. He cautions that:

> If we cannot carry through a divine work, we yet can hamper it. It is not certain that what we can undertake will be blessed by God and endued by Him with efficacy and power, but it is certain, at all events, that if we do nothing, nothing will be done; if we change nothing, nothing will be changed.[160]

Congar points out that the division of Christianity is scandalous particularly because the Church's essential nature is unity, which "is grounded in God as the Trinity; historically given in Christ; the Church his Mystical Body, the People of God, a fellowship, a great sacrament."[161] Additionally, the rupture of this unity contributes to the problem of unbelief because of its inconsistency with the ancient sources of Scripture and tradition. Unbelief, according to Gabriel Flynn, "stands at the focal point of Congar's ecclesiology."[162] Congar begins his discussion of the pastoral issues of the disunity of the Church and unbelief by discussing what should unite the Church, namely, its divinity—its being born from the Trinity. From that divine center the Church "historically given in Christ" emerges among humanity and becomes known as the people of God, the Mystical Body. It is Christ who calls humanity to belief and to unity.

---

[160] Yves Congar, *Divided Christendom; A Catholic Study of the Problem of Reunion*, trans. M. A. Bousfield, 1st English ed. (London: The Centenary Press, 1939), 2.

[161] Fergus Kerr, *Twentieth-Century Catholic Theologians: From Neoscholasticism to Nuptial Mysticism* (Malden, MA: Blackwell, 2007), 39.

[162] Gabriel Flynn, *Yves Congar's Vision of the Church in a World of Unbelief* (Burlington, VT: Ashgate Publishing, 2004), 2.

The divine origin of the Church and the necessity of unity were reinforced for Congar through his study of Scripture and the writings of the Fathers. He emphasizes the need to reestablish the Church's unity when he begins his chapter on "The Oneness of the Church" with this quotation from St. Cyprian:

> The Lord said, "I and the Father are one." And it is also written of the Father, the Son and the Holy Ghost, These three are one. Who then would believe that this unity, deriving from the divine stability and homogeneous with the heavenly mysteries, could be, in the Church, torn and broken by the opposition of wills at variance with one another?[163]

Congar observes that St. Cyprian sees the Church as an extension of the divine life of the Blessed Trinity. "The Church is not merely *a* Society, men associated with God, but the divine *Societas* itself, the life of the Godhead reaching out to humanity and taking up humanity into itself."[164]

The Church receives its life and mission from the Trinity and then imparts this life and mission to the people of God. As Congar writes,

> The Church is not a "natural" entity but a society of spiritualized beings, a community of human persons with divine persons. That a true plurality of persons should yet truly have one life is the mystery of the mystical Body. *Unum corpus, multi sumus.* The unity of the holy and undivided Trinity which is the perfect unity in plurality is the model and principle of the unity of the Church as St. Cyprian forcibly said.[165]

---

[163] Congar, *Divided Christendom*, 48, citing Cyprian, *De Unitate Ecclesiae* 6, CSEL 3.1.

[164] Ibid., 48–49.

[165] Ibid., 58. From this, the question arises as to whether Congar viewed the Roman Catholic Church as deficient because it is not in union with other churches and ecclesial communions. In 1937, when *Divided Christendom* was written, Congar would not have viewed the Roman Catholic Church as deficient as his thought on this issue was not fully developed until after the experience of Vatican II. Gabriel Flynn notes on pages 143–44 of *Yves Congar's Vision of the Church in a World of Unbelief* that Congar's understanding of ecumenism changed from what he wrote in 1937, *Chrétiens désunis*, and what he wrote in 1982, *Diversités et Communion*.

For Congar, then, the Church is sinful to the extent that it is in disunity and division and is holy to the extent that it mirrors the Trinity in its unity.

## True and False Reform

In *True and False Reform of the Church* (first published in French in 1950), Congar describes the critical role of the Spirit in the Church's striving for holiness:

> The root of the holiness of the church is shown to be hidden in God with Christ and the Holy Spirit. There is a visible holiness, seen in the works that demonstrate a sort of proof of holiness. But the essential holiness of the church, deeper than the works of its members, characterizes its very existence. That holiness can be affirmed by faith in the Holy Spirit, whose proper activity this is.[166]

Having established that the Church's holiness is the "divine action attributed to the Holy Spirit," Congar expounds on how that call to holiness is evident in the various definitions operative when using the word "church": the Church as institution; the Church as assembly of the faithful; the Church as hierarchical; and the Church as a mixture of all three of the aforementioned.

He defines the first sense of Church as the institution coming from God. It contains the principles essential to the faith, namely, revealed doctrine, sacraments, apostolicity, and charisms.[167] This first meaning of Church, as a divine institution, highlights the faith of the Church and takes its starting point from God. The "gifts of grace," the sacraments, and the faith all come from God to humanity in and through the Church. In this sense of the word, the Church's claim to holiness rests on essential principles: "the faith of the church cannot deviate, and its sacraments, insofar as Christ is in them, are saving and effective (the meaning of the expression *ex opere operato*)."[168] Furthermore, since these principles do not age and have no limitations, in respect to them, the Church is incapable of

---

[166] Yves Congar, *True and False Reform in the Church*, trans. Paul Philibert (Collegeville, MN: Liturgical Press, 2011), 92.

[167] Ibid., 92–93.

[168] Ibid., 93.

failure and has no need to reform itself.[169] Having argued that the Church's holiness is indefectible from its constituent principles, Congar turns to the question of under what circumstances and in what sense can it be said that the Church is sinful. In this regard, he suggests that the word "church" should be considered from the perspective of those who comprise it.

In the second sense of the word "church," it means the Christian people, those humans who, with all their freedom, their weakness, their instability, and their essential fallibility, comprise the membership of the Church. It is through these people that sin and various other weaknesses penetrate into the Church.[170] This second meaning of the word "church" focuses on the assembly of the faithful. Because the focus is not on God but human beings who are weak and sin, one can refer to the Church as sinful. The acknowledgment of the Church as sinful is not a cause for despair for Congar; rather, it emphasizes the significance of the Holy Spirit's role in the sanctification of the Church and its members.

Congar further observes that acknowledging that there is sin in the Church spurs the members to sanctification through openness to the Spirit. If the Church is only a completely spiritual communion with God, then sinning, in effect, would destroy communion with God in Christ and one would need to leave the Church because of one's sin. But the Church's proper work is precisely to ceaselessly purify sinners from their sin. The Church is itself the place and the instrument for the application of Christ's redemption.[171] The Church's concern for the ongoing purification and sanctifying of its members is critical because it is in this work that the members participate in the redemption gained through the life, death, and resurrection of Jesus Christ.

Of the third meaning of Church—as hierarchical—Congar notes that: "It is easy enough to admit that there are members of the church who sin and who fail. But there are also faults and defects of hierarchical figures— churchmen—who not as individuals but precisely as hierarchical person- ages are at fault in the very exercise of their ecclesiastical functions."[172]

---

[169] Ibid.
[170] Ibid., 95.
[171] Ibid., 98–99.
[172] Ibid., 101.

Congar then describes the various ways throughout the history of the Church that those churchmen failed in their important role.

Congar acknowledges that sin is present in the Church in spite of "the habitual governance of the Holy Spirit over the church."[173] The presence of the Holy Spirit

> does not rule out particular failings, nor does it always supply for the limitations or the ignorance of churchmen, even those placed in highest roles. Even if it is certain that the church as such will never teach error, nonetheless the part left in the church to the activity of human beings means that the church will not necessarily always, at each moment and in each circumstance, enjoy the best manner of teaching or the greatest plenitude of teaching.[174]

In summary, Congar writes:

> Churchmen, charged with hierarchical powers and responsibilities, failed over and over not only in their personal lives, but also in the exercise of their administration. They failed to the degree that they were not pure instruments of the action of God (as in the celebration of the sacraments or the charism of infallibility linked to their function), that is, to the degree that they expressed themselves. The church itself, through the voice of its most important pastors, has several times admitted this.[175]

He cites the example of the legates at Trent as well as many other popes, cardinals, bishops, priests, and religious throughout the history of the Church who have admitted that through their failings, particularly with regard to the exercise of power the Church has suffered. Flynn reminds us how important it is for Congar to hold the infallibility of the magisterium and the errors of Church leaders in a delicate balance:

> Without denying the guarantee of infallibility, under certain determined conditions, for the magisterium of the Church, Congar admits the sinfulness of Church leaders, precisely as leaders and in the manner in which they exercise their authority. Bishops and

---

[173] Ibid., 103.
[174] Ibid.
[175] Ibid., 105–6.

theologians, acting alone as well as in groups (theological schools), can be mistaken in their teaching, thereby contributing to the possibility of weakness (*défaillance*) and poverty (*misère*) in the Church.[176]

Congar also notes the importance of understanding the sins of those in power in the Church in light of "historical conditioning. From the moment that the priesthood, the magisterium itself, but above all the power of government are concretely exercised in history, they are touched by the conditioning of historical situations."[177] Congar is not excusing "these imperfections in the church's history." Drawing on Newman, he observes:

> The church in carrying out its sacred ministries in the framework of human history, was led to allow itself to adopt concrete expressions that were somehow unworthy. In this same perspective, he [Newman] came to distinguish between two conditions of Catholicism (or of Anglicanism). First there was the level of principles, for example, the formal dogmas of the church, and then there was the level of religion lived spontaneously and concretized in the passage of human history—namely, the common doctrine expressed in popular beliefs and practices, deriving from controversies and historical circumstances. In sum, this is the difference between Catholicism (or Anglicanism) *at rest*, and Catholicism *in action*. In changing the frame of reference a bit, we might call this today the difference between "Christianity" and the "Christian world." Newman went on to add that the objections and the oppositions of Anglicans and Protestants to Catholicism were in general due more to Catholicism "in action" than to Catholicism and its principles "at rest."[178]

Given Congar's understanding via Newman of historical conditioning, it is clear that he is trying to respond to the Church's seemingly intransigent position against modernity. Congar notes that Newman's understanding of Catholicism *at rest* and *in action* should not be isolated from each other. Rather, Congar sees that just as his three senses of the Church describe one Church, so too Catholicism *at rest* and *in action* are descriptive of one Church.

[176] Flynn, *Yves Congar's Vision of the Church in a World of Unbelief,* 166.
[177] Congar, *True and False Reform in the Church,* 106.
[178] Ibid., 109–10.

Congar aptly summarizes Newman's thought when he writes, "The very church that a strict historian sees as a human society (second and third senses) possesses, as the faithful know, truly divine internal principles (first sense). They know it is the very church whose mystery consists precisely in this fusion of the divine and human that is so difficult for us to perceive."[179] Congar is trying to explain how these various senses of church bring diverse yet important nuances to one's understanding of the Church.

With these three senses of the Church in mind, Congar reiterates his position that the Church "is both holy and full of sinfulness, both indefectible and fallible, both perfect and still subject to many historical imperfections. In the church, what comes from Christ is holy and without defect, but what comes from the exercise of human freedom is subject to mistakes."[180] As a true student of *ressourcement*, Congar quotes from the Fathers to substantiate his position.

> St. Ambrose who said, "*Immaculata ex maculates*—the Immaculate is made up of the sinful."[181] . . . St. Ephrem who said, "The whole church is the church of penitents and the whole church is the church of those who were perishing."[182]

There is no doubt that for the Fathers of the Church and for Congar, the Church is divine and yet human. The Church is of God and therefore can lay claim to holiness; yet, the Church is of people and can suffer from their sins.

Aspects of these three senses of Church are folded into Congar's fourth sense which Gabriel Flynn describes in this way:

> the assembly of people united with the Father in which Jesus Christ is present through his Spirit, the sacraments and the Word. There is a clear recognition of the essential weakness (*faiblesse*) of the Church in its earthly and visible element.[183]

Congar's fourth sense of Church brings all three senses of Church together, uniting the divine aspects of the institution revealed by God as a divine

---

[179] Ibid., 111.
[180] Ibid., 112.
[181] Ibid., citing Ambrose in *Commentary on the Gospel of Luke* in Lucam 6.21.
[182] Ibid., 112–13.
[183] Flynn, *Yves Congar's Vision of the Church in a World of Unbelief*, 167.

institution with its human aspects as demonstrated by its members and its existence in history.

In his preconciliar writings, Congar clearly recognizes the sin and weakness in the Church visible in its people and structures and simultaneously stands firm in his belief of the holiness of the Church because of its rootedness in the Trinity, sacraments, and the Word. After Vatican II, however, his thought undergoes a development that he acknowledges in his 1979 book, *I Believe in the Holy Spirit*. Gabriel Flynn notes this major shift in Congar's thinking: "Congar's unequivocal acknowledgement in *Je crois en l'Esprit Saint* that the Church is sinful constitutes a clear and definite development in his thought which raises an obvious difficulty: it marks a departure from the carefully formulated theology of sin articulated in Congar's earlier writings, where he defends the Church's holiness."[184] This development in Congar's understanding of the Church as sinful began after Vatican II and is beyond the scope of this study.[185] This postconciliar shift can be seen to have grown out of his continued disturbance at the divisions and disunity of Christianity and developing emphasis on the eschatological nature of the Church. This further development allowed Congar to see the Church more clearly in its pilgrim nature and to see holiness as eschatological, something to strive for with the grace of the Holy Spirit.[186] Additionally, one can deduce that the growth in Congar's theological understanding of the Church was in some ways a by-product of the discussions on the Church's holiness and sinfulness in which he was involved at the council.

In Congar's preconciliar thought, the sinfulness of the Church was not only a by-product of divided Christendom but also closely related to how one exercised his or her membership in the Church. Congar describes membership in these categories:

> There is perfect membership of the Church—and so of Christ—in one who lives according to the principles of the new life of reconciliation with God which Christ has given to His Church. But there is imperfect membership of the Church, and of Christ, in one who

---

[184] Ibid., 169.

[185] Congar's position change will be noted in the discussion that occurs in chap. 2 regarding the influence of Congar's work at/after the council.

[186] Flynn, *Yves Congar's Vision of the Church in a World of Unbelief*, 170.

lives only by one or other of the principles of the new life. It is because the benefits of the New Covenant are many that it is possible
to belong to the Church in varying degree and to claim membership
of it on various grounds.[187]

Congar's understanding that an individual or the "dissident bodies, re-
garded as separate ecclesiastical communities"[188] can be considered by
the one Church to possess membership in it in an imperfect way is very
significant. This idea of imperfect membership allows for dissident Christians[189] to be "in possession of something which belongs to the nature and
integrity of the one Church, some fibres of her very being."[190] This idea
also provides a starting point for leaders of Christian churches to begin
to discuss roads toward reunion.

In addition to "dissident Christians," the concept of imperfect membership can be used to refer to those whose membership is in the one true
Church but who do not fulfill the responsibilities and duties inherent in
being a member. For the dissident Christians, through this concept of
imperfect membership, Congar acknowledges that their community of
faith has some, though not all, elements of sanctification and salvation.
By referring to their membership as imperfect, Congar is recognizing
the elements of holiness within their belief system. For those inactive
Catholics, Congar points out that they are not living the holiness of life to
which their membership in the Church calls them. Because of this, Congar
refers to those inactive in their faith commitment as imperfect members
also. Although both the dissident Christian and the inactive Catholic are
referred to as imperfect members, the discussion of their membership begins at different places. For the dissident Christians, the discussion begins
from the standpoint of holiness; for those baptized but inactive members
of the Church, the discussion begins from the standpoint of sinfulness.[191]

---

[187] Congar, *Divided Christendom*, 227.

[188] Ibid., 241.

[189] Ibid., 246.

[190] Ibid.

[191] From Congar's explanation in *Divided Christendom* on p. 235 that "The bad
Catholic gives no glory to God: on the contrary, he offends Him, and is heading for
final loss. The other does give glory to God, though imperfectly, and is on the way to

Because the idea of imperfect members is another way to refer to the extent of the holiness and sinfulness of a member in the Church, Congar's concept adds an important nuance to the discussion of the holiness and sinfulness of the Church, one of being "on the way," of being on pilgrimage. The concept of perfect and imperfect membership in the Church can be equated with holiness and sinfulness in the Church. Imperfect membership allows for all members to remain in communion with the Church though they are not living according to all that Christ and the Church calls them.

Congar argued that all humanity is invited to participate in the Church's living tradition by being open to the working of the Holy Spirit. Through participation in this living tradition, each human being can receive through the power of the Holy Spirit the grace from God that is necessary to live a life of holiness; thereby, a person can grow from imperfect membership into perfect membership.

In 1965, almost thirty years after he wrote *Divided Christendom*, Congar reflected on this work with these words:

> When I examine the position that I held, there is nothing of importance to alter. The conclusions to which I had been drawn seemed to me to remain valid. Where exactly am I with regard to this? I believe more and more that the essence of ecumenism is for the Catholic Church to live fully and purely her life; to purify herself as much as possible, to increase in loyalty, in good will, and in depth of prayer and union with God. It is in being fully herself, in all force of her vigor, that she should develop her ecumenical power.[192]

For Congar, the Church's holiness is intimately tied to her union with God and her vigorous pursuit of that unity through the work of ecumenism. The Church of the twenty-first century and beyond needs to involve itself deeply in the work of ecumenism, particularly because the scandal of

---

be saved. The one has Catholic nationality, yet has not the Church for his fatherland. The other was born in a far country, and outwardly bears an alien nationality, but his true spiritual fatherland is the Church," one can surmise the differing places from which Congar begins his discussion of each one's membership.

[192] Yves Congar, "The Need for Patience," *Continuum* 2, no. 4 (December 1, 1965): 686.

divisions in Christianity can be a contributing factor in the widespread unbelief in the Christianity.

## Conclusion

In evaluating Congar's work, one can easily conclude that his concerns for the Church are deeply pastoral, i.e., how to reform the Church so that the sinful divisions in Christianity can be overcome. One must be careful, however, as people can hijack Congar's theology, with its strong pneumatological base, to call for changes in the Church without regard for the living, active tradition of the Church or to use reliance on the Spirit as an excuse to maintain the status quo. Neither discontinuity with the tradition nor stagnation is an option in the pneumatological theology of Congar. For Congar, openness to the Holy Spirit implies a dynamism that encompasses a movement from sin toward the holy. This dynamism is reflected in the development of the living, active tradition of the Church throughout its history. To embrace Congar's theology, one must be well versed in the tradition and Scripture so as to discover ways for the historical experience of the Church to address current issues in its life. If a balance is not kept between tradition and Scripture and openness to the promptings of the Spirit, one is not keeping with the true spirit of Congar's theology.

The strength of Congar's work is its applicability to various moments in history. Although he is writing for the pre–Vatican II Church about critical pastoral issues of its time, e.g., sinful divisions within Christianity, the role of the laity, and true and false reform in the Church, they are issues that are always present in the Church. Congar's reliance on the Holy Spirit as the way through problems in every age is profound. It is evident that for him, the Holy Spirit has been an integral grace and gift to the Church from its inception. There is no need to be paralyzed by the problems and scandals facing the Church. Rather, the need is to acknowledge the critical role of the Holy Spirit in the Church as it makes its pilgrimage through this "in-between" time, between creation and the eschaton. With such an openness to the Holy Spirit, Congar is convinced that this pilgrim Church will be able to live a life worthy of its call to holiness. Congar himself grows in his understanding of the role of the Spirit and its effect on the holiness of a sinful Church as is evidenced in his postconciliar work *I Believe in the Holy Spirit*.

Congar's theology was clearly influenced by the divisions and disunity that he experienced in the Church during his childhood. He then tried to articulate ways in which to address this concrete, pastoral problem through bringing the call to unity found in tradition and Scripture to bear on this problem and others that the Church in the twentieth century was facing. Clearly Congar's work, rooted deeply in pneumatology, advances the Church's understanding of itself as having both sinful and holy aspects.

Karl Rahner was also trying to find ways to open the Church to the modern world. In his theological study, Rahner found that there was a need to combine current modern philosophical thought with an understanding of the contemporary experience of God, and thereby open up new possibilities for the Church to be able to communicate and minister to the modern world. It is to these new ways of communicating with the modern world that Rahner offered to theology that we will now turn.

## Karl Rahner and a New Language of Faith: A Church of Sinners

### *Life and Career*

Karl Rahner[193] was born on March 5, 1904, the middle child of a middle-class family in the city of Freiburg in the Black Forest. After finishing secondary school, he entered the Society of Jesus, following his brother Hugo. During his years of Jesuit formation and philosophical and theological study in Austria, Germany, and the Netherlands, he was exposed to the ideas from which he would develop his thought and begin a critical dialogue with the prevailing neoscholastic theology and modern German philosophy. His thought would also bear the influence of the Ignatian spirituality into which he was being initiated.[194]

Of these various early influences on Rahner's theology, Richard Lennan notes the influence of Martin Heidegger—in whose seminars Rahner had participated while a doctoral student at the University of Freiburg in

---

[193] A work that traces the life and writings of Karl Rahner is William V. Dych, *Karl Rahner* (New York: Continuum, 2000).

[194] Declan Marmion and Mary E. Hines, "Introduction," in *The Cambridge Companion to Karl Rahner* (Cambridge, UK: Cambridge University Press, 2005), 2.

Breisgau—whose primary focus was on the subject's experience of God. From him and others, Rahner reclaimed theology of past years that was characterized by its emphasis on identifying God as central to all human experience, rather than to the narrowly "religious" sphere of life.[195] One of Rahner's major contributions to theology was to discover within modernity's turn to the subject the possibility of God's self-communication.[196] This contribution made it possible for Rahner to construct new ways for the Church to communicate more effectively with the modern world by joining elements of modern philosophical thought with peoples' experience of God. Of this, Alister McGrath writes:

> the most important aspect of Rahner's theological program is his "transcendental method," which he saw as a Christian response to the secular loss of the transcendence of God. . . . Rahner argued that the recovery of a sense of the transcendent could only be achieved through a reappropriation of the classical sources of Christian theology, especially Augustine and Thomas Aquinas.[197]

Rahner's desire was to make the Catholic faith more accessible to the humanity of the twentieth century as he "believed that modern men and women were living in a radically changed situation, one that called theologians to find new ways to articulate Catholic theology. We needed a new language of faith."[198] Rahner's new language began with "God who enters into relationship with humans through God's own self-communication, which is his primary understanding of grace, 'uncreated grace.'"[199]

For Rahner, reclaiming the earlier tradition of the Church was critical because this tradition preserved the fact that it is in and through the Church that humanity experiences God's self-communication. Lennan

---

[195] Richard Lennan, *The Ecclesiology of Karl Rahner* (Oxford: Clarendon Press, 1995), 7.

[196] Kevin Vanhoozer, "Human Being, Individual and Social," in *The Cambridge Companion to Christian Doctrine*, ed. Colin E. Gunton (Cambridge, UK: Cambridge University Press, 1997), 171.

[197] Alister E. McGrath, *Historical Theology: An Introduction to the History of Christian Thought* (Malden, MA: Wiley-Blackwell, 1998), 240.

[198] Sullivan, *The Road to Vatican II*, 30.

[199] Marmion and Hines, "Introduction," *The Cambridge Companion to Karl Rahner*, 5.

notes that Rahner understands the Church as a "sacrament of Christ, the means by which his grace was embodied in history."[200] In "Sacramental Piety" (1963), Rahner describes how people experience grace through the sacraments:

> A sacrament takes place . . . as a dialogical unity of the personal acts of God and of the person in the visible sphere of the Church's essential (that is, given to it directly by Christ himself) sanctifying, official actions. In the sacraments, the incarnation and process of becoming historically tangible of grace reach their high-point.[201]

Rahner's emphasis on each believer's response to the gratuitous gift of grace in his or her life lays the groundwork for his 1947 essay on the topic of the "Church of Sinners."[202] In it, he deftly traces the history of the two important aspects of the Church of sinners, that of sinners in the Church and the sinful Church. Rahner's consciousness that the Church is a visible, historical reality in the world is a critical component to his explanation of how sinfulness can be a part of the Church. Unlike de Lubac, who emphasizes the paradoxical aspect of sin and holiness within the Church, Rahner holds that the Church "is not simply a pure paradox since holiness belongs to the church in a different way than its sinfulness. The former is a manifestation of its true nature, whereas the latter is present like a disease in an otherwise healthy body."[203]

Before exploring the sinful aspects of the Church, Rahner asks how one can refer to the Church as sinful if in the Creed we declare her as holy. He questions why the Donatists, who demanded holiness of all those in the Church, were condemned as schismatics in the fourth and fifth centuries. Were they not merely practicing what they preached? Furthermore, wasn't Luther's Reformation just a reaction against sinfulness and corruption within the Church? Was he too not just trying to profess his

---

[200] Lennan, *Ecclesiology of Karl Rahner*, 25.

[201] Karl Rahner, *Theological Investigations*, vol. 2, *Personal and Sacramental Piety*, trans. Karl- H. Kruger (Baltimore, MD: Helicon 1963), 109–34.

[202] Karl Rahner, "The Church of Sinners," *Theological Investigations*, vol. 6: *Concerning Vatican Council II*, trans. Boniface Kruger (Baltimore, MD: Helicon Press, 1969).

[203] Daniel T. Pekarske, *Abstracts of Karl Rahner's Theological Investigations 1–23* (Milwaukee, WI: Marquette University Press, 2003), 197.

belief? As Richard Lennan notes, these questions led Rahner to reflect on the Church's holiness from a different vantage point:

> When Rahner referred to the holiness of the Church, his focus was on the mystery of the Spirit's presence, which established the Church as the sacrament of God's revelation in Jesus. The presence of the Spirit in the Church manifested itself through the gospel and the sacraments, which even the sinful members of the Church could not impair. In addition, it was also "the saints," those characterized by their openness to God and commitment to others, who gave shape to the Spirit's presence. On the other hand, Rahner insisted that the principle of sacramentality implied that it was legitimate to describe the Church as sinful when its members or structures witnessed to something other than the movement of the Spirit.[204]

As a practical theologian who wanted to find new ways to articulate the faith to the modern era, Rahner confronts the serious problem of the presence of sin in the Church. Rahner is not trying to walk a tightrope between the holiness and sinfulness of the Church. Rather, he is acknowledging the presence of sin in the Church and the impact that that sin has on a person's faith. He describes how detrimental to a person's faith the sinfulness of the Church can be:

> Is there anything repeated more frequently than that church-people are not better than others, that the Church too has failed? And these reproaches and the troubled temptations against faith that arise from them have, from the purely human point of view, a certain amount of right on their side. There stands the Church, and she declares herself necessary for salvation, she comes to us in the name of a holy God, she declares herself to be in possession of all truth and grace, she claims to be the one ark of salvation among the flood of sin and corruption, she believes herself commissioned to convert and save all men. And this very Church which comes to us with such claims, why, look at her!—so they will say—look how she seems to use two different yardsticks: she proclaims to poor, troubled humanity the Sermon on the Mount with its "impossible" demands, but her

---

[204] Richard Lennan, "Ecclesiology and Ecumenism," in *The Cambridge Companion to Karl Rahner*, 135.

official representatives seem to let these demands rest very lightly
on their own personal shoulders.[205]

Rahner's theology is deeply rooted in humanity's experience of God
through the grace that permeates reality as it is and not in some uto-
pian form. He realizes the importance of acknowledging the many ways
throughout history that the actions of the Church, particularly those of
her leaders, have been perceived as inconsistent with the holiness that
she ascribes to herself. Lennan further observes that for Rahner the sins
of the Church's hierarchy were not limited to their private lives, because

> the members of the Church could refuse obedience to such author-
> ities only when commanded to do something objectively sinful.
> The belief that a particular directive from a superior was motivated
> by a sinful narrowness was not itself sufficient justification for a
> refusal to obey.[206]

For Rahner, no one, not even the hierarchy, "is protected against the effects
of sin." This fact highlights the role that human freedom plays and opens
new insights into why Rahner, in his preconciliar reflections could write
that the Church can and should be called a "Church of Sinners."

Rahner begins to unpack his theological reflection on the sinfulness
of the Church by stating, "for us the question is not at all one of how we
as Christians who believe in the holiness of the Church manage to deal
with our *purely human* experience of the unholiness of the Church. Rather,
the question is a dogmatic one: namely, what does Revelation itself have
to say about the unholiness of the Church?"[207] For Rahner, the critical
question is not how humanity comes to terms with the unholiness of the
Church but how God's self-communication with humanity in and through
the Church makes the Church a place wherein sinners are accepted, wel-
comed, forgiven, and healed.

Rahner begins to answer these critical questions from the vantage point
of God's self-communication in revelation by simply stating that "It is an

205 Rahner, "Church of Sinners," 254.
206 Lennan, *Ecclesiology of Karl Rahner*, 29.
207 Rahner, "Church of Sinners," 255.

article of faith that sinners are members of the Church. Even sinners who are destined to be lost can truly and really belong to the Church."[208] Rahner cites tradition and Scripture which attest to this belief. In Scripture, there are several gospel passages in which Christ teaches that the righteous and sinners exist together in this world and will be separated in the judgment of the world to come; and perhaps there is no greater example in the tradition of the Church of the acceptance of sinners as members of the Church than that of St. Augustine in his handling of the Donatist controversy in the early fourth century.

In regard to Rahner's insistence that sinners belong to the Church, Lennan comments that the presence of sin does not proclaim that God has forsaken the Church but highlights the mystery of the way God's grace works. Therefore, members should not reject the Church because of its sinfulness but

> hope that the Church would be led through its sinfulness to a deeper conversion. While the Church's sinfulness was a burden for its members, Rahner was emphatic that the Church's sacramental structure precluded the possibility of separating its corrupt human elements from the immaculate Spirit of God.[209]

Rahner makes an important distinction between membership and commitment when he notes that "the sinner does not belong to the Church in the same full sense as the justified person."[210] One can be a member without ever letting what that means affect his or her life. "It is possible," Rahner says, "to have in certain circumstances a 'valid sacrament' which in point of fact does not cause any grace in the recipient of the sacrament."[211] Similarly, membership for some exists only for appearances and does not include striving for holiness of life.

Because all members sin in various ways and to various extents, the Church is sinful. As Lennan reminds us, however, "Rahner stressed that sin in the Church, just as in the life of the individual, was never anything

[208] Ibid., 256.
[209] Lennan, *Ecclesiology of Karl Rahner*, 30–31.
[210] Rahner, "Church of Sinners," 258.
[211] Ibid., 259.

other than a contradiction of its own deepest reality."[212] Rahner sums up
the presence of sin in the Church in these words:

> she is something real, and if her members are sinners and as sinners
> remain members, she is herself sinful. Then the sins of her children
> are a blot and a blemish on the holy mystical Body of Christ itself.
> The Church is a sinful Church: this is a truth of faith, not an elemen-
> tary fact of experience. And it is a shattering truth.[213]

Rahner is careful to point out that the members who are sinners are not limited to one category of member. Lay, religious, cleric—all have at times been
a part of that shattering truth. No state in life is exempt. Rahner notes that

> sin happens in opposition to the impulse of the Spirit and the norms
> and the laws always proclaimed by the Church. But this is surely
> what is so great about this *faith* in the sinful Church, that she can
> really do all these things and yet (unlike all human organizations
> falling away from their ideals) remain the bride of Christ and the
> vessel of the Holy Spirit, the only means of grace, from which no
> one can separate himself by appealing to her own ideal, accusing
> her of no longer being what she "once" was (she never was it), or
> what she ought and claims to be.[214]

Rahner emphatically holds that the Church, though a Church of sinners,
though a sinful Church, never loses her holiness with regard to her connection to Christ, her sacraments, her dogma, and the lives of many of
her members: "Thus, even the sinful Church did not cease to proclaim,
through the indwelling Spirit, the holiness of God."[215]

Having laid out the rationale for how a Church whose very essence
is holy can also lay claim to being composed of sinners, Rahner turns to
the climactic point of his essay: "What must be our own attitude in order
that this eternal scandal of the Church does not become a scandal for us
but rather an edification of our own Christian life and so contribute for

---

[212] Lennan, *Ecclesiology of Karl Rahner*, 31.
[213] Rahner, "Church of Sinners," 260.
[214] Ibid., 261.
[215] Lennan, *Ecclesiology of Karl Rahner*, 31.

our part also to the building up of the Church?"[216] His answer is simple: each member of the Church must contemplate his or her own sin, short-comings, or contribution to this eternal scandal. It is only from that very personal vantage point that we can experience the grace of conversion for our own individual lives. Only through such experiences of grace can one go forth and help others to experience the grace of conversion and thereby build up the Church in the world.

### Conclusion

In evaluating Rahner's work, one might try to criticize him for being so intensely focused on the individual, on the subject and his or her re-lationship with God, that there seems to be little or no need for the faith to be mediated by the Church. As Richard Lennan points out, however, this critique is not valid. Lennan observes that Rahner "stressed that the Church's existence as the sacrament of Christ's presence in history iden-tified the Church as more than a human response to grace. Although it was not the source of salvation, the Church was certainly the channel through which salvation was offered to the world."[217] So, the Church, though sinful, as the means through which humanity experiences grace in history, is essential and nonnegotiable in Rahner's ecclesiology and in the life of the believer.

The strength of this major essay on our subject, "Church of Sinners," is that Rahner has handled not only "one of the most agonizing questions of ecclesiology which persistently recurs throughout the history of dogma, but also a question of deep significance for the individual's life of faith."[218] Rahner's contribution to the discussion of the holiness of the Church is of particular import because he pursues this question from the vantage point of the existence of sin in the Church. Most important, however, Rahner calls the reader to reflect on the presence of sin in his or her own life. By doing so, he is the consummate pastor who tries to provide places for a human being to be open to his or her own personal experience of

---

[216] Rahner, "Church of Sinners," 265.
[217] Lennan, *Ecclesiology of Karl Rahner*, 33.
[218] Rahner, "Church of Sinners," 253.

the grace of God. Rahner's contribution takes lofty, provocative questions about sin and holiness in the Church, and in the end, makes them very personal—perhaps on the basis of his experience of Ignatian spirituality.

Rahner, unlike the other theologians under consideration here, makes the bold claim that the Church is a Church of sinners. Because Rahner's theology is concerned with the individual's experience of the transcendent God, he does not dwell on the Church as Bride of Christ or the Mystical Body of Christ. Rather, Rahner begins with the individual's experience of the grace of God in the Church that allows the individual to acknowledge his or her sin. By beginning with the individual who can and does sin, Rahner is trying to find ways to explain how the Church can be a Church of sinners. Because his theological starting point is the individual, the Church must acknowledge that it is sinful simply because it is composed of people who can and do sin.

Rahner's theological reflections on sin in the Church opened up a new language for the Church to deal with that undeniable aspect of its nature. Without people, there is no Church. People sin. Therefore, sin in the Church is a reality with which all the members, clergy and laity, must deal. Rahner's blunt assertion that the Church is a Church of sinners was viewed as extremely controversial and certainly not in keeping with the way theology was being done through the use of neoscholastic manuals.

In order for the leaders of the Church to be open to the ideas about the holiness and sinfulness of the Church put forth in the writings of the theologians considered in this study thus far, someone had to bridge the gap that was beginning to form between the neoscholastic manual mode of doing theology and the new methods of doing theology that had roots in *ressourcement*. Charles Journet, who found ways to use the neoscholastic categories along with Scripture and patristic sources in his theological works, was instrumental in bridging this gap.

## Charles Journet: A Bridge to Vatican II

The theology of Charles Journet does not fit neatly into the category of *ressourcement* because, while he references the scriptural and patristic sources in his writing, he uses the language of neoscholasticism. His book, *The Theology of the Church*, written in 1958 just prior to the convocation of the Second Vatican Council, however, has been included because it looks at the Church through the lens of pneumatology and offers an important insight into how sin and sinners are in the Church. This ecclesiological work also demonstrates the divide that had to be overcome between theologies that were steeped in neoscholasticism and those that were proponents of *ressourcement*. In his study of both Yves Congar and Charles Journet, Dennis Doyle describes the struggle that the Church was soon to undertake in Vatican II by juxtaposing Congar's theology, which focused on the Holy Spirit and attended to the dynamic, historically developing Church to Journet's, which focused on the Church as an objective, aesthetically engaging given.[219] Although the theology of both men was clearly focused on the life of the Church, they had very different ideas of how that life should be lived out under the inspiration of the Holy Spirit. Both men were influential in the days leading up to Vatican II. Because the fathers of Vatican II chose to embrace many of the ideas of the *ressourcement* theologians, Journet's theology is not as well known today as Congar's. Since, however, Journet is the last ecclesiologist of note prior to the Second Vatican Council, a brief overview of his life and work is part of the story recounted here.

## Life and Career

Charles Journet[220] was born on January 26, 1891, in Genève, Switzerland. He studied theology at the seminary in Fribourg and was ordained to the priesthood for the diocese of Fribourg on July 15, 1917. For the first seven years of his priesthood, he was involved with pastoral work in the diocese. After that, from 1924 to 1965, Journet was assigned to the seminary of Fribourg as a faculty member. During his time as "professor at the Grand Seminaire in Fribourg, Journet made magnificent contributions which have served to orient modern theology into a full-blown ecclesiology."[221] Journet's desire to explore the mystery of the Church in his theological writing was shared with his contemporaries de Lubac and

---

[219] Doyle, *Communion Ecclesiology*, 38.

[220] A work that traces the life and writings of Charles Journet is Guy Boissard, *Charles Journet (1891–1975): biographie* (Paris: Salvator, 2008).

[221] Connolly, *The Voices of France*, 96.

Congar, whose works also helped to open the way for "the Church herself to become the object of patient reflection and thought."[222]

During the years in which Journet taught at the seminary, Church leaders continued to react strongly against the Modernist movement. They insisted that ecclesiology be taught through the ecclesiastically accepted method of neoscholastic manuals. Avery Dulles notes that

> these Latin manuals showed a predilection for juridical catego-
> ries. Christ was seen as the founder of the Church; the Church
> was presented as a "perfect society" in which the officeholders had
> jurisdiction over the members; the pope, as vicar of Christ, was
> depicted as ruler of the entire society. The functions of the Church
> were studied primarily under the rubric of power. Two powers were
> generally recognized: order and jurisdiction.[223]

Given the tremendous influence that the fear of Modernism was having on the world of theology, Church leaders believed it necessary to cling to what they knew, namely, the neoscholastic model of order and jurisdiction, so that the Church would be safeguarded from Modernist errors.

Charles Journet, however, had a different idea regarding how ecclesiology should be presented. Thomas O'Meara notes that Journet's theology demonstrated a distinctive and original neoscholastic ecclesiology. Journet, an independent thinker, drew from the individual scholastic schools—Jesuit, Dominican, German, Roman—and expanded his research to include other sources: patristic, canonical, Baroque scholastic, manualist, and papal texts.[224] In many ways, Journet's theology was very much in keeping with the "both/and" principle that is operative in the Catholic tradition. He tried to take the neoscholastic categories and find their foundations in Scripture and the writings of the patristic authors. Dennis Doyle points out that "Journet retained much of the Thomistic terms and concepts even as he transformed their applications. He did this, though, by reading Aquinas's understanding of the Church against the

---

[222] Ibid., 97.

[223] Avery Dulles, "A Half Century of Ecclesiology," *Theological Studies* 50, no. 3 (1989): 420.

[224] Thomas O'Meara, "The Teaching Office of Bishops in the Ecclesiology of Charles Journet," *Jurist* 49, no. 1 (1989): 24.

background of the patristic tradition."[225] Journet himself explained that "in Augustine and Aquinas, I found a theology of the Church more living, more far-reaching and more liberating than that commonly contained in manuals. In them we feel the active presence of a vision of the Mystery of the Church understood as an extension of the Incarnation."[226]

In his survey of seminary manuals, Daniel A. Triulzi, SM, observes that "they used Aristotelian categories of causality (some explicitly, some implicitly) to describe the Church. The formal cause of the Church is the hierarchy; its material cause is the laity; its remote efficient cause is the Trinity and its immediate, efficient cause is Christ; its final cause is the beatific vision."[227] Given this neoscholastic understanding of the Church, Journet's "rethinking of the formal cause of the Church, that which makes it what it is, that which determines its essence is not the hierarchy, but the Holy Spirit"[228] becomes a link between neoscholasticism and *ressourcement*. Of this shift, Doyle comments, "in Journet's approach, to recognize the Holy Spirit as the formal cause of the Church is to move behind the seminary manuals to the real St. Thomas."[229]

This background information on the work of Journet is critical in order to appreciate his contribution to how the Church understood its holiness and sinfulness as it entered the threshold of Vatican II. Journet's insights about the Church's holiness were a significant development in the field of ecclesiology because they took into account the scholastic and neoscholastic seminary manual method, the scriptural and patristic writings and the societal milieu. Journet's theological reflection tried to put various theological methods, particularly the manual method and *ressourcement*, into dialogue and thereby bridge the gap between scholasticism/neoscholasticism and Scripture and the patristic authors. Dennis Doyle points out that "for all of his limitations from a contemporary perspective, Journet

[225] Doyle, *Communion Ecclesiology*, 41, citing Journet, *Church of the Word Incarnate*, vol. 1, xxx.

[226] Charles Journet, *The Church of the Word Incarnate: An Essay in Speculative Theology*, trans. A. H. C. Downes (London: Sheed and Ward, 1955), xxx.

[227] Doyle, *Communion Ecclesiology*, 41.

[228] Ibid., 42.

[229] Dennis M. Doyle, "Journet, Congar, and the Roots of Communion Ecclesiology," *Theological Studies* 58, no. 3 (S 1997): 466.

evoked a sense of awe, mystery, and love concerning the Church as the mystical Body of Christ and as the presence of the Holy Spirit among Christians."[230] We will now turn to Journet's thought on the nature and mission of the Church.

In his preface to Journet's *Theology of the Church* (1958), Bishop Pierre Mamie writes, "The Church, 'holy and immaculate,' is at the heart of Cardinal Journet's theology. She was also the center of his life."[231] Before one can get to the heart of Journet's theology, one must grapple with how Journet understood the nature of the Church. For Journet, the most profound way of "regarding the Church is with the eyes of faith. Then, the Church is seen in her mystery, in her profound reality, as the Body of Christ, inhabited by the Holy Spirit, who directs her and dwells in her as her Guest."[232] The role of the Holy Spirit in the Church is of major importance in Journet's works, but not in the same manner as that of the *ressourcement* theologians.

For example, Journet's understanding of the role of the Holy Spirit is not the same as that of Yves Congar. Congar sees the Holy Spirit as expressive of the dynamism in the living, active, developing tradition of the Church. Journet emphasizes the Holy Spirit as dwelling and rooted particularly in the ordained ministers of the Church who exercise the role of dispensing the sacraments. The dynamism of the Spirit in Journet's theology is curtailed because he is trying so hard to fit the Spirit into the neoscholastic categories of causality. Yet, his gift to the Church at this time is that he attempts to present almost a middle ground between neoscholasticism and *ressourcement*.

Journet points out that "the Church appears to us as a reality that is a visible mystery. She is a mystery because of the life that animates her and that is totally divine. She is visible by the brilliance that shines forth from that life and by means of which that life is announced and communicated."[233] The Church is a mystery because within her dwells the Holy Spirit

[230] Ibid.

[231] Charles Journet, *The Theology of the Church*, trans. Victor Szczurek (San Francisco: Ignatius Press, 2004), xxxv.

[232] Ibid., 3.

[233] Ibid., 8.

as the uncreated Soul of the Church and the Church is visible because
that divine life is

> like a created soul in her. It descends upon men from on high. It is
> incarnated in them. It animates them, gathers them in Christ and
> transforms them interiorly. The permanent virtues and hidden
> powers that it confers on them will be for them the principle of
> a new mode of being and acting. Thence, both in the measure in
> which they allow themselves to be "animated" by the Spirit of God
> and by the gifts that he pours upon them, a change is produced
> even in their exterior condition and comportment. These external
> manifestations, taken together, are the body of the Church, that by
> which she becomes visible to the world.[234]

Francis Sullivan explicates Journet's theology as it describes the life of
the Church:

> The Church is made visible through its body, which consists of the
> activity of its members that is animated by the soul of the Church,
> that is, by charity that is given and nourished by the sacraments,
> and is guided by the hierarchy. Since it is the ordained who dispense
> the sacraments and provide the leadership of the Church, they have
> a special role in making possible the activity that is animated by
> charity that is "sacramental and oriented."[235]

When Journet gives the ordained the role of guiding the Church in its
exercise of charity, Sullivan sees this as an attempt to go "beyond the
manuals by making the Holy Spirit the Church's formal cause and by
relegating the hierarchy to the category of immediate efficient cause,[236]
thereby reclaiming an earlier understanding of the role of the Spirit in
the life of the Church.

To substantiate his claim that the Holy Spirit is the Church's formal
cause, Journet looks to the scriptural and patristic understandings of

---

[234] Ibid., 9.

[235] Francis A. Sullivan, "Charles Journet," personal communication with author,
July 16, 2010.

[236] Doyle, *Communion Ecclesiology*, 42.

the foundation of the Church. He writes, "It is the Holy Spirit who, in Scripture, is designated as the efficient principle of the Church. The Spirit animates the Church and makes her known."[237] He draws on three Scripture passage to support his understanding of the Holy Spirit as the formal cause of the Church: Acts 2:1-4, which relates the coming of the Spirit at Pentecost; 2 Cor 13:14, which relates the unity with which the Spirit gifts the Church; and 1 Cor 12:7-13, which details the various charisms that the Spirit pours out on believers for the benefit of the Church. "*The Spirit is the Supreme responsible subject of the Church's activities*. It is the Spirit, therefore, who, through the humanity of Jesus, forms the Church and introduces her to the world."[238] The Spirit's ultimate responsibility for the Church's activities is exercised when the Spirit descends on the apostles at Pentecost and sends them forth to preach the Gospel. Journet also contends that "*the Spirit rules the Church by a special providence*."[239] By this, he is referring to the fact that the Spirit works through the ordained who are dispensers of the sacraments and entrusted with the leadership of the Church by giving them the gifts necessary for these aforementioned roles. Finally, he states that the "*Holy Spirit fills and moves the Church*."[240] This is the place in which Journet might have embraced a more dynamic understanding of the role of the Holy Spirit in the Church. His commitment to the neoscholastic categories, however, is so great that he is not able to move beyond inserting the Spirit into hierarchical categories.

Journet notes that the Spirit moves hearts to embrace the Church and her teaching. Through the instrumental role of the ordained, the Spirit guides the Church and her teaching in the way of truth. "He sends the rays of his grace, even into the deepest darkness to illumine our minds, to bring them the first lights of faith, to dispose them to welcome in due course the message of his teaching Church: to warm hearts once again, to purify them, to prepare them to receive the graces of consummation he gives only in the sacraments, in the Eucharist most especially."[241] The Spirit is clearly the

---

[237] Journet, *The Theology of the Church*, 69.
[238] Ibid., 70.
[239] Ibid., 71.
[240] Ibid., 73.
[241] Ibid.

animating life force of the Church; however, for Journet the Spirit's work in and through the ordained is of paramount importance to the Church.

Understanding how Journet sees the Holy Spirit working in the Church as the uncreated soul of the Church, we can now look at what has come to be known as the chief insight of his ecclesiology:

> The Church, which is not without sinners, is nevertheless without sin: "Sinners are members of the Christ and his Church, but not in the same way as the just. The former *belong* to the Church in which one finds the just, but they are incapable themselves of *constituting the Church*."[242]

Although Journet agrees that there are sinners within the Church, because of his understanding of the role of the Holy Spirit, he cannot agree with theologians such as Rahner who claim that those sinners make the Church itself sinful. Journet contends that the Church as a body is not sinful, yet can have individual members of the body who sin. Those individual members who sin remain in the Church by virtue of the grace of their baptism which never leaves them. Journet summarizes his position by stating that both the just and sinners are members of the Church only because of what is holy in them. Therefore, the Church is totally holy. In sinners, sanctity is imperfect, fettered; in the just, it is perfect, free. The just are members in themselves and in a salutary manner; sinners are members to a lesser degree and in a nonsalutary way. "Christ continually looks down from heaven with a special love upon his immaculate Bride, *intemeratam Spousam*, who struggles in exile in this world."[243] For Journet, understanding that the just are perfect members of the Church and sinners are imperfect members allows for her sanctity to always be present while acknowledging sinners in her midst.

The reference to the Church as the immaculate Bride that struggles in this world is significant because Journet is acknowledging that

> the imperfect sanctity is authentic and, sometimes, profound. By its very nature (and not always consciously) it is ordered toward the

---

[242] Ibid., xxviii.
[243] Ibid., 216–17.

fuller sanctity of the Church, like a stem to its flower and a flower to its fruit. Truly proceeding from Christ, it truly tends toward the perfection of his Mystical Body, which is not possible except where the hierarchy is complete and the primacy of Peter recognized.[244]

For Journet, perfect sanctity is tied to whether or not people accept the primacy of Peter and the role of the hierarchy. Since Christ himself chose Peter as the rock upon which he built his Church, and since the Spirit came upon Peter and the others at Pentecost, giving them the power to go forth and preach the Gospel, Journet believes that the instrumental role of the papacy and the hierarchy is necessary for the sanctity of the Church. Although the pope and the members of the hierarchy can be imperfect and sinful, Journet explains that the "power of order itself, which is a pure instrument in the hands of God, is not sullied or diminished. St. Augustine writes on John 1:33: 'When Peter baptizes, it is Christ who baptizes; when Judas baptizes, it is Christ who baptizes.'"[245] In the area of the jurisdictional powers of the ordained, however, Journet cautions that although they are not the subject of the Church's sanctity, sanctity is fitting to the ordained, not by their own merit, but "tendentially," by reference to the Church's sanctity. This tendential, ministerial sanctity can be subject to error and injustice, though this does not alter the sanctity of the Church.[246] Therefore, even though members of the Church can sin, even though those who exercise sacramental powers can be weak and sinful, and even though the jurisdictional decisions made by the ordained can be in error, none of these sins detracts from the holiness of the Church. The Church remains without sin. Francis Sullivan sums it up best when he comments on Journet's theology of the sinfulness and holiness of the Church:

> Sinners belong to the body of the Church in a purely material sense, but since no sin is animated by charity, their sins are not part of the body of the Church. Obviously, if the sins of its members do not belong to the body of the Church, they cannot affect its holiness,

[244] Ibid., 217.
[245] Ibid., 219.
[246] Ibid., 223.

which is manifested by that activity of its members which is animated by the Church's soul.[247]

Journet's use of the neoscholastic categories cast the Church as completely without sin. Because of this starting point, he is clearly on a very different trajectory than the other theologians whose theological reflections on the holiness and sinfulness of the Church have been traced in this chapter.

## Conclusion

In evaluating Journet's work, his weakness can be seen as his continued use of the categories of neoscholasticism. Though he does rethink the formal cause of the Church and reclaims the Holy Spirit as the essence of the Church and as the source of holiness of the Church, his continued exaltation of the role of the ordained does not lend itself to seeing the myriad ways that the Holy Spirit is active in the life of all the members of the Church. Journet's theological reflection does, however, begin to set the stage for the Spirit as the source of the Church's claim to indefectible holiness and the members, lay and ordained, as the material source of the Church's sinfulness.

A major contribution of Journet's theology is that it challenged the leaders of the Church at that time to see that the Holy Spirit, not the hierarchy, was the formal cause of the Church. This insight that he reclaimed from the tradition provided a way to breathe new life into the neoscholastic categories which clung to the institutional structure as the formal cause of the Church. His writings are significant because they begin to create a bridge between the two methods of doing theology, neoscholastic and *ressourcement*.

## Major Preconciliar Contributions

From this survey of six theologians between the years 1910 and 1960, one can see how ecclesiology was developing and drawing on new methods

---

[247] Francis Sullivan, "Do the Sins of Its Members Affect the Holiness of the Church?" in *In God's Hands: Essays on the Church and Ecumenism in Honour of Michael A. Fahey, SJ*, ed. Michael S. Attridge and Jaroslav Z. Skira, Bibliotheca Ephemeridum Theologicarum Lovaniensium 199 (Leuven: Leuven University Press, 2006), 253.

of doing theology. Clarifying how the Church understood itself and its claim to be simultaneously indefectibly holy and composed of members who are sinners was one of the important contributions that these theologians made during these years.

In 1910, the neoscholastic manual method presented an understanding of the Church that was deeply rooted in its institutional structure. A defensive, apologetic posture was taken by the Church. Modernity was seen as something not to be engaged but avoided. The historical methods that many other Christian denominations were advocating were considered a danger to magisterial teaching, tradition, and the Catholic understanding of Scripture.

Between 1910 and 1960, the works of these six theologians helped prepare the way for Vatican II to deal with the Church in general and the question of her sinfulness in particular. Mersch by his work retrieving the scriptural and patristic sources for the Mystical Body of Christ doctrine; de Lubac by his use of paradox to bring the humanity and divinity of the Church into conversation; von Balthasar by his application of spirituality to these sources; Congar by his call for unity in Christendom; Rahner by his plea to make the faith accessible to the modern mind and his new approach to Thomism; and Journet by reworking of the neoscholastic categories in terms of the Holy Spirit: all encouraged an engagement with, rather than a retreat from, modernity. As a result, during this period, the defensive stance of the Church toward modernity slowly began to change. How?

First of all, the social and political turmoil during the era of 1910 to 1950 that included the Great Depression and two world wars exercised a significant influence on the lives of the six theologians discussed in this study. Their works advocated a new method of doing theology that can be seen in part as a response to the traumatic history of the world at that time and the concomitant inability of neoscholastic theology to address this context. Through uncovering the historical and scriptural foundations of the Church, they were trying to rediscover how the Church had understood itself in the past in order to find ways to apply Scripture and tradition to the urgent questions emerging in this century.

Despite being considered suspect by Church leaders because of their new theological methods, these six theologians set the stage not only for a change in the way theology was done but also for the Church to discuss its nature in terms of holiness and sinfulness. Although the paradox of a holy and sinful Church can never be resolved, retrieval of biblical and patristic understandings of the Church as the Mystical Body of Christ by some of these theologians allowed for new understandings of the nature and mission of the Church. For example, the christological view of the Church as Christ's Mystical Body helped the Church come to terms with its own historicity. Because of its rootedness in the life, death, and resurrection of Christ, the Church is not a stagnant institution but a living organism that has grown and developed since its inception. This christological emphasis also developed into a more expansive understanding of the Church's holiness and sinfulness because the Church as the Mystical Body of Christ incorporates the visible and invisible, temporal and eternal aspects of the Church. These paradoxes found in the Christology of the early Fathers helped open in new ways the Church's mission of making Christ present to all humanity in the twentieth century.

Second, this christological foundation of the Church also brought with it a deeply spiritual component. It uncovered a renewed understanding based on the writings of the Fathers that God was living and active within history and theology and within the individual lives of people. This development gave theology and history a concrete and practical significance.

Third, the pneumatological foundation of the Church also emerged in new ways during the fifty years from 1910 to 1960. Because these theologians used new methods to do their theology, they were able to put a renewed emphasis on the dynamic role of the Holy Spirit in the life of the Church. Their preconciliar work would enable Church leaders during the sessions of Vatican II to begin to address, albeit slowly, scandalous issues such as the divisions and disunity that existed in Christianity. By delving into the historical reasons for such disunity among Christians, theologians retrieved the idea of the Church as being on a pilgrimage. Consequently, the idea of the pilgrim Church opened up new ways to address the sinfulness of disunity in the Church and the need to heed the call to unity and holiness. If the Church is on pilgrimage on earth, there is room for dialogue and for trying to find ways to reform the Church through the study of history, tradition, and Scripture. The role of the Holy Spirit in the life of the Church proved to be critical in such discussions about how a pilgrim Church can live and grow into a life worthy of its call to holiness.

The role of the Spirit in the Church, however, is not limited to institutional issues of unity and the reform necessary to achieve such unity.

The new understanding of the Spirit's role in the life of the Church also had a profound effect on understanding how individuals respond to the grace freely given to humanity through the Spirit. Seeing the Church as the means by which this grace is embodied in history was another major development during these fifty years. The Church began to be seen more as an instrument of grace in people's lives and not primarily as a juridical institution. This existential aspect of ecclesiology was instrumental in making the faith more present in the real lives of people in the world. Emphasizing that grace is a gift freely given which the recipient can choose to accept or decline also brought into play the way in which each individual's response contributes to the holiness and sinfulness of humanity in the Church's life. This existential aspect of ecclesiology contributed to helping the Church engage modern philosophical thought with theology, thereby helping to prepare it for the questions that would be posed at Vatican II.

As evidenced by studying the work of Charles Journet, not all of the theologians during this period were able to move beyond neoscholastic categories in their understanding of the nature and mission of the Church. Nevertheless, even those who used the neoscholastic categories tried to rework them so that new christological and pneumatological understandings of the Church could be incorporated into their theology.

Although the issue of how the Church can lay claim to its holiness while being composed of people who can and do sin was not resolved once and for all, the writings of these theologians with their emphases on the christological and/or pneumatological foundations of the Church helped advance this conversation.

Prior to the retrieval of these historical and scriptural foundations of the early Church, the role of the hierarchy and the ordained was so stressed that it left little or no room for the role of the laity in the ongoing life of the Church. The work of the theologians discussed in this chapter contributed to the renewed understanding of the nature and mission of the Church as articulated at Vatican II, in which the laity assume a more integral role in the Church's life and have a unique competency in regard to the evangelization of the secular and civil order. The emergence of a much more dynamic role for the laity helped the Church to define itself more forcefully in light of all its members. This new awareness of the Church as composed of lay and clerical members who can and do sin made it possible to describe the Church as sinful. At the same time, awareness of the pilgrim nature of the Church underscored the necessity that all its members seek to grow in holiness.

In chapter 2, I will trace the contributions that the work of the six theologians discussed here made in the preparation, discussions, and final promulgation of *Lumen Gentium*, the Dogmatic Constitution on the Church (1964) at Vatican II. Only some of these theologians were present, in person, at the sessions of Vatican II: Mersch died in 1940; von Balthasar was not invited; Journet, de Lubac, Congar, and Rahner were in attendance at the council in varying capacities. But their works presented two possible routes for the fathers of Vatican II to take: on the one hand, Journet's steadfast insistence that the Church herself is not sinful, or the trajectory launched by the other five theologians. We will now proceed to discuss the route taken and the impact it had on the proceedings of the council.

# CHAPTER TWO

# *Lumen Gentium* on the Holiness and Sinfulness of the Church

## The Contributions of the Preconciliar Theologians

*For the vision still has its time, presses on to fulfillment, and will not disappoint. If it delays, wait for it, it will surely come, it will not be late.*

—Habakkuk 2:3

As we have seen, between 1910 and 1960 the way of doing theology began to move beyond the method of the neoscholastic manuals to a more pastoral and experiential approach. The new theologies proposed by the theologians discussed in chapter 1 were part of a larger movement known as *ressourcement*. Although they were initially met with suspicion, these new theologies found a reception at Vatican II. It took much struggle during the deliberations of the Second Vatican Council, but the bishops and other Church leaders finally acknowledged and began to embrace these new methods. Because the council fathers began to consult with some of the theologians discussed in chapter 1, the Church was able to experience a major shift in its understanding of its nature and mission and embrace a much more pastoral orientation.[1]

---

[1] Giuseppe Alberigo and Joseph A. Komonchak, eds., *The History of Vatican II*, vol. 3, *The Mature Council, Second Period and Intersession, September 1963–September 1964* (Maryknoll, NY: Orbis Books, 2000), 511; "European theologians, encouraged by the fruitful conciliar experience during the second period, were laying the foundation for continuing their collaboration after the celebration of Vatican II. The isolation and distrust that Congar and Rahner, De Lubac and Metz, Schillebeeckx and Chenu had suffered during the 1950's seemed light years away."

In order to understand this major theological shift, it is important to consider some brief historical background as well as some hermeneutical principles for reading *Lumen Gentium*. Then we will be in a position to consider the contribution the preconciliar theologies made to the understanding of the holiness and sinfulness[2] of the Church in *Lumen Gentium*, one of the four constitutions of the council.

## The Council in Context

When Angelo Giuseppe Roncalli was elected pope at seventy-seven years old and took the name of John XXIII on October 28, 1958, no one could have imagined that just three months later, on January 25, 1959, he would announce his plans to call a general council for the universal Church. The announcement, which was made at the Basilica of St. Paul Outside the Walls at the end of the Week of Prayer for Christian Unity, stirred up worldwide interest.

> The news spread all over the world in just a few hours, arousing attention, interest, and expectations with such a range of both fundamental and subtle differences that even the most accurate account cannot fully document them. The most immediate general impression was that a profound change was taking place in the heart of Catholicism; everyone had a different idea of which outcomes and developments were most important, but what is really striking is the hope and expectation created in so many circles.[3]

Hopes and expectations about the council were further augmented by the fact that John XXIII "did not give birth to a fully formed council, like Minerva springing from the brain of Jupiter. Its aims and nature were

[2] Bernard E. Yetzer, *Holiness and Sin in the Church: An Examination of* "Lumen Gentium" *and* "Unitatis Redingratio" *of the Second Vatican Council* (Ann Arbor, MI: UMI, 1991), 4. It is important to keep in mind Yetzer's caveat that "the complexity of the question of the sinfulness of the Church precludes a simple yes or no." There are many nuances that must be tended to so that the Church is not empty of meaning or members or so that the members are not emptied of their sinfulness.

[3] Giuseppe Alberigo, *A Brief History of Vatican II* (Maryknoll, NY: Orbis Books, 2006), 4.

gradually sketched out, tested, and deepened in terms of their weight and implications as the pope continued to reflect upon them."[4]

Openness to the ideas and opinions of others about what issues and concerns should be handled in this council was made evident when the pope solicited the input of the bishops from around the world to elicit the problems and topics that the council should consider. A further indication of the openness that John XXIII wanted in the dialogue between the Preparatory Commission and the bishops worldwide was shown when he

> entrusted responsibility for this phase to the secretariat of state and not to the feared—and sometimes hated—Supreme Congregation of the Holy Office (formerly the Inquisition). By doing this, he prevented the "supreme congregation" from enjoying a monopoly over the Council. This decision clearly showed the pope's preference that the Council not be prepared in the traditionally doctrinaire style and intransigent atmosphere of the Holy Office.[5]

The decision about who would be responsible for the preparatory phase of the council was not universally applauded. Some wanted it to remain in the hands of the Holy Office; others wanted it to be entrusted to a commission outside of the Curia.[6] John's decision to place the preparation of the council in the care of the secretariat of state, however, opened an entry point for the involvement of theologians such as de Lubac, Congar, and Rahner at the council. If the Holy Office had been given this responsibility, these theologians, whom they had heretofore silenced, would probably not have been given a hearing.

Of those theologians in attendance at Vatican II, Abbot Christopher Butler (1902–1986), a Scripture scholar present at the council as a *peritus*, writes:

> There were at hand to advise its [the council's] members and to collaborate with its commissions not only canon lawyers and strict Thomists who enjoyed the favour of the curia, but a host of others of a very different type, including men like de Lubac, Karl Rahner, and

---

[4] Ibid., 9.
[5] Ibid., 11.
[6] Ibid.

Congar, who had all suffered for their convictions, but who became, in fact, in large measure the artificers of the theology of Vatican II.[7]

The presence of these previously suspect theologians who were now invited to serve the council fathers as *periti* certainly added to the expectation about the work that the council would be undertaking.

The tone that John XXIII set for the council was contained in the opening address, which he wrote in his own hand. John asked the council to be pastoral, to apply the medicine of compassion. He also cautioned the council fathers not to engage in scholastic disputation, arguing fine points of specific doctrines. Rather, he asked that they direct their efforts toward a fundamental renewal of the universal Church in living dialogue with the present time and its needs.[8] Pope John was clearly doing all that was in his power to set the stage for a pastoral council to ensue. With this brief historical overview of the announcement and preparations for the council, we will now turn to some hermeneutical principles that are important to keep in mind while studying Vatican II's Dogmatic Constitution on the Church, *Lumen Gentium*.

## Some Hermeneutical Considerations

Before delving into *Lumen Gentium*, I will consider some hermeneutical principles proposed by Ormond Rush in *Still Interpreting Vatican II* with regard to the council's documents. His method encompasses three elements: (1) a hermeneutics of the author, (2) a hermeneutics of the text, and (3) a hermeneutics of the receiver.[9] For the purposes of this study, it is the hermeneutics of the authors and texts that are most important.

Rush explains the hermeneutics of the author as an attempt to reconstruct the intention of the author or authors of a text. In the case of Vatican

---

[7] Basil Christopher Butler, *The Theology of Vatican II*, rev. ed. (Westminster, MD: Christian Classics, 1981), 14–15.

[8] John XXIII, "Allocutio in Sollemni SS. Concilii Inauguratione," Speech Given October 11, 1962, http://w2.vatican.va/content/john-xxiii/la/speeches/1962/documents/hf_j-xxiii_spe_19621011_opening-council.html.

[9] Ormond Rush, *Still Interpreting Vatican II: Some Hermeneutical Principles* (Mahwah, NJ: Paulist Press, 2004), xi.

II, this means trying to discover what the bishops intended to communicate.[10] Using Paul Ricoeur's hermeneutical categories, Rush notes that "a hermeneutics focused on the authors looks to 'the world behind the text' and the historical factors that conditioned its formulation."[11]

> Vatican II was an event that can be understood as an attempt by the bishops to restate the church's self-understanding by re-interpreting the Catholic tradition in the light of contemporary challenges. Its reception of the tradition was multifaceted. The reality which it "received," in the above sense, was the living tradition, including the elements of scripture, doctrinal formulations, previous councils as events, the scholarly work of past and contemporary theologians, and so on. Ultimately, of course, the reality that it was receiving was what had been initially entrusted to the church: *revelation*, that is, the Gospel, the Christ event, God's self-communication and self-disclosure, God reaching out to humanity through Christ in the power of the Spirit. It had been from the beginning the mission of the church to tradition what it had received.[12]

In reinterpreting the tradition for the modern world, the works of the *ressourcement* theologians of the twentieth century, which go back to the sources of the tradition, became of critical import to the task at hand. Rush observes the results of this work:

> With a focus on *ressourcement* of the riches of the pre-Scholastic tradition, these approaches had come to be broadly characterized as the *nouvelle théologie*. In receiving the insights of these approaches, the Council was coming to grips with "history" as impacting its self-understanding and the very nature of its documents.[13]

Two major shifts occurred when the bishops embraced the new historical consciousness. First, the bishops themselves became conscious "of the dramatic nature of what they were involved with and of what they were doing. They were making 'history.' And, in the second sense, 'history as

[10] Ibid., 1.
[11] Ibid.
[12] Ibid., 3–4.
[13] Ibid., 8.

lived experience,' the bishops began to come to grips with the relationship of faith and history."[14] Understanding in new ways that faith is lived out in history helped the bishops view the Church and its role in the world in a more dynamic manner. The Church needed to be involved with the world and help shape history. Isolation from the world was no longer an option. The time for a more serious engagement with the world had arrived.

Because the *ressourcement* theologians helped the bishops to be at ease with this new historical consciousness, Rush notes that "the Council can also be seen as an event of ecclesial reception of consensus in contemporary theological scholarship."[15] He describes this aspect of the council's work:

> Over four years of conciliar debate, there is evidence of an explicit widening of approach beyond the narrow perspective of the Counter-Reformation Catholicism and later neo-Scholastic frameworks, and a reception of the fruits of decades of research of biblical, patristic, liturgical, historical, and ecumenical *ressourcement* theologians. Vatican II's innovation was to break not only with the church's exclusive recourse to the neo-Scholastic framework and to embrace other methodologies, but also with the style of Catholicism that had surrounded the neo-Scholastic mentality. In this sense, it could described as a micro-rupture—a desire to break with the attitudes to theological scholarship characterizing the era of Pius X and the Modernist crisis.[16]

In understanding the effect this attitudinal change had on opening the Church to a new mode of doing theology, it is important to consider the hermeneutic of the text, especially matters "of genre, rhetoric, style, structure, intratextuality, and intertextuality."[17]

The genre, rhetoric, and style of the conciliar documents are very much related. Rush observes that "the genre of Vatican II's documents is unique in the history of conciliar teaching. Pastoral in intent, the council deliberately intended not to attack specific errors but to renew the church in the

---

[14] Ibid., 8–9.
[15] Ibid., 11.
[16] Ibid.
[17] Ibid., 36.

light of urgent contemporary issues."[18] The new rhetoric and style in these documents were marked by the use of both persuasion and dialogue. By citing John O'Malley's work on the style of Vatican II, Rush explains the stylistic changes in these words:

> "For the first time in history, official ecclesiastical documents promoted respectful listening as the preferred mode of proceeding, as a new ecclesiastical 'way,' a new ecclesiastical style." Collaboration rather than mere consultation, captured in Vatican II's teaching on "collegiality," although with deep roots in the history of the church, "indicates a break with a long-standing and then current style of ecclesiastical dealing." The pastoral intention of the popes and bishops is therefore best exemplified in the challenge they set themselves: *to pastor in a new way.*[19]

This "pastoring in a new way" is evident from a close analysis of how the conciliar documents were finally put together. Careful consideration was given to the placement of chapters, sentences, and even words, so that the entire document exuded a consistent pastoral intent behind the words being written.

In one of the earlier drafts of *De Ecclesia*, for example, the chapter on the hierarchy preceded that of the chapter on the people of God and the laity. As Alberigo and Komonchak report, however, Cardinal Suenens (1904–1996), archbishop of Mechelen in Belgium, in his capacity as one of the four moderators of the council, "proposed the division of chapter III of the schema on the Church into two parts, one on the People of God in general, to be placed before the chapter on the hierarchy, and the other on the laity, to be made the fourth chapter, after the treatment of the hierarchy."[20] Because of Suenens's intervention, in the final version of *Lumen Gentium*, "The Mystery of the Church" and "The People of God" preceded

---

[18] Ibid.

[19] John W. O'Malley, "Vatican II: A Matter of Syle," in *Weston Jesuit School of Theology 2003 President's Letter* (Cambridge, MA: Weston Jesuit School of Theology, 2003), 5, quoted in Rush, *Still Interpreting Vatican II*, 39. O'Malley's argument is more fully developed in *What Happened at Vatican II* (Cambridge, MA: Harvard University Press, 2008).

[20] Alberigo and Komonchak, *The History of Vatican II*, 3:24.

the chapters on the hierarchy and the laity. This ordering of the chapters marks a significant shift in theology and in how the Church understood itself. In Vatican I, the hierarchy were presented as the primary receivers of the Word of God. In Vatican II, the whole People of God, laity and hierarchy, are the primary receivers of the Word of God. The placement of these chapters was a monumental shift in understanding the Church, its nature and mission.[21]

Careful attention to structure was taken within *Lumen Gentium* and each conciliar document, and also among all of the documents. Rush observes that intratextuality and intertextuality of the conciliar documents are also what

> the supplementary hermeneutical principle enunciated by the 1985 Synod of Bishops called for: "The theological interpretation of the conciliar doctrine must consider *all the documents both in themselves and in their close interrelationship*, so that the integral meaning of the Council's affirmations—often very complex—might be understood and expressed."[22]

Rush also points out the need for a hermeneutics of the receivers. He notes the need to interpret the documents of Vatican II by recalling that when John XXIII first announced the council, he often referred to it as a "new Pentecost." If this is so, he argues, "a new Pentecost demands a new pneumatology, a pneumatology of reception."[23] He offers a sketch of such a reception pneumatology, which begins with the dynamism that occurs when God the Father takes on human flesh in the person of Christ Jesus. In that interaction, when the Father gives himself to the Son and the Son in his humanity receives the divine life of the Father, Rush notes, the Holy Spirit is at work. It is from this trinitarian foundation that the Church emanates, and through the mission and ministry of the Church humanity is invited into a sharing in the divine life of the Trinity.[24] Although Rush values the hermeneutics of the authors and of the texts in interpreting

---

[21] Rush, *Still Interpreting Vatican II*, 39–40.

[22] Synod of Bishops, "Final Report," 22, quoted in Rush, *Still Interpreting Vatican II*, 46, emphasis mine.

[23] Rush, *Still Interpreting Vatican II*, 69.

[24] Alberigo and Komonchak, *The History of Vatican II*, 3:48.

the documents of Vatican II, for Rush, the most important principle of hermeneutics is an openness and reliance on the Spirit who is "the dynamic of giving (*traditio*) and receiving (*reception*) between Father and Son, and between the Triune God and humanity."[25] This pneumatological hermeneutic is the foundation of the documents of Vatican II.

Keeping in mind Rush's acknowledgment that the role of the Spirit in the preparation and promulgation of the documents of Vatican II was indispensable, it is nevertheless important to note that currently there is a debate taking place within the Church on the hermeneutics of the postconciliar reception of the documents. This debate took on greater urgency after the election of Joseph Ratzinger, Benedict XVI.[26] In December, 2005, not even a year into his pontificate, Pope Benedict XVI gave a Christmas address to the Curia[27] in which he set out the hermeneutical issues regarding the reception of Vatican II:

> There is an interpretation that I would call "a hermeneutic of discontinuity and rupture"; it has frequently availed itself of the sympathies of the mass media, and also one trend of modern theology. On the other, there is the "hermeneutic of reform," of renewal in the continuity of the one subject-Church which the Lord has given to us. She is a subject which increases in time and develops, yet always remaining the same, the one subject of the journeying People of God.[28]

As Massimo Faggioli observes in *Vatican II: The Battle for Meaning*,[29] the pope's words fueled the current debate on the hermeneutics of Vatican II. Faggioli contends that "a correct hermeneutical approach to the issue of continuity/discontinuity calls for a non-originalist reception of the Vatican II,"[30] that is, interpreting the council in light of the "law of unintended

---

[25] Rush, *Still Interpreting Vatican II*, 70.

[26] Massimo Faggioli, *Vatican II: The Battle for Meaning* (Mahwah, NJ: Paulist Press, 2012), 1.

[27] "Christmas Address of His Holiness Benedict XVI to the Roman Curia," December 22, 2005, http://w2.vatican.va/content/benedict-xvi/en/speeches/2005/december /documents/hf_ben_xvi_spe_20051222_roman-curia.html.

[28] Ibid.

[29] Faggioli, *Vatican II*, 1.

[30] Ibid., 137.

consequences,"[31] a concept that John O'Malley uses to describe some of the unexpected effects that the council had on the postconciliar world of Catholicism. Indeed, such a hermeneutic is aptly described by Faggioli as "non-originalist." Roberto De Mattei, however, counters Faggioli's proposal by upholding Pope Benedict's assertion that the council must be interpreted through the lens of history, by which Benedict means only in continuity with the past.[32] This study will argue that there may be a third way, namely, the hermeneutic of development of understanding through a retrieval of the patristic and biblical sources of the tradition.

## Vatican II: The Context

The convoking of a second Vatican Council came upon the Church as a complete surprise. Vatican I, which opened on December 8, 1869, had to end abruptly in October 1870 because of the invasion and capture of Rome by the army of the Italian government during the Franco-Prussian War.[33] During this brief council, only two major doctrinal statements, one of which was the doctrinal definition of papal infallibility, were completed. There was an obvious need for another council.

Because Vatican I had ended so abruptly, the lingering question of whether Vatican II was a continuation of Vatican I had to be addressed prior to John XXIII's formal opening of the Second Vatican Council on October 11, 1962. Since Vatican I had hastily disbanded without an official act of closure when the Italians seized Rome on September 20, 1870, one of the first things John XXIII did, once he had made up his mind to hold Vatican II, was to declare Vatican I definitively closed.

### Opening of the Second Vatican Council

On October 11, 1962, at St. Peter's Basilica, John XXIII formally opened the Second Vatican Council. In his opening remarks, he stated that "the greatest concern of the Ecumenical Council is this: that the sacred deposit

---

[31] Faggioli, *Vatican II*, 140.

[32] See Roberto De Mattei, *Il Concilio Vaticano II. Una Storia Mai Scritta* (Bavaria: Lindau, 2010).

[33] *Catholic Encyclopedia*, s.v. "First Vatican Council," 1913.

of Christian doctrine should be guarded and taught more efficaciously."[34] Additionally, he noted that this concern of presenting the faith in the language of the modern world should be addressed by applying the medicine of mercy rather than that of severity.

Although John XXIII had made it clear that he wanted the nature of the council to be both pastoral and practical, his death on June 3, 1963, and the subsequent election of Cardinal Giovanni Montini (1897–1978), who took the name Paul VI, brought with it many questions as to how the council would proceed. As Alberigo and Komonchak note, it is not inappropriate to think of the second period of the council at the end of September 1963 as a new beginning since one of its chief novel factors was the presence of a new Bishop of Rome.[35]

Paul VI's style was definitely different from that of John XXIII. Congar remarks in his journal that there was a lack of symmetry between the council-as-light of John XXIII, for whom the otherness of the Church and world is overcome by the gift of grace, and the council-as-dialogue of Paul VI, which builds a bridge, but in doing so acknowledges the gap.[36] One can see this difference in the manner in which Paul VI chose to guide the council. He decided to create a college of moderators, whose outlooks, though extraordinarily diverse, were significant in exercising a positive influence on the council and thereby guiding it in the direction it would take.[37] It has been noted that John XXIII had refrained from laying out a specific "plan" for the moderators of the council, whereas Paul VI tended to be "programmatic."[38]

Even with the changes inherent with a new pope who had different ways of proceeding, both the pastoral and practical nature of the council started by John XXIII and inherited by Paul VI is evident in the constitution on the Church, *Lumen Gentium*. This document would become the "central document of the whole council and the one which exerted the most pervasive influence on those subsequently debated."[39]

---

[34] John XXIII, "Allocutio in Sollemni SS. Concilii Inauguratione," October 11, 1962.

[35] Alberigo and Komonchak, *The History of Vatican II*, 3:492.

[36] Ibid., 38.

[37] Ibid., 493.

[38] Ibid., 496.

[39] Butler, *The Theology of Vatican II*, 52.

One of the main reasons *Lumen Gentium* was expected to have a "pervasive influence" was because a full treatment of the Church had been so long awaited. "Vatican I had had ambitions in that direction, but broke off its work, after dealing directly only with papal supremacy and infallibility,"[40] due to the outbreak of war. The abrupt halting of Vatican I meant that the opportunity to discuss ecclesiology on a conciliar level was lost. Understandably, one must note that, since the Reformation, "Catholic theological writing on the Church had tended to be controversial or polemical, and had concentrated on the visible, authoritarian, juridical and legal aspects of the subject" and, therefore, Catholic theologians "said little about the 'invisible,' or 'mystical' or 'mysterious' aspects of the Church."[41] With the convocation of the Second Vatican Council, however, these neglected aspects of the nature and mission of the Church now had the chance to come to the fore.

## The Church as the Theme of the Council

Although *Lumen Gentium* is the second of four constitutions that the council fathers promulgated at Vatican II, early in the first session the Church became the focus of the council, the lens through which to view all its decrees. This was due in no small part to the work of Cardinal Léon-Joseph Suenens.

Prior to the opening of the council in October 1962, Cardinal Suenens had been asked to serve as a member of the Central Preparatory Commission and emerged as an important figure in these preconciliar discussions. Although his experience on this commission dismayed him because of the uncoordinated and unfocused documents being produced, it also gave him a position of great influence on the council.[42]

During the Lenten season of 1962, Suenens wrote a letter about the council to his diocese that caught the attention of John XXIII and very likely changed the work and focus of the council.[43] In his Lenten letter, Suenens "expressed the conviction that the council should emphasize,

---

[40] Ibid.
[41] Ibid., 54.
[42] O'Malley, *What Happened at Vatican II*, 157.
[43] Ibid.

in the tense international situation of the times, what unites Catholics with others, not what separates them."[44] This conviction, coupled with Suenens's distinction between the Church looking inward (*ad intra*) and looking outward to the world (*ad extra*), became central to the subsequent exchanges between John XXIII and Suenens about the shape that the work of the council should take.

In October 1962 the council opened. On November 14, the draft constitution on the Sacred Liturgy was approved. On November 20–21, however, the draft schema on the sources of revelation fell short of the two-thirds majority required to approve continuation of discussion of the schema as presented—of the 2,209 votes cast, 1,368 were for discontinuing debate, 822 for continuing. This move by the council fathers demonstrated the division and dissatisfaction among many of them, as well as their efforts to make the council *their* council and not the Curia's council. The next day Pope John sent a message to the council expressing his concern regarding the need to reconcile the various opinions that had emerged. To this end, John referred the revision of the document to a "mixed commission" made up of members of the Doctrinal Commission and the Secretariat for Christian Unity.[45]

The division of the council fathers on the schema on the sources of revelation was symptomatic of a greater division among them, namely, the need for a central theme around which to unite their work. To address this, on December 4, 1962, Cardinal Suenens, with the approval of Pope John, took to the council floor to deliver an intervention. Of this intervention, O'Malley writes:

> Suenens asserted that what the council needed was a central theme that would lend it a basic orientation. Let that theme be, as the pope put it on September 11, "the church of Christ, light to the world," *Ecclesia Christi, Lumen Gentium.* That theme has two parts, the first of which looks to the inner reality of the church and asks the question, "What do you say of yourself?" The second part concerns the relationship of the church to the world outside of it, and asks

---

[44] Ibid.
[45] Ibid., 150.

questions about the human person, about social justice, about evangelization of the poor, about world peace.[46]

Suenens's intervention paved the way for the council fathers to make the Church the connecting and orienting theme of the whole council. Having the Church as the overarching theme allowed the council fathers to consider how the Church reflects the holiness of the light of Christ as well as how it fails to do so. Addressing the Church's nature helped the council fathers to articulate what the Church's mission is in the world.

In what follows, we will examine the development and structure of *Lumen Gentium*, key sections on the holiness and sinfulness of the Church, the reflection of these themes in later conciliar documents, and the unfinished agenda in regards to the development of the Church's theology of its holiness and sinfulness.

## From *De Ecclesia* to *Lumen Gentium*

What we know today as *Lumen Gentium* (the Dogmatic Constitution on the Church) began as a relatively comprehensive draft in eleven chapters (or twelve, if the appendix on the Virgin Mary is considered a chapter) produced by the Preparatory Commission, though without any very clear intrinsic structure. The chapters had the following headings:

1. The nature of the Church militant.
2. The members of the Church and the necessity of the Church for salvation.
3. The episcopate as the highest grade of the sacrament of orders: the priesthood.
4. Residential bishops.
5. The states of evangelical perfection.
6. The laity.
7. The teaching office (magisterium) of the Church.
8. Authority and obedience in the Church.

---

[46] Ibid., 157–58.

9. Relationships between the Church and State and religious tolerance.
10. The necessity of proclaiming the gospel to all peoples and in the whole world.
11. Ecumenism.[47]

Even upon a cursory reading of the schema, one can see that the committee members were trying in chapters 9, 10, and 11 to bring out aspects of the Church that were in urgent need of clarification from a pastoral standpoint, as they knew these issues would be discussed more thoroughly at the next session. The commission as well as the other council fathers were in agreement on one point, that the constitution on the Church would be the center and climax of the council.[48] As Vorgrimler notes, however, the preparatory draft of *De Ecclesia* was rejected because the fathers saw a disconnect among the eleven chapters as well as an absence of a pastoral spirit. Their rejection made it necessary for both a different commission and a different approach to be taken. The rejection of the draft also shows, however, how much the theological atmosphere was already changing.[49] The effect of the schema's rejection is summed up well by Bishop Elchinger (1908–1998) of Strasbourg, France:

> Yesterday the Church was considered above all as an institution, today it is experienced as a community. Yesterday it was the Pope who was mainly in view, today the Pope is thought of as united to the bishops. Yesterday the bishop alone was considered, today all of the bishops together. Yesterday theology stressed the importance of the hierarchy, today it is discovering the people of God. Yesterday it was chiefly concerned with what divided, today it voices all that unites. Yesterday the theology of the Church was mainly preoccupied with the inward life of the Church, today it sees the Church as orientated to the outside world.[50]

Bishop Elchinger's words capture the new understanding of the Church's nature and mission that was beginning to emerge.

---

[47] Herbert Vorgrimler, ed., *Commentary on the Documents of Vatican II*, vol. 1 (New York: Herder and Herder, 1968), 106.

[48] Ibid., 107.

[49] See O'Malley, *What Happened at Vatican II*, 153–59.

[50] As quoted from Vorgrimler, *Commentary on the Documents of Vatican II*, 108.

Much discussion among the fathers was still needed about how to articulate this new understanding of the Church. Several key theological issues kept arising. For example, should the chapter on the hierarchical nature of the Church precede the chapter on the people of God, the laity? How would the collegial character of the bishops interface with the primacy of Peter? What role does conscience play in light of the authority and obedience of the magisterium? How can the Church that professes the fullness of faith be involved with ecumenical efforts without offending other Christian communities? Should there be a separate chapter in this document or a separate document on the role of Mary? If so, how would that affect ecumenical efforts? With so many issues and concerns coming to the fore, the first draft was sent back for revision.[51]

In 1963, the second draft of the text was composed under the direction of the newly appointed Coordinating Commission, whose task was to expedite the agenda, resolve conflicts among the heads of the commissions, and see that the documents reflected the aims of Pope John.[52] This commission, taking into account the many suggestions of the council fathers regarding the first draft, presented the second draft on September 30, 1963, following this outline:

Fascicle 1:

  I. The Mystery of the Church

  II. The Hierarchical Constitution of the Church and the Episcopate

Fascicle 2:

  III. The People of God and the Laity in Particular

  IV. The Call to Holiness in the Church.[53]

---

[51] See O'Malley, *What Happened at Vatican II*, 153–59 for the debate about *De Ecclesia*.

[52] Ibid., 161. The Coordinating Commission in this case was mediating between the concerns of *Cardinal* Alfredo *Ottaviani as president of the Preparatory Theological Commission and the Doctrinal Commission and Cardinal Augustin Bea, the secretariat for Christian unity.*

[53] Vorgrimler, *Commentary on the Documents of Vatican II*, 110.

The most significant change that had occurred from the Preparatory Commission's first draft was the introduction of "mystery" as the first way to put forth the idea of Church. The concept of mystery would, as we shall see, have implications for how the Church understands itself as both holy and sinful and also for how the hierarchy and the laity are called to participate in the life and mission of the Church. Placing the Church in the context of mystery may have helped to answer the question as to how chapters 2 and 3, one emphasizing the hierarchical constitution of the Church and the other the role of the laity in constituting the Church, would relate to each other, but the text did not suggest how. Just questioning the hierarchy's placement in the constitution of the Church, however, reflects a major shift in thinking about the Church. In the second draft, the hierarchy is placed side by side with the laity. In this draft the hierarchy is beginning to be seen as equal with, not superior to the laity. Replacement of juridical categories such as referring to the Church by grades of orders, with a call to all to holiness and with describing the Church as a mystery, underscores the inward supernatural reality of the Church.[54] Of this new draft, John O'Malley notes:

> The Fathers were glad to see that the structure of the draft had been improved, that it displayed an ecumenical and pastoral approach, that it avoided juridical severity and made much use of biblical imagery. It was emphasized, however, that the dynamic and eschatological aspect of the Church needed to be brought out more strongly.[55]

With these critiques and many others, the fathers sent this new draft back to the Theological Commission for further revisions.

In September 1964, what would become the final version was presented to the council. Over the next months, there continued to be considerable deliberation about certain controversial points such as the people of God preceding the hierarchy, the collegiality of the bishops, and the inclusion of a final chapter on the Blessed Virgin. On November 21, 1964, *Lumen Gentium*, the Dogmatic Constitution on the Church, was finally promulgated by Pope Paul VI with the consent of the fathers of the council.

---

[54] Ibid., 111.
[55] Ibid.

## The Evolution of Vatican II's *Lumen Gentium* (The Dogmatic Constitution on the Church) [56]

### First Draft (1962)

1. The Nature of the Church Militant
2. Membership in the Church and its Necessity for Salvation
3. Office of Bishop as the Highest Degree of Ordination
4. Residential Bishops
5. The States of Evangelical Perfection
6. The Laity
7. The Magisterium
8. Authority and Obedience in the Church
9. Relations between Church and State
10. The Necessity of Evangelization
11. Ecumenism

Appendix: Virgin Mary, Mother of God and Mother of Men

### Second Draft (1963)

1. The Mystery of the Church
2. The Hierarchical Constitution of the Church and the Episcopate in Particular
3. The People of God and the Laity in Particular
4. The Call to Holiness in the Church

### Final Version (1964)

1. The Mystery of the Church
2. The People of God
3. The Hierarchical Constitution of the Church and the

### Episcopate in Particular

4. The Laity
5. The Call of the Whole Church to Holiness
6. Religious
7. The Pilgrim Church
8. The Blessed Virgin Mary

[56] Edward P. Hahnenberg, *Ministries: A Relational Approach* (New York: The Cross-road Publishing Company, 2003), 113. Though Hahnenberg refers to the drafts as first, second, and final, it would be more precise to refer to the first draft as that of the Preparatory Commission, the second draft as the new draft of the Theological Commission, and the final version as that of the council fathers.

This chart reproduced from Edward P. Hahnenberg's *Ministries: A Relational Approach* shows the drafts of Vatican II's constitution on the Church and provides a visual representation of the shift that was taking place in the council fathers' understanding of the nature and mission of the Church during the discussions that led to the promulgation of *Lumen Gentium*. Of particular note is that the title and placement of the chapters in the first draft of *Lumen Gentium* reflect the juridical, apologetic, and authoritative understanding of the Church that was present at the commencement of Vatican II. The titles and placement of the chapters in the final version demonstrate a much more pastoral understanding of the Church. This progression in how the council fathers came to a more pastoral and scriptural understanding of the nature and mission of the Church, was, in part, a result of the theological reflection of six preconciliar theologians whose writings I have discussed previously, as well as by the work of the council fathers, the new Theological Commission, and the assistance of the *periti* at the council. The experiences of Church that the bishops brought to the council were also influential in the process of writing and approving *Lumen Gentium*.

We turn now to consider *Lumen Gentium* on the holiness and sinfulness of the Church.

## *Lumen Gentium* on the Holiness and Sinfulness of the Church

The titles of the chapters of the final version of *Lumen Gentium* point in various ways to the theme of the holiness and sinfulness of the Church. Beginning with the Church as mystery, accentuating its holiness and then continuing to discuss how that holiness is lived out through a universal call to holiness of the people of God—the hierarchy, laity, and religious—suggests a dynamism and a growth in holiness. Growth, in turn, implies incompleteness and creates an opening for considering sinfulness. The chapter on the pilgrim Church addresses how the Church and its members are in this world but not of it. While in this world, however, the people of God are called from sin to holiness. The final chapter on Mary gives an example of how the call to holiness was lived out in the life of the Blessed Virgin Mary. Within these chapters, there are seven key passages that advance the discussion of the theme of the holiness and sinfulness of the Church.

*Lumen Gentium* begins with a chapter on mystery. Within that chapter, the council fathers discuss the holiness of the Church as emanating from a trinitarian foundation and the Church as the sacrament of Christ in the world. Section 7 of this chapter then explores how the Church as the body of Christ existing in history and on pilgrimage in this world is in need of the Spirit's grace to continuously choose to be conformed to Christ, that is, to grow in holiness. In section 8, the council fathers acknowledge the disunity and division of Christianity and the need to work toward unity. At the end of section 8, the council fathers explicitly state that that the "church, clasping sinners to its bosom, [is] at once holy and always in need of purification" (LG 8).

The next chapter, on the people of God, makes the connection of the Church to Israel, the people of God. This image in itself suggests continuity with Israel and that, like Israel, the Church in its covenantal relationship with God will always be in need of forgiveness and conversion for its infidelities.

This theme is expanded in chapter 5, wherein the council fathers discuss the universal call to holiness for all people. The call in itself suggests that all of us need to move from our sins, failings, and weaknesses to a state of holiness and fidelity to God. Finally, in chapter 7, the council fathers complete what they began in chapter 1. In chapter 1, the Church as mystery, as sacrament, and as trinitarian is holy; in chapter 7, the council fathers explain that the Church is also on pilgrimage in this world, has not reached perfection in holiness, and is, therefore, sinful. The Church in this world is subject to sin and, simultaneously, the Church is not of this world, and therefore, eschatologically holy.

I maintain that these seven passages delineate that one of the overarching themes present in *Lumen Gentium* is that of the holiness and sinfulness of the Church. We will now turn to discovering how the theologians discussed in chapter 1 were instrumental in advancing these themes.

## Theological Influences: The Holiness and Sinfulness of the Church in *Lumen Gentium*

The works of the theologians discussed in chapter 1 of this study helped pave the way for the discussions of the holiness and sinfulness of the Church that ensued at Vatican II. The theological insights of these preconciliar theologians were of invaluable assistance in the preparation, deliberation, and final promulgation of *Lumen Gentium*.

Before making the case for each theologian's influence on *Lumen Gentium*, it is important to take note of the following pertinent remarks made by Karl-Heinz Neufeld about such an endeavor:

> In the case of many Councils, and especially that of Vatican II, it is well known that there was a great deal of work by theologians behind the drafts, proposals, and recommendations, without their contribution ever being clearly acknowledged in the official documents. Of course, occasionally some theological influence of a particular stamp cannot be missed, but this remains more or less a matter of chance. . . . However decisive the influence of theologians on the work of the Second Vatican Council may have been, their work nevertheless remained outside the Council Hall, and thus outside the event itself. It was essentially hidden service, despite all the sensational journalistic reports.[57]

Neufield nevertheless maintains that, despite the problems inherent in assigning this or that idea in a conciliar document to a specific theologian, it should not "prevent us from giving an overview that bundles them all together just as the reality of the Council's work did."[58] Although the problem of certitude remains, one can make some reasonable assumptions regarding the influence of these preconciliar theologians to the preparation of *Lumen Gentium*. For example, Emile Mersch's work has been seen as an important foundation for Pius XII's encyclical.[59] De Lubac's work also contributed to recovering a sense of the importance of the Mystical Body of Christ. Additionally, his service as a *peritus* at the council allowed for his theological thought to be influential at the council fathers' discussions of the nature and mission of the Church. Von Balthasar's work, though influenced by de Lubac, was not as influential on the council fathers as the others because he was not present at the council. His work, however, will be seen to be extremely important to John Paul II's millennial statement

---

[57] Karl H. Neufeld, "In the Service of the Council: Bishops and Theologians at the Second Vatican Council (for Cardinal Henri De Lubac on His 90th Birthday)," In *Vatican II: Assessment and Perspectives Twenty Five Years After (1962–1987)*, ed. René Latourelle (Mahwah, NJ: Paulist Press, 1988), 75.

[58] Ibid., 76.

[59] Jürgen Mettepenningen, *Nouvelle Theologie—New Theology: Inheritor of Modernism, Precursor of Vatican II* (London: T. & T. Clark International, 2010), 27.

of repentance, which will be discussed in chapter 3 of this work. In his memoirs written during his service as a *peritus* at the council, Congar himself discusses the particular sections of *Lumen Gentium* that his theological work had influenced. The influence of Rahner's work can also be deduced from both his work as a *peritus* as well as his own reflection on the council and his work for it. Finally, Journet's service on the Preparatory Commission connotes that he had an opportunity to directly influence the council. As we have seen, however, the preparatory draft on which he worked was rejected by the council fathers in the first session.

In the following section, I make a case for the influence of these theologians on *Lumen Gentium* in regard to the holiness and sinfulness of the Church. In a few instances direct influence can be shown; in others, influence can reasonably be inferred. We turn then to key sections in *Lumen Gentium* regarding the holiness and sinfulness of the Church and the ways in which they reflect the influence of the preconciliar theologians and their connection to other conciliar documents.

## *Lumen Gentium* Section One:
## Church as Mystery, Sacrament, and Sign

> Since the church, in Christ, is a sacrament—a sign and instrument, that is, of communion with God and of the unity of the entire human race—it here proposes, for the benefit of the faithful of the entire world, to describe more clearly, and in the tradition laid down by earlier council, its own nature and universal mission. (LG 1)

By choosing to describe the Church as a mystery and a sacrament in Christ, the council fathers begin *Lumen Gentium* with an emphasis on the Church's connection to the salvific mission of Christ and on its inherent holiness. They continue to explicate the mystery of the Church in sections 2 to 8 of this chapter. The fathers were pleased with the shift in language from previous drafts of this chapter as "it displayed an ecumenical and pastoral approach, that avoided juridical severity and made much use of biblical imagery."[60] Additionally, the "notion of the Church as sacrament forms a close link with patristic and modern ecclesiology."[61]

---

[60] Vorgrimler, *Commentary on the Documents of Vatican II*, 111.
[61] Ibid., 138.

Henri de Lubac's retrieval of the patristic and scriptural understanding of the Church in Christ as both mystery and sacrament influenced the council fathers in their writing of *Lumen Gentium* 1. The council fathers emphasize that the Church is by its nature holy because of its relationship to Christ. Christ's life, death, and resurrection broke the bonds of sin and offered salvation to all humankind; the Church as the sacrament of Christ continues this salvific mission of Christ until he comes. Understanding the Church as the continuation of Christ's salvific mission underscores a dynamism within the nature and mission of the Church. The Church for de Lubac and for the council fathers is on pilgrimage and must grow in the holiness to which its relationship with Christ beckons.

Karl Rahner's understanding that the Church does not simply make the sacraments available but is itself a sacrament is reflected in the council fathers' description of the Church as sacrament. Rahner's insight that the Church is sacrament for the world also carries with it a dynamism. The Church walking in history brings the grace of Christ to the world and is a means of infusing the world with grace, thereby making the world holy.

## Henri de Lubac

Through the use of the paradoxical understanding that the Church is ever ancient, ever new, de Lubac's theology helped retrieve the history of the Church found in the writings of the early Fathers. The fathers of the Vatican Council were able to use that history as a lens to view the Church in the current milieu. With a strong emphasis on paradox, de Lubac's theological reflection opened up an expansive understanding of the mystery of the Church's holiness and sinfulness. This mystery for de Lubac was seen through the lens of sacramentality, which views the Church as the place in which the visible and invisible, the temporal and eternal aspects of relationship to God converge. Because of the convergence of time and eternity, the Church can be seen as sinful as it exists in time and as holy because it exists beyond time. The simultaneous reality of sinfulness and holiness underscores the mysterious nature of the Church.

How these paradoxes are worked out in the mission and nature of the Church we shall see in the content of *Lumen Gentium*. Both Karl-Heinz Neufeld and Paul McPartlan have identified contributions that de Lubac's theological insights made to the final draft of the document. Neufeld notes:

G. Philips mentions that the French Jesuit had already in 1963 described the Church as a sacrament of Jesus Christ, just as Jesus Christ as Man is for us the sacrament of God. This is the expression of one of the principles of the Council's view of the Church. De Lubac developed this from his idea of the Church as mystery, which he had used as a title in his *Méditation sur l'Eglise* and which he was to discuss in detail after the Council in his *Paradoxe et Mystère de l'Eglise*. But *Catholicism* and *Corpus Mysticum* had already taken important preparatory steps in this direction. However, it was above all the *Méditation sur l'Eglise* with which the Council Fathers were familiar as a source of theological ideas and as inspiration for the spiritual life.[62]

Clearly, the fathers of Vatican II were not only aware of de Lubac's work but also saw it as a source of inspiration for the task at hand, that of writing a dogmatic constitution on the Church and in an important sense complete the unfinished work of Vatican I. McPartlan credits de Lubac's work even more directly through his work at the council.

De Lubac steered through to its ratification the crucial conciliar document on the Church, *Lumen Gentium*, which bears significant signs of the influence of de Lubac's book, most of all in the way it begins its exposition. The draft text, first presented to the council in 1962, opened with a chapter on "The Nature of the Church Militant." By 1964, the strident tone had gone and the first chapter of the final text bore the title, "The Mystery of the Church," directly in line with the first chapter of de Lubac's *Méditation*, entitled, as the basis of all that was to follow, "The Church is a Mystery."[63]

One of the greatest expositions of this mystery for de Lubac is how the Church lives out its sacramental nature in the face of the sinfulness of its members.

The mystery that is the Church is first put forth in the second sentence of *Lumen Gentium* where the fathers of the council define the Church as

---

[62] Karl H. Neufeld, "In the Service of the Council: Bishops and Theologians at the Second Vatican Council (for Cardinal Henri De Lubac on His 90th Birthday)," in Latourelle, 94.

[63] Paul McPartlan, *Sacrament of Salvation: An Introduction to Eucharistic Ecclesiology* (Edinburgh: T. & T. Clark, 1995), 59.

being "in Christ like a sacrament." The use of the word "sacrament," as defined in the *Catechism of the Catholic Church* (1131) as "efficacious signs of grace, instituted by Christ and entrusted to the Church, by which divine life is dispensed to us," not only connotes mystery, sharing in divine life, but also paradox, bringing the human and divine together.

De Lubac's definition of the Church as sacrament makes the Church expansive because it draws together all time, the temporal as well as the eternal. He also emphasizes that our supernatural dignity springs from our common human dignity, that is, grace builds on nature. In the case of the Church, grace building on nature means that the Church is built on a natural unity, the unity of all humanity. Because we share in this common humanity, we can now say that we share in a common call to holiness. The *call to holiness* implies that *sinfulness* prevents us from attaining supernatural life in communion with God and humankind. For de Lubac, we are truly one body and what affects one, affects all, living and deceased. The sacramental life of the Church also brings the acknowledgment that when a member fails to live up to his or her supernatural dignity, that failure affects all of us because we are all united in Christ to each other (LG 11). Paul McPartlan explains this theological insight of de Lubac in this manner:

> De Lubac is probably the one who deserves the credit for invit-
> ing us to think *big* and recognize the Church herself as "the great
> sacrament which contains and vitalizes all the others" (*Splendor*,
> p. 203). . . . If grace was previously understood as something
> invisible, dispensed sacramentally to individuals, with de Lubac's
> encouragement it was increasingly recognized as something cor-
> porate, namely the life of the Church, and moreover as something
> *concrete*, for that life centres upon the celebration of the Eucharist,
> where the Church is dramatically revealed.[64]

De Lubac's writing on sacrament and his recognition of the Church as "the great sacrament" is brought to bear on the life of the Church during the writing of *Lumen Gentium*. Dennis Doyle observes that "when in its opening paragraph, *Lumen Gentium* refers to the Church as a sacrament,

---

[64] Ibid., 41.

the voice of de Lubac in *Catholicism* can be heard."[65] The title as well as the first few lines of chapter 1 of *Lumen Gentium* are a clear indication of the amount of influence that de Lubac's theology wielded at the council.

The sacramentally centered ecclesiology of *Lumen Gentium*, "the Church is in Christ like a sacrament" (LG 1), can be seen to originate in De Lubac's ecclesiology based on the Church's call to be "for us the sacrament of Christ." Both de Lubac and the council fathers are highlighting the Church's call to bear Christ to the world.

This mystery of the life of the Church is renewed each time a sacrament is celebrated. It is in and through the sacramental life of the Church that a bridge is crossed between the temporal and the eternal, the sinful and the holy. Therefore, as de Lubac said so emphatically, "The Church is a mystery; that is to say that she is also a sacrament. She is the 'total *locus* of the Christian sacraments,' and she is herself the great sacrament that contains and vitalizes all others. In this world, she is the sacrament of Christ, as Christ himself, in his humanity, is for us the sacrament of God." And later, "her whole end is to show us Christ, lead us to him and communicate his grace to us. . . . If the world lost the Church, it would lose the Redemption, too."[66]

From his study of the biblical and patristic foundations of the Church, de Lubac was able to retrieve a sense of the individual and corporate dimensions of baptism, by which members are incorporated into the mystical Body of Christ.

> That is the constant teaching of the Church, though it must be confessed that in practice it is too little known. Just as redemption and revelation, even though they reach every individual soul, are none the less fundamentally not individual but social, so grace which is produced and maintained by the sacraments does not set up a purely individual relationship between the soul and God or Christ; rather does each individual receive such grace in proportion as he is joined, socially to that one body whence flows this saving life-stream.[67]

---

[65] Henri de Lubac, *Catholicism*, trans. Lancelot C. Sheppard (London: Burns and Oates, 1950 [orig. 1938], 29, quoted in Dennis M. Doyle, *Communion Ecclesiology: Vision and Versions* (Maryknoll, NY: Orbis Books, 2000), 65.

[66] Henri de Lubac, *The Splendor of the Church*, 203.

[67] De Lubac, *Catholicism*, 82.

From his study of the scriptural and patristic foundations of the Church, de Lubac realized that there was a need to retrieve this communal aspect of the sacraments because it was a means of opening the Church to the world.

The fathers of the council also understood the pastoral importance of retrieving the communal aspect of the sacraments so that the Church could "unfold more fully to the faithful of the Church and to the whole world its own inner nature and universal mission." De Lubac's retrieval of the communal aspect of the sacraments paved the way for the fathers of the council to follow suit and thereby begin to make the Church more accessible to the world by reinvigorating the social dimension of the Church.

De Lubac's sacramental ecclesiology, however, does not make the Church immune to sinfulness. The dynamic of the sinfulness of one member in the Church affects the whole body. De Lubac saw this dynamic reflected in the "double functions" of the sacrament of penance in which there was a need for both inner purification and some visible sign of the sinner's restoration to communion with the Church. For de Lubac, the "primitive" Church's practice of public penance and reconciliation of sinners with the community demonstrated the Church's acceptance of sinners in her midst. Retrieving the practice and theology of penance made it possible for de Lubac to assert that sin affects the whole community and is present in the Church without ever affecting its holiness. Recognition of the Church's sinfulness and holiness is another important aspect of de Lubac's theology that the fathers of the council tried to adopt. The insight that the Church is not for just some chosen few but for all people is translated by the council fathers in what becomes known as the first paragraph of *Lumen Gentium*.

## Karl Rahner

For Rahner, it is in and through the Church that humanity experiences God's self-communication. One of the primary means of experiencing the transcendent God is the sacramental life of the Church. The Church is able to facilitate this encounter because it is "the continuance, the contemporary presence, of that real, eschatologically triumphant and irrevocably established presence in the world, in Christ of God's salvific will. The Church is the abiding presence of that primal sacramental word of definitive grace, which is Christ in the world." For Rahner, "the Church is truly the fundamental sacrament."[68] In and through the sacraments and the Word, humanity is able to experience God in the person of Jesus Christ through the outpouring of the grace of their Spirit. For Rahner, this is the reason for the Church's existence. As Lennan notes, Rahner understands that the Church "was the sacrament of Christ, the means by which his grace was embodied in history."[69]

## *Lumen Gentium* Section Four: One People and the Spirit's Role in the Mission

> The Spirit dwells in the church and in the hearts of the faithful, as in a temple. . . . He guides the church in the way of all truth (see Jn 16:13) and, uniting it in fellowship and ministry, bestows upon it different hierarchic and charismatic gifts. . . . By the power of the Gospel he rejuvenates the church, constantly renewing it and leading it to perfect union with its spouse. (LG 4)

By highlighting the important role of the Spirit in the life and mission of the Church, the council fathers acknowledge that there is a need to be open to the Spirit in order to share in the holiness of the Church. "The Church's holiness is not derived from the subjective holiness of its members. Rather, it is through participation in the holiness of the Church that the individual member is made holy."[70] Furthermore, the council fathers also acknowledge that the Church and its members at times fall short of holiness and need sanctification and renewal by the Holy Spirit.[71] The significance of the Holy Spirit's continual renewing, rejuvenating, and leading the Church to perfection not only allows for the presence of sin within the Church but also seems to assume it.

Yves Congar, Karl Rahner, and Charles Journet, though with different purposes, write about the importance of the dynamic role of the Spirit in the life and mission of the Church. The renewed emphasis on the role of the Spirit that the council fathers note in this section demonstrates that the Church exists in history and is in need of the outpouring of the Spirit

---

[68] Karl Rahner, *The Church and the Sacraments* (New York: Herder and Herder, 1963), 18.

[69] Richard Lennan, *Ecclesiology of Karl Rahner* (Oxford: Clarendon Press, 2002), 25.

[70] Yetzer, *Holiness and Sin in the Church*, 116.

[71] Vorgrimler, *Commentary on the Documents of Vatican II*, 142.

for it to be true to its mission of bringing Christ to the world. All three theologians acknowledge that the gifts of the Spirit are given to all members of the Church, not just the hierarchy, and they are crucial aids to the Church as it makes its journey. In and through the workings of the Spirit in the Church, people are called from divisions, failings, and weaknesses to union with Christ and each other, to holiness.

### Yves Congar

In *Lumen Gentium* the council fathers speak to the sinfulness of this disunity by expounding on the holiness to be attained through the oneness to which the Church is called. Among the many images the council fathers employ to express this unity is the Trinity: "Thus, the Church has been seen as 'a people made one with the unity of the Father, the Son, and the Holy Spirit'" (LG 4). In a footnote, the council fathers document their reliance on patristic sources for the trinitarian grounding of the Church's unity.[72] Congar emphasizes the role of the Spirit in the Church while keeping in mind its trinitarian foundation. The Spirit is given to the Church corporately because it is not just the people of God but the Body of Christ.

> The gift of the Spirit as a principle of life in the Church changes the conditions under which it is possible to speak of sin, lying, and repentance in connection with the Church. In one way or another, a distinction is introduced between the Church, inasmuch as it is a certain superimposed reality united to Christ by the bonds of an unbreakable union—spouse, Body of Christ, and the Church inasmuch as it is the totality of Christians who, each and all, are sinful and weak.[73]

[72] In *Lumen Gentium*, par. 4, footnote 4, the council fathers cite Cyprian, *De Orat. Dom.* 23: PL 4, 553; Augustine, *Serm.* 71, 20, 33: PL 38, 463; St. John Damascene, *Adv. Iconocl.* 12: PG 96 1358 D. For this footnote, see *Vatican Council II: The Conciliar and Postconciliar Documents* (Collegeville, MN: Liturgical Press, 2014), 352. See also Ph. Denis, "Archbishop Hurley's Contribution to the Second Vatican Council," *Bulletin for Contextual Theology in Southern African and Africa* 4, no. 1 (1997), 11, quoted in Alberigo and Komonchak, *The History of Vatican II*, 3:48.

[73] Yves Congar, "The Church: The People of God," trans. Kathryn Sullivan, in *The Church and Mankind: Dogma*, vol. 1, *Concilium*, ed. Edward Schillebeeckx (Glen Rock, NJ: Paulist Press, 1965), 33.

Congar's attention to the role of the Spirit underscores the Church's innate holiness as the Body of Christ and its sinfulness as composed of people who can and do sin. The Spirit is not only the source of the Church's indefectible holiness but also the source of its growth in holiness. It is important to notice the conditions under which Congar acknowledges the Church's claim to holiness:

> the Church is not yet completely holy, as St. Augustine acknowledged when considering the interpretation of Eph. 5, 27 ("without spot or wrinkle"). Here we have one of the many and very fruitful applications of the truth in dialectical form in which is described the condition of the Church *in via* between Pentecost and the Parousia, what *is now* and what is *not yet*.[74]

### Karl Rahner

Karl Rahner also emphasized the role of the Spirit in the Church. He believed that if Vatican II was to have any lasting impact on the Church, the council fathers would have to open themselves to the grace and inspiration of the Holy Spirit. In his theological thought prior to the council, Rahner put forth his conviction that the Church needed to be opened to the Spirit and risk changing the language we use to speak about faith.[75] As Maureen Sullivan comments, "The traditional language of faith did not—perhaps could not—address this crisis [of faith]."[76] Rahner was astutely reading the signs of the times and knew that it was necessary to present the faith in a different manner to modern men and women. The Church needed to embrace the whole world, not merely Western Europe. Additionally, the Church needed to find new ways to minister in a global

---

[74] Ibid.

[75] See Karl Rahner, "History of the World and Salvation History," in *Theological Investigations*, vol. 5, *Later Writings* (New York: The Crossroad Publishing Company, 1970); Rahner, "Christianity in the New Man," in *Theological Investigations*, vol. 5, *Later Writings* (New York: The Crossroad Publishing Company, 1970); and Rahner, "What is Heresy?" in *Theological Investigations*, vol. 5, *Later Writings* (New York: The Crossroad Publishing Company, 1970).

[76] Maureen Sullivan, *The Road to Vatican II: Key Changes in Theology* (New York: Paulist Press, 2007), 30–31.

context. The manner in which the Church had been trying to hand on the faith was not working. Rahner saw a need to retrieve from the early Fathers and from Scripture some "ever ancient, yet ever new" ways to hand on the faith to the current generation.[77] As Maureen Sullivan notes, "What becomes very clear from a reading of Rahner's preconciliar writings is that before John XXIII had called for an *aggiornamento*, Rahner himself was committed to the need for change in the church."[78] For Rahner, such a change was necessary in order to carry out the mission and ministry of the Church in modernity.

### Charles Journet

In *Lumen Gentium* 4, the council fathers describe the Spirit as dwelling in the Church and guiding, rejuvenating, and renewing it so as to lead the Church to "perfect union with its spouse." This understanding of the Spirit's role as effecting the movement of the Church toward perfect union with Christ also reflects a renewed emphasis on the inherent eschatological nature of the Church. Both of these aspects on the Spirit's work in the Church resonate with Journet's writings. The idea of moving toward perfect union implies that the Church, on pilgrimage in this world, is not perfect yet, which in turn implies sin or the possibility of sin. For Journet, the holiness of the Church is related to the Spirit's role in moving members of the Church to perfection and holiness from places of sin and shortcomings. The movement of the Church toward holiness and union with Christ is related to Journet's identification of the Spirit as the formal cause of the Church. Inherent in this understanding of the Church is the eschatological nature of the Church to which the council fathers devote chapter 7 of *Lumen Gentium*.

---

[77] To articulate the faith more authentically, Rahner saw the need for the Church to acknowledge its composition. See Karl Rahner, "The Church of Sinners," *Theological Investigations*, vol. 6, *Concerning Vatican Council II* (Baltimore, MD: Helicon Press, 1969), 260ff.

[78] Sullivan, *The Road to Vatican II*, 88.

## *Lumen Gentium* Section Seven: Church as Body of Christ

By communicating his Spirit, Christ mystically constitutes as his body his brothers and sisters who are called together from every nation. In this body the life of Christ is communicated to those who believe and who, through the sacraments, are united in a hidden and real way to Christ in his passion and glorification. . . . As all the members of the human body, though they are many, form one body, so also do the faithful in Christ. . . . The same Spirit who of himself is the principle of unity in the body, by his own power and by the interior cohesion of the members produces and stimulates love among the faithful. From this it follows that if one member suffers in any way, all members suffer, and if one member is honored, all the members together rejoice. . . . On earth, still as pilgrims in a strange land, following in trial and in oppression the paths he trod, we are associated with his sufferings as the body with its head, suffering with him, that with him we may be glorified. (LG 7)

The image of the Mystical Body of Christ demonstrates how the Church is not only ever holy because its head is Christ but also subject to sin because its members are human, weak, and sinners. Vorgrimler sums up the importance of retrieving this image that encompasses the holiness and sinfulness of the Church when he observes that the Church must become ever more truly the body of Christ and attain to the fullness of God.[79] If, as Vorgrimler notes, the Church must become more like Christ, then it can be inferred that it is presently less because of its sinfulness.

Emile Mersch, Pius XII, Henri de Lubac, and Yves Congar rely on the Pauline corpus to discuss the Church as the Mystical Body of Christ. If the Church is the Body of Christ, then the holiness of the Church is unquestionable. If, however, the members of the Church are the Body of Christ, then the existence of sin in the Church is a reality. These two aforementioned understandings of the Mystical Body of Christ need to be united with the concept that the Church is on pilgrimage and in the process of being conformed to Christ, in the process of growing in holiness.

---

[79] Vorgrimler, *Commentary on the Documents of Vatican II*, 145.

## Emile Mersch: Mystical Body

Mersch's research retrieved the scriptural underpinnings for the Church's understanding of itself as the Mystical Body of Christ. He draws on the letters of Paul and the Gospel of John for his understanding of the Mystical Body of Christ as having four aspects, the first of which has four forms:

> Christ is the head, we are the members; He is the Vine, we are the branches; He is Life in its source, and we are animated by that life; He is Unity, and we many are one in Him who is One. Between Him and ourselves all is common.[80]

Mersch's appeal to biblical imagery allows him to assert that humanity is made holy by its union with Christ the Head. This understanding of the divine nature of the Church is also what the fathers of the Vatican Council are trying to capture in *Lumen Gentium* 7. This relationship is not just one way: indeed, the members do receive holiness from Christ; but Christ also receives from the members by taking upon himself the sinfulness of the members. This unity between Head and members referenced in *Lumen Gentium* is the point that Mersch is making when he writes:

> As His excellences pass into men and transfigure them, so do their miseries pass into Him and are there consumed. In Him, by His Blood and by His Cross, sin has been destroyed . . . in Him and in Him alone is the restoration and the ennobling of man.[81]

Finally, this union of humanity with God and with each other "imposes an obligation, we must live for God and for our brethren, since we are to live with them in Christ."[82] By this transformation into being adopted sons and daughters of God comes the obligation to care for all humanity. When humanity falls short of this obligation, sin and disunity occur. Thus the holiness and unity of the body of Christ are affected.

---

[80] Emile Mersch, *The Whole Christ: The Historical Development of the Doctrine of the Mystical Body in Scripture and Tradition*, trans. by John R. Kelly (Milwaukee, WI: Bruce Publ., 1938), 4.

[81] Ibid.

[82] Ibid., 5.

Mersch's work emphasized the divinity of the Mystical Body of Christ and how humanity is transformed by participation in it. Although he did not stress the sin that is present in and affects the holiness of the Church, the Body of Christ, he certainly recognized sin's existence in the Church and the need for it to be transformed in and through Christ. So too the council fathers in the first chapter of *Lumen Gentium*, in writing about the mystery of the Church, acknowledge that while on pilgrimage on this earth, there is an opening for sin to affect and infect humanity. Because of this, members can and do sin and need to have that sin transformed in Christ. The council fathers recognize the presence of sin in the world when they describe how, as pilgrims on this earth, we experience trials and oppression both in and outside the Church that are often the result of sin. The pain of those trials and oppression, as well as the sin that frequently caused them, needs to be united to the Lord so that it can be glorified in him. The presence of sin among believers in the Church is implied not only in the image of pilgrims but also in the need for renewal by the Spirit. His Mystical Body, an idea Mersch proposed in the early twentieth century, is evidence that Mersch's work had some, even if small, influence on the thought of the fathers in preparing *Lumen Gentium*.

Mersch's understanding of the Church as the Mystical Body of Christ was later built on by Henri de Lubac. Mersch's work on the history and theology of the Mystical Body of Christ was an important preparatory step for de Lubac's subsequent work and it also had an influence of *Mystici Corporis.*

## Pius XII, Mystici Corporis

Following on Mersch's important contribution in retrieving the scriptural and patristic underpinnings for the understanding of the Church as the Mystical Body of Christ, it would be remiss not call attention to Pius XII's 1943 encyclical, *Mystici Corporis.*[83] Although Jürgen Mettepenningen

---

[83] See Avery Dulles, "A Half Century of Ecclesiology," *Theological Studies* 50, no. 3 (1989): 421–23 for further explanation of Mersch's influence on the retrieval of the theology of the Mystical Body, as well as a discussion of the issues regarding Pius XII's insistence that the Church could not be a body unless it were visible and the implications for ecumenism that thereby arose.

notes that Mersch can be considered the main protagonist in the elaboration of this vision of the Church as the Mystical Body of Christ,[84] he also acknowledges that Pius's encyclical underscores the interest, even at the highest levels of the Church, of focusing on the significance of understanding the Church as the Mystical Body of Christ.

Given that *Mystici Corporis* was the last major official pronouncement on ecclesiology before the Second Vatican Council, and that John XXIII appointed Father Sebastian Tromp, Pius XII's chief collaborator in the writing of *Mystici Corporis*, as the secretary to the Preparatory Theological Commission of Vatican II, it is important to take account of the encyclical and the way in which it addressed the meaning of the Church as Christ's Mystical Body. Perhaps the biggest concern the encyclical raised for the council fathers was the fact that Pius XII understood the Mystical Body "not merely as an image but as a concept."[85] On the positive side, this concept helped the council fathers see the Church as a whole, including the saints in heaven; at the same time, it was problematic because the concept equated only those who were members of the institutional, visible Church with the members of the Mystical Body. Of this Butler observes,

> the encyclical's trend seems to be to establish a simple dichotomy between those who belong visibly to the Roman Catholic communion, and everyone else, be he Christian or non-Christian, religious or irreligious, man of good will or man of bad will. All the former are "really" members of the Church, the body of Christ; none of the latter class is.[86]

According to Butler, the Mystical Body theology developed by Pius's understanding of the Mystical Body of Christ would need further understanding and nuancing in the developing ecclesiology of the fathers of Vatican II.[87]

---

[84] Gregory E. Malankowski, *Emile Mersch, S.J. (1890–1940): Un christocentrisme unifié*, in *Nouvelle revue théologique* 112 (1990) 44–66, quoted in Jürgen Mettepenningen, *Nouvelle Theologie—New Theology: Inheritor of Modernism, Precursor of Vatican II* (London: T. & T. Clark International, 2010).

[85] Butler, *The Theology of Vatican II*, 54.

[86] Ibid., 54–55.

[87] Ibid., 55.

Although the council fathers use the image that Mersch retrieved in *The Whole Christ* and that Pius XII wrote about in *Mystici Corporis*, they are careful not to embrace the use of this image in the way in which Pius XII did. The fathers expand the theological reflections of Mersch and Pius XII through their reliance also on de Lubac's and Congar's writings on this image. De Lubac's writings on this subject are more expansive as his use of paradox opens the Mystical Body image to a more communal understanding. What happens to one person in the Mystical Body affects the entire Body. This allows for sinfulness to be included in the Church's members who make up the Mystical Body of Christ. Congar's pneumatological emphasis in his writing on the Mystical Body furthers the possibility of sin existing within the Body of Christ. In this way, Congar opens the way for the council fathers to speak of the sin of division and disunity in Christianity in light of the understanding that all are on pilgrimage in this world and in need of the Spirit to grow in holiness of life.

### Henri de Lubac

De Lubac builds on Mersch's work by developing a theological description of the communal nature of the sacraments and the completeness of salvation as we have previously seen. He used the example of the efficacy of the sacrament of penance in explaining how one member affects the whole. The fathers chose to use the example of the Spirit and its charisms to explain the same point, that is, the corporate nature of the sacraments—"it follows that if one member suffers in any way, all the members suffer, and if one member is honored, all the members together rejoice (see 1 Cor 12:26)" (LG 7). Although the fathers of Vatican II embraced de Lubac's retrieval of Paul's insight in 1 Corinthians 12:26, they used a pneumatological lens rather than a christological one to express the corporate nature of the Church. De Lubac deepened the significance of the corporate nature of humanity when he maintained that our supernatural dignity issues forth from our natural dignity of being made in the image and likeness of God, thereby expanding the Mystical Body of Christ to envelop all people.[88]

---

[88] See page 112 above.

## Yves Congar

The council fathers drew out various scriptural images to describe the Church in *Lumen Gentium* 6: sheepfold, farm, field, building, the Jerusalem from above, our mother. They explain in section 7 how these images help in understanding the nature of the Church. The image of Christ taking on our human nature to redeem humanity and then through the Spirit making us all members of his one Body is by far the most comprehensive description of the nature of the Church in the document. Implicit in this image of the Church as one Body in Christ is an inherent call to holiness. For Congar, one crucial way to follow this call is through taking concrete steps toward Christian unity. The implication of Congar's Body of Christ imagery is reflected in section 8 of *Lumen Gentium* where it is applied it to the question of the unity and disunity of the churches.

## *Lumen Gentium* Section Eight: Elements of the Church

The earthly church and the church endowed with heavenly riches, are not to be thought of as two realities. On the contrary, they form one complex reality comprising a human and divine element. For this reason the church is compared, in no mean analogy, to the mystery of the incarnate Word. (LG 8)

This is the unique church of Christ. . . .This church, constituted and organized as a society in the present world, subsists in the Catholic Church, which is governed by the successor of Peter and by the bishops in communion with him. Nevertheless, many elements of sanctification and of truth are found outside its visible confines. Since these are gifts belonging to the church of Christ, they are forces impelling towards catholic unity. (LG 8)

The church, however, clasping sinners to its bosom, at once holy and always in need of purification, follows constantly the path of penance and renewal. The church, "like a stranger in a foreign land, presses forward amid the persecutions of the world and the consolations of God," announcing the cross and death of the Lord until he comes. But by the power of the risen Lord it is given strength to overcome, in patience and in love, its sorrows and its difficulties. (LG 8)

This section of *Lumen Gentium* brings together the human and divine aspects of the Church as "one complex reality." It acknowledges that the Church in time also possesses characteristics that are beyond time, that are eternal. Because of this, the Church, though not a hypostatic union as Christ is, can in some ways be seen to mirror Christ. The Church cannot lay claim to being the same as Christ because unlike Christ, the Church is always in need of purification. Bernard Yetzer expounds on the important subtleties being addressed by the council fathers when he writes:

> In contrast to Christ who is personally sinless, the Church "embraces sinners in its bosom." The Church is not sinless: it is a Church of sinners; its members are sinful; sin enters into the Church in its concrete historical existence. The contrast is thus one of personal sinlessness with sinful membership (and perhaps sinfulness). Sin is a part of the actual historical existence of the Church at least insofar as the Church exists in and as a sinful people and numbers sinners among its members.[89]

As Yetzer notes, one can see the council fathers' efforts to hold in tension the eschatological holiness of the Church with the sinfulness that occurs because it is composed of human beings and shares in their historical existence. A renewed awareness of the historicity of the Church makes it possible to acknowledge the Church's need for purification. By recognizing that there are elements of truth and sanctification outside the Catholic Church, this section also opens the way for efforts to restore the unity of the Christian churches. The importance of this breakthrough for ecumenism is noted by Vorgrimler: "the Church is the deposit of the whole of salvation, of revealed truth and of sanctification." Then the question follows, "where is this Church?"[90] The council's answer, that it subsists in the Catholic Church and that elements of sanctification can be found outside its visible confines, was of supreme importance to future discussions about the reunion of Christianity.

Henri de Lubac, Yves Congar, and Karl Rahner contribute in different ways to the thinking of the council fathers in this section. De Lubac's

---

[89] Yetzer, *Holiness and Sin in the Church*, 133.
[90] Vorgrimler, *Commentary on the Documents of Vatican II*, 149.

paradoxical themes of the Church being human and divine, in time and beyond time, visible and invisible, help to underscore the complexity of the nature of the Church. Congar's stress on the importance of finding ways to unite Christianity is apparent in the council fathers' recognition that there are elements of sanctification and truth outside the Church that impel toward unity. Rahner's understanding that sin exists in the Church through its members is seen not as a liability but rather as retrieving the need for and importance of grace in the life of its members.

### Henri de Lubac

An integral aspect of de Lubac's theology of paradox is the intersection of time and sacramentality. For de Lubac, the tension between the temporal and the eternal is reflective of the tension between sinfulness and holiness or, as Paul O'Callaghan describes it, "the paradox of the Church at once holy and in tension towards a greater holiness."[91] O'Callaghan explains that the council fathers expressed this paradox when they used the formula *the Church at once holy and always in need of purification* (LG 8) and reiterated expressions of a similar kind in the first section of chapter 7 on "the Pilgrim Church" (LG 48).[92] These texts are important because they "speak unequivocally of the *sanctity of the Church* as being *imperfect*."[93]

What the council fathers wrote in *Lumen Gentium* 8 (and also 48) regarding the idea that the Church's holiness is not stagnant but rather a dynamic call to greater holiness was worked out by de Lubac in *Splendor of the Church* when he wrote about the Church as being at once in time and beyond time. The mystery inherent in the Church being simultaneously in time and beyond time allowed for de Lubac to argue that the Church's nature includes "both the sanctifying Church and the Church of the sanctified, that is, of those who are 'called to be saints' and have in fact become such in Christ; all this always by reference to him who alone is 'the holy one.'"[94] De Lubac's conception of time and the Church

---

[91] Paul O'Callaghan, "The Holiness of the Church in *Lumen Gentium*," *The Thomist* 52 (October 1988): 690.

[92] Ibid., 690–91.

[93] Ibid., 693.

[94] Henri de Lubac, *The Splendor of the Church*, trans. Michael Mason (San Francisco: Ignatius Press, 1986), 106–7.

is clearly echoed when the council fathers speak of a Church "embracing in its bosom sinners, at the same time holy and always in need of being purified" (LG 8) and of a Church "on earth endowed with a sanctity that is real though imperfect" (LG 48).

De Lubac reminds us that we cannot claim holiness for the Church without acknowledging that at the same time there are people within the Church who sin. He writes that "in this world the Church is a mixed community and will stay like that to the very end—unthreshed corn, the ark with both clean and unclean animals, a ship full of unruly passengers who always seem to be on the point of wrecking it."[95] Lest anyone of us believes we have arrived at sanctification, de Lubac warns that "even the best of her children are themselves never any more than in the way of sanctification, and their sanctity is always liable to shipwreck; all alike have to flee from the evil of the times to the mercy of God. Thus it is that the Church which we are, must say daily as with one voice and without exception: 'And forgive us our trespasses.'"[96]

These theological insights on the holiness and the sinfulness of the Church, written by de Lubac prior to the council, helped the fathers acknowledge in *Lumen Gentium* 8 and 48 that the Church is a mystery that can lay claim to being in time and beyond time, of being sinful and yet indefectibly holy.

### Yves Congar

The council fathers' acknowledgment that "many elements of sanctification and of truth are found outside its visible structure" and "impel towards unity" was a major development in understanding the Church in its relation to other Christian denominations.[97] With Congar, the council fathers recognized that the Church's growth in sanctification was necessarily tied to its attitude toward other Christian denominations. In his concern for renewal of the Catholic Church and restoring unity among the churches, Congar sought a point of departure in places in which the theologies of the various Christian denominations converge. For him, the

---

[95] Ibid., 112–13.

[96] Ibid., 114–15.

[97] Francis A. Sullivan, "The Meaning of '*Subsistit in*' as Explained by the Congregation for the Doctrine of the Faith," *Theological Studies* 69, no. 1 (March 2008): 116–24.

premier place of convergence was baptism. The council fathers likewise recognized that the grace of God is operative not only in the Church but also in the various ecclesial communities that share the grace of baptism and the devotion to the Scriptures with the Catholic Church.

In the first few years after the council, there was much debate as to what the fathers meant when they used the word "subsists" to describe the relationship between "the unique Church of Christ" and the Catholic Church.[98] This debate and its implications for the ecclesiological status of Protestant churches and for ecumenism continue today.

### *Karl Rahner*

Rahner's "new language" of theology for a new generation of believers, coupled with his refusal to separate grace and nature, led him to speak of a "graced nature" that is at the core of the human condition.[99] The mission of the Church and its sacraments is to be the visible means by which God's grace is imparted in history. His departure from the traditional understanding of grace gave him the freedom to speak of sinners in the Church and the sinful Church.[100] Although Rahner had been the object of suspicion from the Roman Curia in the years prior to Vatican II,[101] he was vindicated not only by being called to serve as a *peritus* at the council but also by the acknowledgment in *Lumen Gentium* 8 that the Church is "at once holy and always in need of purification."

### *Lumen Gentium* Section Nine: People of God

> Christ instituted this new covenant, the new covenant in his blood (see 1 Cor 11:25); he called a people together made up of Jews and Gentiles which would be one, not according to the flesh, but in the Spirit, and it would be the new people of God. (LG 9)

---

[98] Joseph Ratzinger, "Responses to Some Questions Regarding Certain Aspects of the Doctrine on the Church," June 29, 2007, http://www.vatican.va/roman_curia/congregations /cfaith/documents/rc_con_cfaith_doc_20070629_responsa-quaestiones_en.html. This document explains how the Church has come to define the use of the word "subsist."

[99] Sullivan, *The Road to Vatican II*, 33.

[100] Rahner, "Church of Sinners."

[101] Sullivan, *The Road to Vatican II*, 34.

> Advancing through trials and tribulations, the church is strength-
> ened by God's grace, promised to it by the Lord so that it may not
> waver, through the weakness of the flesh, from perfect fidelity, but
> remain the worthy bride of the Lord, ceaselessly renewing itself
> through the action of the holy Spirit until, through the cross, it may
> arrive at the light which knows no setting. (LG 9)

Embracing the image of the Church as the people of God, a people
on a pilgrimage, the council fathers are able to discuss the Church as an
institution in history. Like the Israelites, the Church as the people of God
is capable of weakness, sin, and infidelity. This dynamic image of God's
people on a journey in history is significant because it is a reminder to
each historical time period that "God does not bind his election to certain
periods of history and to membership."[102] Rather, God, at every moment
from the beginning of time, has always been calling humanity away from
sin, weakness, and infidelity toward holiness, salvation, and faithfulness.
This shift in paradigm from a Mystical Body that must be the pure, sinless
Body of Christ to one of covenant which allows for human sinfulness
and God's faithfulness is an important development in the Church's self-
understanding. This paradigm shift also opens the way for a more dynamic
role of the Spirit in ecclesiology.

Yves Congar's biblical and theological study was very influential in the
council fathers embrace of the image of the Church as a people on a journey.
This image highlights the connection of the Church with the history of the
first chosen people, the Israelites, and reveals the new people of God in Christ.

## Yves Congar

The image of the Church as the people of God, the new Israel, is significant because it highlights that, like the people of Israel, the Church is
on a pilgrimage, a journey. During this pilgrimage in time, the people of
God who are members of the Church can and do sin yet always remain
God's people. In an essay published in *Concilium* about a month after the
promulgation of *Lumen Gentium*, Congar wrote about the importance of
the "Renewal of the Idea of the People of God in Contemporary Theology":

---

[102] Vorgrimler, *Commentary on the Documents of Vatican II*, 154.

It is not always possible to pinpoint the first expression, the origin of the ideas, which, in a few years, have won general acceptance. Between 1937 and 1942 the idea of the People of God was firmly reestablished in Catholic theology. This rediscovery was the work of men who wished to go beyond the rather juridical concept of the foundation of the Church made once by Christ, and they sought in the whole Bible a development of God's Plan. This led them to rediscover the continuity of the Church with Israel, to locate the fact of the Church in the larger perspective of history of salvation and to see the Church as the People of God of messianic times. This was connected with the rediscovery of the nature or the historic dimension and the salvific institution of revelation, which culminated in the rediscovery of eschatology.[103]

For Congar and for the council fathers, the Church's continuity with Israel accentuates the fact that the Church is not at rest, but rather, on a journey. It is a pilgrim Church.

In Congar's rediscovery of the eschatological end of the Church, he sees sacraments as assisting the Church, the people of God, to turn from sin while on pilgrimage in this world. "This People is called to give witness to Christ and to his charity. It is a People composed of sinners who do penance and try to walk along the path of conversion. This is a point that many 'classical' presentations of the Church neglect, static and juridical as they often are."[104]

In *Lumen Gentium* 9, the fathers of the council do not present the Church as "static and juridical"; rather, they acknowledge the dynamism at work in the Church through the grace of the sacraments which renew the Church on its pilgrim journey. The connection between Congar's theo-

---

[103] Congar, "The Church: The People of God," in *The Church and Mankind*, 1:14. On p. 11 of this work, Congar states, "As a result of an intervention made by the Co-ordinating Commission of Vatican II . . ." From this, one can infer that Congar was present at the Coordinating Commission meetings. One can also see Congar's recently published *My Journal of the Council*, pp. xiv–xvii, in which he speaks of his involvement with writing the schema *De Ecclesia* to confer this inference. Additionally, on p. 14 of Congar's "The Church: The People of God," Congar notes that he had written in May 1937 about the idea of the people of God in his study published in French in *Esquisses du Mystère de l'Eglise* (Paris, 1941), 11f.

[104] Congar, "The Church: The People of God," in *The Church and Mankind*, 1:27.

logical reflection on the Church as the people of God on pilgrimage and the council fathers' understanding of the Church "moving forward through trial and tribulation" is obvious. Because the Church needs to purify and renew itself as it walks through trial and tribulation, the council fathers underscore the role of the Holy Spirit in the life of the pilgrim people of God. Congar's retrieval of the image of the Church as a people on a journey in need of the grace of the Spirit to grow in holiness opened up a space for the council fathers not only to acknowledge that sin is present in the Church but also to call the Church to renewal and conversion from sinfulness.

## *Lumen Gentium* Sections Thirty-Nine and Forty: Universal Call to Holiness

> Therefore, all in the church, whether they belong to the hierarchy or are cared for by it, are called to holiness. (LG 39)

> It is therefore quite clear that all Christians in whatever state or walk in life are called to the fullness of Christian life and to the perfection of charity, and this holiness is conducive to a more human way of living even in society here on earth. In order to reach this perfection the faithful should use the strength dealt out to them by Christ's gift. Thus the holiness of the people of God will grow in fruitful abundance, as is clearly shown in the history of the church by the lives of many saints. (LG 40)

Chapter 5 introduces two significant developments in the understanding of the Church. The first is that the call to holiness is universal, not just for saints, not just for ordained or religious, but fundamentally for all Christians, and it is rooted in baptism. It follows from the call to holiness that we're not there yet. Thereby, this call to holiness leaves room for the acknowledgment of sin and the call to conversion. The second development is that saints aren't perfect. Their holiness does not result from works but from God's love and grace. Vorgrimler notes the importance of these developments when he notes that Christian holiness is not concerned primarily with moral perfection or heroic human virtue but with the glory and love of God given freely to the redeemed without any merit on their part.[105]

---

[105] Vorgrimler, *Commentary on the Documents of Vatican II*, 263.

Charles Journet, a member of the Preparatory Commission, desired to see the document on the Church articulate clearly that the Church's mission was about calling all people to holiness. Hence, the Holy Spirit and not the hierarchy is the formal cause of the Church. This section of *Lumen Gentium* affirms that the call to holiness of all the Church's members is the goal of their lives. Living this call to holiness is critical, so that when one's pilgrimage on earth is over, one can share in the beatific vision. Journet's influence is quite apparent. Additionally, Henri de Lubac's retrieval of the patristic and scriptural understanding that our supernatural dignity rests on our natural dignity can also be seen as a lens through which the council fathers see the importance of placing within *Lumen Gentium* a chapter on the universal call to holiness.

## Charles Journet

> The universal call to holiness in Chapter Five of *Lumen Gentium* (#39–42) "expresses well Journet's concern that the spiritual life be not something extra, added over and above an institutional Church, but rather that which constitutes the Church's very core.[106]

The fathers of the council refer to the Church as being "indefectibly holy" through the Spirit who brings it to perfection. Here they are in accord with Journet's identification of the Spirit as the formal cause of the Church. In the hierarchy's care for the faithful, there may be an echo of Journet's designation of the hierarchy's role as the efficient cause in assisting all members of the Church on their way to sanctity.

## Henri de Lubac

De Lubac's retrieval of the patristic and biblical groundwork that grace builds on nature enabled the council fathers to see that the Church is built on a natural unity, the unity of all humanity. By sharing in this common humanity, all therefore are summoned to embrace a common or universal call to holiness. For de Lubac, humanity is one body and what affects one, affects all. Therefore, by issuing a universal call to holiness, the council

---

[106] Doyle, *Communion Ecclesiology*, 44.

fathers are calling all humanity to the grace needed to participate in the
supernatural dignity of the life of Christ.

### *Lumen Gentium* Section Forty-Eight: Church as Pilgrim

The pilgrim church, in its sacraments and institutions, which belong
to this present age . . . carries the mark of this world which will
pass, and it takes its place among the creatures which groan and
until now suffer the pains of childbirth and await the revelation of
the children of God (see Rom 8:19-22). (LG 48)

The council fathers' recognition that the Church is on a pilgrimage
opens up a way to embrace both the holiness and sinfulness of the Church.
The "pilgrim" nature of the Church acknowledges the historical existence
of the Church, its being in time, as well as recognizes that the Church's
final destination is beyond history and is eternal. This eschatological understanding of the Church allows the council fathers to account for ways
in which the Church in history has been the source of pains, anguish,
weakness, failings, and sin and has also suffered from the failings and
sins of others. At the same time, they emphasize that the Church is the
sacrament of salvation and that it offers to a sinful world the promise of
something more lasting through the grace of its sacraments and its faith
in Jesus Christ. Section 48 ties together many of the earlier themes of
*Lumen Gentium*, particularly section 1, the Church as sacrament, section
8, the Church as a "stranger in a foreign land," and section 9, the role of
the Spirit as the Church makes its journey. All of these themes accentuate
that the members of the Church are on a pilgrimage heading toward the
kingdom of God. The significance of the Church's eschatological character, according to Vorgrimler, is that in the Church, Christ's redemptive
grace has engulfed every dimension of human existence so that all will
eventually be renewed in Christ.[107]

The writings of Yves Congar and Karl Rahner contributed to this section
of *Lumen Gentium*. Congar's desire to see a reunion of Christianity not
only connotes that a holy Church must strive for unity among Christian

[107] Vorgrimler, *Commentary on the Documents of Vatican II*, 281.

churches but also presupposes the historical dimension of the Church. The image of the Church as the People of God imbued with the Holy Spirit is implied in embracing a pilgrim Church. Karl Rahner's writing on humanity as threatened by guilt is a clear reference to the sinfulness of the members of the Church. Rahner's writings on grace as God's self-communication open new vistas for understanding the Church as the instrument of that grace in the lives of humanity as it makes its pilgrimage to that transcendent God who is beyond all time and place.

## Yves Congar

In order to underscore that the Church is on pilgrimage, Congar connects the Church's history with the history of the people first called and chosen to be the people of God, Israel. Like Israel, the Church is the people of God, a people on a journey "toward the future and finally toward eschatology."[108] The renewed emphasis on eschatology was important in understanding how sinfulness and holiness exist in the Church. If the Church exists in a place of "already, but not yet," there is room for the Holy Spirit to operate in the lives of the people of God so that they can experience the grace of conversion: "This People possesses life and is advancing toward an end established for it by God."[109] The Church as the people of God, the new Israel, on a pilgrimage introduces a dynamism into the life of the Church that can account for both fidelity and sinfulness. For Congar, the Church's historicity means that there is an inherent intersection of the holiness of the Church that emanates from its foundation in the unity of the Trinity and the sinfulness of the Church which is the result of being composed of members who can and do sin. To be faithful to its nature, the Church must lay claim to both aspects, its holiness and its sinfulness.

## Karl Rahner

Like Congar, Rahner is very cognizant that the pilgrim Church exists in world history, and he was extremely careful to take that history into account in his theological writing. When he writes "The Church

---

[108] Congar, "The Church: The People of God," in *The Church and Mankind*, 1:20.
[109] Ibid., 20–21.

of Sinners" in 1947, one of the first tasks he undertakes is to look at this question of the sinfulness and holiness of the Church from the vantage point of history. A key question for Rahner is whether one can refer to the Church as sinful when in the Creed we declare her as holy. He answers this question by citing the Donatist controversy in the fourth century and the Reformation in the sixteenth century as valiant attempts to protect the holiness of the Church which ultimately demonstrated that the Church has always considered itself a refuge of sinners as well as a home for those who remain sinless and holy. The Church is the means for helping people as they strive to live a life of holiness.

Richard Lennan calls attention to Rahner's reliance on the Holy Spirit as the source for growth in holiness. "The presence of the Spirit in the Church manifested itself through the gospel and the sacraments, which even the sinful members of the Church could not impair."[110] Through the language of the Spirit, Rahner rethinks the traditional categories of sacrament, sin, and grace in order to address the problem of sin's existence in the Church. His new categories, imbued with the Spirit, opened up new ways for understanding the sinfulness of the Church in its members and leaders. Rahner argues that the categories can help to make sense of sin in the Church rather than leaving people scandalized and disillusioned. At the same time, he acknowledges the impact that the sins of the clergy in particular can have on the faith of individual members. *Lumen Gentium* 48 explicitly refers to sin in the Church and in its members as the "mark of the world" which the pilgrim Church carries.

## The Preconciliar Theologians at the Council

### Charles Journet

As a member of the Preparatory Theological Commission, Journet was influential in the preparations for the subsequent deliberations on *Lumen Gentium*. His work can be seen as an attempt to bridge the gap between the neoscholastic method of theology that emphasized certitude and

---

[110] Richard Lennan, "Ecclesiology and Ecumenism," in *The Cambridge Companion to Karl Rahner*, ed. Mary E. Hines and Declan Marmion (Cambridge, UK: Cambridge University Press, 2005), 135.

authoritative teaching with that of *ressourcement* theology that accentuated the scriptural and patristic sources.

Since the time of the Council of Trent, the Church had operated out of a heavily juridical model. One has merely to read the final decrees and canons of Trent to notice how dogmatic and polemical they were, often using words such as "condemn" and "*anathema sit.*"[111] This polemical, juridical style had guided the Church throughout the Modernist controversy; it was familiar to many of the fathers of Vatican II and favored by many on the Preparatory Commission.

For the minds and hearts of the fathers at the council to be open to new ways of thinking about theology, some middle ground had to be established. Charles Journet was instrumental in doing just that. Dennis Doyle describes Journet's crucial role as a member of the Preparatory Theological Commission that produced the first version of the text *De Ecclesia*. Journet fought against juridicism even as he operated within neoscholastic categories in his own works. He focused his ecclesiology on the importance of the Church as the Mystical Body of Christ. Doyle argues that Journet's theology found a significant place in *Lumen Gentium*:

> There was much in *Lumen Gentium* to which Journet could lay claim as compatible with his own advances. Foremost among these is having the mystery of the Church be the topic for the opening chapter with the Mystical Body of Christ as its primary image. This focus was the main point of Journet's life work. Also reflective of Journet is the first chapter's use of a broad range of scriptural images to speak of the mystery of the Church. That the chapter on the hierarchy comes third, being contextualized by the Church as mystery, is another point characteristic of Journet.[112]

Doyle suggests that Journet was able to present to the council fathers this new way of doing theology because he combined neoscholastic categories with the newly retrieved images of the Church from the *ressourcement* method. Thereby, he was able to advocate for the Mystical Body of Christ

---

[111] These observations on rhetorical style, now commonly used, are from John W. O'Malley, *Four Cultures of the West* (Cambridge, MA: Harvard University Press, 2004).

[112] Doyle, *Communion Ecclesiology*, 44.

as the primary referent image for the Church in chapter 1 of *Lumen Gentium* while simultaneously assuring the council fathers that the hierarchy would still have its role, though it had to be "contextualized" as a part of the mystery of the Church.

One can also reasonably conclude that Journet's theological writings on the holiness of the Church, in which he reworked neoscholastic categories, began to create a space wherein the fathers of Vatican II would be able to discuss issues such as the nature and mission of the Church and use both theological methods of *ressourcement* and neoscholasticism. His theological thought on how the Church can be composed of sinners, yet not sinful, was not as influential as that of other theologians on what became the final draft of *Lumen Gentium*. Dennis Doyle explains that the reason could be that "Journet's work did not anticipate a stress on the Church being always in need of reform and renewal,"[113] an idea that the council fathers embraced. Rather, Journet believed that although there are sinners within the Church, those sinners are not able to make the Church sinful. Journet contended that the Church as a body is not sinful, yet can have individual members of the body who do sin. Those individual members who sin remain in the Church by virtue of the grace of their baptism which never leaves them.

### Henri de Lubac

De Lubac's theology, which retrieved the expansive understanding of the Church in the patristic sources, was influential in helping the fathers at the council understand that the Church is the sacrament of Christ to the whole human race and that the Church is a pilgrim Church, a people on the way, "signed with a sanctity which is real although imperfect" (LG 48). His theological insights, though tending toward the divinity of the Church, were central in helping the fathers articulate how the Church can lay claim to being indefectibly holy while at the same time acknowledging that it is composed of members who sin. De Lubac's understanding of the Church's mission while on pilgrimage in this world is to be "Jesus Christ spread abroad and communicated" accentuated the sacramental nature

---

[113] Ibid.

of the Church. Describing the nature and mission of the Church in such a way helped the council fathers hold onto the holiness of the Church because in its sacraments it makes Christ present in the world while continuing to acknowledge the sinfulness of the Church because it exists in history and is composed of members who can and do sin.

## Yves Congar

The fathers of the council affirm the critical role of the Holy Spirit in the life of the Church, since it is in and through the Spirit that the Church renews herself. Through participation in the living tradition of the Church, the people of God receive from God, through the power of the Holy Spirit, grace that is necessary to live a life of holiness. This grace comes in a particularly powerful way from the sacramental life of the Church. The council fathers focus the second chapter of *Lumen Gentium* on the people of God. Since the people of God follows the chapter on the Mystery of the Church, the great sacrament of Christ, one might infer that the council fathers were trying to demonstrate how the Church's call to holiness is lived by a people who are in need of the grace of God that comes from the Holy Spirit in the sacramental life of the Church.

Congar's retrieval of the early Fathers' and scriptural insight that the Spirit is the "principle of life in the Church" opened up for the fathers of Vatican II a way to address the sinfulness and the holiness of the Church because it emphasized that the Church is on a pilgrimage in history. Because the Spirit's role is to guide the Church between "what is now and what is not yet," the Church can understand itself in terms of being called to holiness as the Body of Christ and of being weak and sinful as being composed of members who can and do sin.

Congar's extensive writing on a myriad of issues[114] that affected the Church prior to the council had a tremendous impact on the council fathers. That influence came to a climax in the fathers' understanding of

---

[114] Alberigo and Komonchak, *The History of Vatican II*, 3:260–61 references the role that Congar played as a member of the working group for the *Decree on Ecumenism, Unitatis Redintegratio*. Though this document is not being handled within the scope of this dissertation, the tremendous contribution that Congar made during the council to the furthering of ecumenism should be noted.

the Church as the people of God, a pilgrim people. Congar's starting point in his work *Divided Christendom* arose from his personal reflection on the scandal that the disunity of Christians was and is for the Church. Perhaps because his theology began from such a practical and real problematic situation for the Church, that of disunity, he was able to respond with concrete and pastoral insights.

The implementation of such insights brought with it a broader understanding of the nature and mission of the Church. The influence of Congar's theological reflections can be seen in the title that the fathers give to chapter 2 of *Lumen Gentium*, "The People of God." Additionally, its presentation of the Church as in one sense ever holy, the Body of Christ, and in another sense ever in need of conversion, a people on the way, clearly harkens back to Congar's thoughts on the fact the Church can and must at times be reformed. Helping the fathers of the council become more embedded in the living tradition of the Church that, from the beginning, has acknowledged the Spirit's role in moving the Church forward through trial and tribulation and aiding in her renewal, is one of the most significant and lasting contributions that Congar made to the council and to the Church's self-understanding.

### Karl Rahner

Rahner saw the need for an ecumenical council in the Church, but he was unsure of the impact it might have. Richard Lennan notes:

> Despite Rahner's positive assessment of both the value of ecclesial faith and its meaning for modern society, he was pessimistic on the eve of Vatican II about the contribution that even a council could make to the life of the church in the world. . . . The beginning of the Second Vatican Council, then, found Rahner in a less than buoyant mood. His negativity, however, arose from his reflection on the ways that Christians lived their faith, rather than from a fundamental doubt about the capacity of that faith to address, and offer hope to, the inhabitants of the modern world.[115]

---

[115] Richard Lennan, "Faith in Context: Rahner on the Possibility of Belief," *Philosophy & Theology* 17, no. 1 (January 1, 2005): 240–41.

For Rahner, the concern was less about how faith and God's grace could be communicated to the modern world and more about the ability of Christians of the modern era to incorporate the reality of God's self-communication into how they chose to live their lives. Rahner's hope was that this transcendental, anthropological method might be the new language needed to make the Catholic faith more accessible to the people of the twentieth century.

Although Rahner's theology was influential at the council, it is hard to pinpoint exactly where his impact was made because of the genre in which he wrote. Of his manner of doing theology, Leo O'Donovan commented, "Rahner has not presented any systematic or comprehensive treatise on ecclesiology, but rather has responded to significant issues and concerns as they emerge in the ongoing life of the Church."[116] Because one of the major issues that the council fathers were trying to address was *aggiornamento*, Rahner's theological reflections about how the Church needed to respond to the issues of the current social milieu were of import to the fathers' deliberations. Similarly, Vorgrimler observes that it is difficult to credit Rahner with particular influence on specific documents of Vatican II, though he does make some educated guesses about those places, especially in *Lumen Gentium*, wherein Rahner's theology may have had an impact on the thinking of the fathers at the council.

> If we ask ourselves today, in which conciliar texts traces of Rahner influence are to be found, it is not altogether easy to give an answer. Rahner made himself an integral part of the intensive and laborious team effort which led to the Council's texts. He had a large part in the making of *Lumen Gentium*, marked as that document is by his favorite themes: the sacramentality of the Church and its eschatological character, the collegiality of the bishops, the meaning of the local Church community, the ecclesial rather than individualistic nature of the sacraments, the salvation of non-Christians, the diaconate, and not least Mary's membership of the Church.[117]

[116] Leo J. O'Donovan, "A Changing Ecclesiology in a Changing Church: a Symposium on Development in the Ecclesiology of Karl Rahner," *Theological Studies* 38, no. 4 (December 1, 1977): 738.

[117] Herbert Vorgrimler, "Karl Rahner: The Theologian's Contribution," in *Vatican Two Revisited: By Those Who Were There*, ed. Alberic Stacpoole (San Francisco: Harper San Francisco, 1986), 44.

All of the themes in *Lumen Gentium* that Vorgrimler notes as "favorites" of Rahner could have become part of *Lumen Gentium* because of the influence of Rahner's theological reflections on the Church. What is interesting about these themes is how they tend to wed the divine and human aspects of the Church together. By doing so, the foundation of Rahner's theology, grace and its ongoing need in the life of a pilgrim Church, is evident.

## Holiness and Sinfulness in Other Documents of Vatican II

The council fathers' theme of the Church and the topic of the holiness and sinfulness of the Church discussed in *Lumen Gentium* (1964) are reflected and supported in the documents that followed: *Unitatis Redintegratio* (1964), *Nostra Aetate* (1965), *Dignitatis Humanae* (1965), and *Gaudium et Spes* (1965). The connection between the theme and topics found in *Lumen Gentium* and these subsequent four documents raises some of the hermeneutical issues about change and continuity. Rush's approach in interpreting Vatican II, which includes the hermeneutics of the text, authors, and receivers suggests that careful attention should be paid to the intratextuality and intertextuality of the conciliar documents, since all five documents reflect developments in thinking about the Church. This section also takes into account the 1985 Synod of Bishops' recommendation that called for attention to the close interrelationship among the council documents in theological interpretation of them.

*Unitatis Redintegratio*, promulgated on the same day as *Lumen Gentium*, expands on what the council fathers began to address in *Lumen Gentium* 8, the scandal and sinfulness of the divisions of Christianity. In the first paragraph of *Unitatis Redintegratio*, the fathers write that this "division openly contradicts the will of Christ, scandalizes the world, and damages the sacred cause of preaching the Gospel to every creature."

Not even a year later, on October 28, 1965, the council fathers again, building on *Lumen Gentium* chapter 2, on the people of God, promulgated a decree specifically discussing the Church's relationship to non-Christian religions, *Nostra Aetate*. In section 9 of *Lumen Gentium*, the council fathers discuss that the Church's foundation rests upon Israel. In section 16 they note that the Moslems "profess to hold the faith of Abraham" and that God is not "remote from those [who] in shadows and images seek the unknown God." Although the council fathers in *Lumen Gentium* speak about overcoming the sins of the past with regard to non-Christian religions, in *Nostra Aetate* section 2, there is a specific call to the Church's "sons and daughters to enter with prudence and charity into discussion and collaboration with members of other religions." And, in section 3, there is an acknowledgment of the "quarrels and dissensions between Christians and Muslims" and the need to forget the past and move forward. Clearly, the sin of the Church in such quarrels and dissensions is suggested, although perhaps not as forcefully as some might have wanted.

*Lumen Gentium* also sets the stage for *Dignitatis Humanae* and *Gaudium et Spes*, both of which were promulgated on December 7, 1965. In *Lumen Gentium* 16, the council fathers call attention to those who "through no fault of their own, do not know the Gospel of Christ or his church, but who nevertheless seek God with a sincere heart, and, moved by grace, try in their actions to do his will as they know it through the dictates of their conscience." In *Dignitatis Humanae* 12, the council fathers not only expand on the principle of religious freedom but also note the following:

> Although, in the life of the people of God in its pilgrimage, through the vicissitudes of human history, there have at times appeared patterns of behavior which was not in keeping with the spirit of the Gospel and were opposed to it, it has always remained the teaching of the church that no one is to be coerced into believing.

The council fathers want to make it abundantly clear that the mandate to preach and spread the Gospel never included forcing people to believe and be baptized. Again, some would argue that the acknowledgment of the sinfulness of allowing such things to happen in the past could have been more forthright. The council fathers' articulation of the principle of religious freedom and the Church's support of it are, however, major developments and can be connected to the groundwork laid in *Lumen Gentium*.

Finally, the discussion of the Church which began with the promulgation of *Lumen Gentium* culminated in the promulgation of *Gaudium et Spes*. Following Cardinal Suenens's suggestion about discussing the Church in itself (*ad intra*) and its mission (*ad extra*) in *Lumen Gentium*, the council fathers considered how the Church could understand its nature and mission better. The titles of the chapters of *Lumen Gentium* stress the internal workings of the Church and its membership. In the preface of *Gaudium et Spes*, the council fathers begin by noting that "the joys and hopes, the grief and anguish of the people of our time" are also those of the followers of Christ. Clearly, the Church is in the world and wants to bring the light of Christ to the world. In this respect, *Gaudium et Spes* completes *Lumen Gentium*. Studying the mystery of the Church in *Lumen Gentium* lays the foundation for expressing the Church's presence and function in the world for the benefit of all people, not just its members.

## Conclusion: An Unfinished Agenda

The theologians discussed in chapter 1 laid the foundation for many of the themes discussed at Vatican II, namely, the Church as the Mystical Body of Christ, the Church as sacrament to the world, the Church as the people of God, the dynamic role of the Spirit in the life of the Church, the scandal of divided Christendom, and the Church on pilgrimage. These themes became part of *Lumen Gentium* and helped advance the discussion of the theology of the holiness and sinfulness of the Church. But as Bernard Yetzer has pointed out, while these conciliar documents offer the most comprehensive and critically incisive magisterial statement to date on the question of sin in the holy Church, they do not explicitly and systematically deal with the question of the existence of sin in the holy Church.[118] Rather, there is a movement toward the understanding advanced by Congar that the Church is itself sinless, but insofar as it exists in history, is composed of members who sin, its holiness always imperfect.[119]

The council fathers clearly did not make a definitive judgment on how sin exists in a holy Church. They did, however, embrace themes and images that set the stage for further exploration of this question. As the Church walks in history, the "how" of interpreting what is meant by a holy Church composed of sinners is part of the unfinished agenda of Vatican II. We will see in chapter 3 how the millennial program of Pope John Paul II is one example of the Church working on this unfinished agenda.

---

[118] Yetzer, *Holiness and Sin in the Church*, 257–58.
[119] Ibid., 263.

## After Vatican II

The impact of Rahner's forthright recognition of this issue of the presence of sin in the Church, particularly the Church's leaders, was not endorsed by the fathers of the council as fully as Rahner would have liked. The importance of his attempt in confronting this issue, however, should not be underestimated. Lennan explains that despite his disappointment that the fathers of the council did not address the issue of sin in the Church forthrightly, Rahner did see:

> in the Council's stress on "the pilgrim Church" the potential for a deeper awareness of the sinful nature of that Church. This was so because acknowledgment of the Church's pilgrim status implied that the Church was neither a heavenly entity untouched by history nor an "institute of salvation" which cared for people while not identifying itself with them. Similarly, Rahner suggested that the resonances of "the people of God" as a synonym for the Church could, more obviously than allusion to "the mystical body," accommodate a sinful Church. Rahner claimed that calls for renewal of the Church—a popular conciliar motif best represented by the reference in *Lumen Gentium* to the Church as *semper purificanda* (LG 8)—had meaning only if it was first accepted that the Church was indeed the subject of sin and guilt.[120]

There are places in *Lumen Gentium* in which one can infer the council fathers' response to the sinfulness of the Church. Rahner points out, however, in an essay on "The Sinful Church in the Decrees of Vatican II," that "the Constitution on the Church does not treat this question with the explicit clarity, intensity and detail which one could expect."[121] In the essay, however, he does "attempt to show that the Constitution on the Church does in fact offer some very noteworthy points of departure for a theology of sin in the Church as such."[122]

Rahner attributes the deficiency on the subject of sin in the Church to the fact that the council fathers did not set out to write "a balanced and systematically complete summary of a whole ecclesiology."[123] Rather, the

---

[120] Lennan, *Ecclesiology of Karl Rahner*, 150–51.

[121] Rahner, *Theological Investigations*, vol. 6, 279.

[122] Ibid., 280.

[123] Ibid.

constitution on the Church grew out of topics of pastoral and ecumenical concern which the council fathers had indicated needed attention. Furthermore, he notes that the Constitution's reserve on the matter of a sinful Church was also due to the fact that "in the traditional ecclesiology of the past century this topic was not far enough evolved (beyond the doctrine that sinners are members of the Church) as to make it appear to a majority of the Theological Commission or of the Council Fathers self-evidently a topic to be treated expressly."[124] With that as background, however, Rahner does point out that "the framework which is in fact given in the Constitution for the doctrine of the Church of sinners is the doctrine of the pilgrim Church."[125] He observes that the theme of a Church on pilgrimage highlights the Church's existence in history and as such is subject to trials, tribulations, suffering, persecution, etc. For Rahner, the Church on pilgrimage is clearly distinguishable in *Lumen Gentium* from the Church of the eternal consummation. He also calls attention to the image of the Church as the people of God, which makes room for the idea of the Church sinners. Although to Rahner's dismay, *Lumen Gentium* avoids using the expression "sinful Church." He observes that it brings out the fact behind the expression that the Church is herself affected by the sins of her members.[126]

The failure of the council fathers to consider explicitly the question of how the Church can simultaneously be sinful and holy has serious implications for the life of the Church. Rahner writes:

> Only if the Church recognizes herself to be the Church of sinners will she be permanently convinced of the fact, and aware of the full force of the obligation it entails, that she has a constant need of being cleansed, that she must always strive to do penance and achieve inner reform. Otherwise all demands for reform will become merely presumptuous prescriptions and inefficacious desires all of which, while they can perfect the legal system of an institution and develop a pastoral technique on the grand scale, are not in touch with real life, true faith and the human Church. Once it is kept clearly in mind that the Church on earth is *always* the Church of sinners, then it becomes intelligible how and why she is the holy Church: namely

[124] Ibid., 281.
[125] Ibid.
[126] Ibid., 284.

> by the grace of God, which alone does not permit the Church as
> a whole to fall away from God's grace and truth and so makes her
> indefectibly holy.[127]

Again, Rahner is trying to assist the Church in finding ways to become more credible with people of the current milieu. By admitting sin, being pastoral, and embracing reform, the Church will open itself more fully to the grace of God and, thereby, in a strange twist, become ever more holy. Unfortunately, the council fathers' articulation of the Church's need of ongoing conversion by acknowledging the pilgrim nature of the Church and by imaging the Church through the lens of the people of God stopped short of embracing the idea of the Church as a Church of sinners.

## Hans Urs von Balthasar:
## A Vision that Still Needs Time

Von Balthasar delves into the question of how the sin of the members affects the Church's holiness in his essay, "*Casta Meretrix*."[128] Though he was strongly influenced by the work of de Lubac, his manner of handling sin in the Church differed greatly. Von Balthasar saw a living, active God at work within history and theology in the spiritual lives of individual people, including their sinfulness. He was able to find God at work in all things, including and especially in the places wherein people need forgiveness and healing. Because people in the Church can and do sin, von Balthasar makes no excuse for the imperfection or sin in the Church; rather, he just accepts it as a reality, there is sin in the Church.

There are a few reasons that von Balthasar's writing on this issue was not more influential on the council fathers. First, von Balthasar was not present at the council as a *peritus*, although his mentor, de Lubac, was.[129] Second, his

---

[127] Ibid., 292.

[128] Hans Urs von Balthasar, *Explorations in Theology: Spouse of the Word* (San Francisco: Ignatius Press, 1991), 198.

[129] Jared Wicks, "Further Light on Vatican Council II," *Catholic Historical Review* 95, no. 3 (2009): 554n24 calls attention to de Lubac's own lament, late in Vatican II, that no one had thought to involve von Balthasar: "The Church thus deprived itself of its best theologian." (November 11, 1965; *Carnets* 2:456).

understanding of the Church as a *casta meretrix* was a vision that was a bit startling to embrace. The council fathers do acknowledge that the Church is on pilgrimage and, therefore, could be seen at times as sinful through the actions of its members. But it was not possible for the council fathers to move in the direction of embracing von Balthasar's prophetic attitude of asserting the Church's sinfulness[130] without offering the qualification that its sin is due to members who sin or to the realities of being on pilgrimage in this world.

At the turn of the twenty-first century, however, John Paul II, in his millennial program, sought forgiveness for the sins of the Church and brought the Church closer to embracing von Balthasar's understanding of the Church as a *casta meretrix*. My contention is that von Balthasar's theological reflections had a significant influence on Pope John Paul and were in part responsible for his millennial program in which he asks for forgiveness of the sins of the Church. For this reason, I have included von Balthasar's work in this study. Its influence will be explored in the following chapter.

---

[130] Ephraim Radner, *A Brutal Unity: The Spiritual Politics of the Christian Church* (Waco, TX: Baylor University Press, 2012), 157. In the chapter "The Sins of the Church," Radner notes that "the traditional ecclesial representation of *casta meretrix* is misunderstood if it is applied in terms of a chronological succession—first 'whore' then 'chaste.' Rather, as we shall see like Balthasar, he views the Church as the whore taken by the Lord and in her takenness lies her ecclesiality. That is, she is always the sinful whore whose holiness is in her surrender to the Lord."

# CHAPTER THREE

# Preconciliar Theologians and *Lumen Gentium*

## Usher in Pope John Paul II's Millennial Program

As the turn of the twenty-first century approached, theologians were more apt to use the inductive method as well as a pastoral mode in doing theology, as these methods had been employed by the council fathers in writing the documents of Vatican II. The use of methods such as these could be seen as having helped to lay the groundwork for Pope John Paul II's desire to include as part of the millennial celebration a papal statement seeking forgiveness for the historic faults and failings of the Church since the birth of Christ. The documents written for this jubilee celebration, *Tertio Millennio Adveniente* and *Novo Millennio Ineunte*, as well as the papal litany of repentance offered on March 12, 2000, can be seen as the fruit of Vatican II's new self-understanding of the Church that was articulated in *Lumen Gentium*.

John Paul II's millennial documents, while in continuity with the nature and mission of the Church as portrayed by the council fathers in *Lumen Gentium*, developed a further understanding of the pilgrim nature of the Church which includes an explicit striving for holiness while being very aware of its members' sinfulness. Admitting that the Church in its members has sinned and needs to seek forgiveness is at the heart of the millennial program of John Paul II and also at the heart of the Church's mission.

Not only understanding that sin exists in the Church through its members but also that the pope as representative of the Church can seek forgiveness for such sin was a different experience for Catholics. This "new" experience would not have been possible at the beginning of the twentieth century, a time when theology was manual based, juridical, and defensive in nature. Through the retrieval of patristic theologies of the Church at Vatican II, there emerged a renewed understanding of Church. Instead of defending itself from the world, the Church could see its mission as bringing Christ to the world in and through the work of the Holy Spirit. These renewed christological and pneumatological understandings of the nature of the Church can be viewed as assisting Church leaders to reflect on the actions or inactions of its members and when they were not in concert with the Church's christological and pneumatological foundations.

## Background and Influences on Pope John Paul II's Millennial Program of Repentance

Pope John Paul's desire to mark the two thousand years which have passed since the birth of Christ by asking for forgiveness and pardon for the sins of the children of the Church was not a new concept in his thought.

Perhaps one of the most influential experiences of forgiveness and pardon in the life of Karol Wojtyla occurred just about twenty days prior to his election as pope.[1] In September 1978 an initiative of forgiveness, begun shortly after Vatican II, culminated in the meeting of a Polish delegation of bishops with their German colleagues. Then-Archbishop Wojtyla was a participant in the reconciliation meeting on Sept. 27, 1978, in Mainz. The theme of this meeting was "Forgive and Ask Forgiveness." At this 1978 meeting, the bishops of each country sought forgiveness for the many difficulties between their people throughout history, but particularly for the atrocities of World War II. This event, as we shall see, had a lasting impact on the life of Wojtyla and the importance he put on asking for and receiving forgiveness.

In 1988, Avery Dulles asked "Should the Church Repent?" in an article in which he observes that apologizing for faults in the Church had become a hallmark of the papacy of John Paul II.[2] One poignant example of John Paul II's ability to see and respond to the need for the Church to apologize for its historic faults and failings occurred early in his pontificate when

---

[1] Luigi Accattoli, *When a Pope Asks Forgiveness: The Mea Culpa's of Pope John Paul II* (Pauline Books & Media, 1998), 48–49.

[2] Avery Dulles, "Should the Church Repent?" *First Things*, no. 88 (December 1, 1998): 36–41.

he established a committee to reassess the condemnation of Galileo. The result of its work was the retraction by the Church of its 1633 denunciation of Galileo. The reopening of this case is significant because it marks the encounter between the Church and the modern age and indicates a dissatisfaction with the act of reparation found in *Gaudium et Spes* (GS 36) which attempted to make amends without mentioning Galileo's name. The decision to return to this case reveals the pope's confidence that historical faults and failings can be discussed and, at times, clarified.[3] Further, in John Paul II's opening address to the Extraordinary Consistory on June 13–14, 1994, he clearly articulated his desire to call the Church to acknowledging its need for repentance:

> With the approach of this Great Jubilee the Church needs a *meta-noia*, that is, a discernment of the historical faults and failures of her members in responding to the demands of the gospel. Only the courageous admission of the faults and omissions of which Christians are judged to be guilty in some degree, and also the generous intention to make amends, with God's help, can provide an efficacious initiative for the new evangelization and make the path to unity easier.[4]

John Paul II was not afraid that such a statement during the millennial celebration might be misinterpreted by people as an acknowledgment that the Church itself was sinful.

In *When the Pope Asks Forgiveness*, Luigi Accattoli suggests that John Paul II's fearlessness about this apologetic millennial statement can be seen to emanate from the influence that Hans Urs von Balthasar's writings had on him.[5] Von Balthasar's writings were instrumental in John Paul II's staying the course on his program of *metanoia* for the Church, even when faced with opposition.[6] Accattoli, describing von Balthasar's effect on John Paul's millennial statement, writes:

---

[3] Accattoli, *When a Pope Asks Forgiveness*, 125–26.

[4] Avery Dulles, *Church and Society: The Laurence J. McGinley Lectures, 1988–2007* (New York: Fordham University Press, 2008), 263.

[5] Accattoli, *When a Pope Asks Forgiveness*, 5.

[6] Ibid. Accattoli infers that von Balthasar's writing in 1965 at the close of Vatican II calling for a full confession could have had a profound impact on Bishop Wojtyla

Balthasar was surely one of the most influential promoters of a "confession" of the sins committed by the Church throughout the centuries. The burden does not exist for other men and it is decidedly very light for Protestants, for they are not responsible for the first fifteen centuries of the Church. Neither is it a burden for the Orthodox Christians, who must answer only for their own particular Church. But the Catholic has not escaped.[7]

Von Balthasar believed that the Catholic Church, more than all other Christian denominations, bore the culpability for the divisions of Christianity precisely because of its failure to keep Christendom united. Von Balthasar enumerates the errors that caused such division:

Forcible baptisms, inquisitions and *auto-da-fé's*, the Saint Bartholomew's Day massacre, the conquest of new worlds with fire and sword as if the release of brutal exploitation were also the way of the religion of the cross and of love; unasked for and utterly absurd meddling in the problems of developing natural science; proscriptions and excommunications by a spiritual authority which behaves as if it were political, and even demands recognition as such.[8]

With this rationale for the confession of sin and a list of sins committed by the Church, von Balthasar proposed what such a confession should entail, namely, no defense, a full confession, and a caveat to not throw stones "when no one is alive to stand up and plead justification."[9]

Von Balthasar's writings on the history and tradition of the Church reflected on some of the darkest and most sinful moments in the life of the Church. He saw the seamy side of the Church's missionary efforts made manifest in forced baptisms, in the brutal exploitation of peoples in new worlds, and in the overarching ambition and control exerted by Church leaders in the political sphere. His concern was that if these issues of the

---

who, in the same year, became involved in the asking and giving of pardon between the Polish and German bishops for the struggle between the two nations which resulted in the genocide that took place in the Second World War.

[7] Hans Urs von Balthasar, *Who Is a Christian?*, trans. J. Cumming (New York: Newman Press, 1967),14–15ff, quoted in Accattoli, *When a Pope Asks Forgiveness*, 3.

[8] Ibid., 4.

[9] Ibid.

sinful past of the Church were not addressed and named for what they were, "sinful," the Church's credibility would continue to be questioned.

Von Balthasar's retrieval of the writings of the early Fathers that recognized the Church's sinfulness demonstrated that the idea of acknowledging the Church as sinful was in keeping with the tradition of the Church. As von Balthasar argued in "*Casta Meretrix*," the struggle between holiness and sinfulness is both internal as well as external:

> The seriousness of the issue dawns on us when we stop seeing the bride's infidelity as something largely outside her, in heresy, and realize that it exists inside her. All Christians are sinners, and if the Church does not sin as Church, she does sin, in all her members and through the mouths of all her members she must confess her guilt.[10]

In admitting that sin exists in the Church, von Balthasar was not making a judgment about the Church but merely stating the fact that sin must exist in the Church as she is composed of members who are sinners. To achieve salvation, Christ, the sinless one, must fully assume our sinful humanity. Because of this, for von Balthasar, the Church being sinful is not an abnormality but rather the means of our salvation. For von Balthasar, "in the divine aesthetic, the beautiful does not simply appear despite sin, but in sin itself."[11] Von Balthasar's belief is that the Church, like Christ, assumes the sinfulness of its members. Von Balthasar can envision the existence of a sinful Church because the destiny of the Church and its members are intertwined,[12] and he is not alone in seeing this compatibility of holiness and sin in the Church. As noted in chapter 1 of this study, von Balthasar cites the writings of St. Bernard, St. Eusebius, and St. Augustine on the existence of sin within the Church. They admitted the reality of sin in the Church "without defense, judgment and/or throwing stones." John Paul's millennial program makes a similar admission that sin exists in the Church. His admission, however, is more nuanced than that of his

---

[10] Ibid., 244–45.

[11] William T. Cavanaugh, *Migrations of the Holy: God, State, and the Political Meaning of the Church* (Grand Rapids, MI: Eerdmans, 2011), 160.

[12] Jeremy M. Bergen, *Ecclesial Repentance: The Churches Confront Their Sinful Pasts* (London/ New York: T. & T. Clark International, 2011), 235.

mentor, von Balthasar, as John Paul II acknowledges sin only in the sons and daughters of the Church.

Another important influence on John Paul II's thoughts was the documents of Vatican II. As Dennis Doyle comments:

> A fresh testimony to the ongoing relevance of Vatican II is given by John Paul II in his 1994 "As the Third Millennium Draws Near." This apostolic letter, which details preparation for the celebration of the year 2000, relies heavily upon the documents of Vatican II. Over fifty percent (22 of 41) of the letter's citations are to six of the Council's sixteen documents. It is not just the quantity, however, but the quality and force of the references that make them so integral and important to John Paul II's vision of the Church in the year 2000.[13]

In addition, as we shall see below, John Paul will link John XXIII's call for a new Pentecost at the outset of Vatican II to his call for a new Advent as a way to prepare for the third millennium. Along with the fact that twenty-two of the forty-one citations in John Paul II's millennial letter refer to the documents of Vatican II, the appeal to John XXIII makes a good case that the council had a tremendous influence on the program that John Paul set for the millennial celebration.

Before we turn to the documents John Paul II wrote for the millennial celebration, we will look at material he presented in preparation for the upcoming observation of the beginning of the third millennium since the birth of Christ.

## The Anonymous Memo

Prior to the release of *Tertio Millennio Adveniente* in November 1994, a twenty-three page internal memorandum (referred to as "only a work sheet") titled "Reflections on the Great Jubilee of the Year Two Thousand" was sent to all the cardinals who were to attend an Extraordinary Consistory on June 13, 1994.[14] This memorandum has neither a precise date nor an acknowledged author. Some of its contents seem to have been leaked to the Italian newspaper *La Stampa*, as it published an interview

---

[13] Dennis M. Doyle, *Communion Ecclesiology: Visions and Versions* (New York: Orbis Books, 2000), 79.

[14] Accattoli, *When a Pope Asks Forgiveness*, 55.

with Jas Gawronski on November 2, 1993, in which he reported that, "at the end of this second millennium we must make an examination of conscience: where we are, where Christ has brought us, where we have deviated from the Gospel."[15] That is all that is known of this mysterious document which sought written responses from all the cardinals about the proposed ways to celebrate the Jubilee.[16] Nevertheless, here we find proof of the dramatic change that had occurred in the way in which the Church operated after Vatican II.

Although at first it was not clear who wrote this memorandum, later, on two occasions during the Consistory, Pope John Paul revealed that he was the author: "As I pointed out in the memorandum" and "In the cited memorandum I have emphasized."[17] Prior to Vatican II, the pope usually issued edicts from the Vatican. At the turn of the century, however, the pope, in a spirit of collegiality, sent a proposal to all the cardinals to elicit their support for his millennial program.

This memorandum has come to be seen as a precursor to Pope John Paul II's *Tertio Millennio Adveniente*. In it the pope outlined his intention that the Church acknowledge the "faults and failures of her members in responding to the demands of the Gospel."[18] The proposal presented in the memorandum was not well received by the cardinals. As a matter of fact, Accattoli notes that "the Pope repeated his proposal energetically because it had aroused doubts and objections among the cardinals in a previous consultation conducted by mail. And there were doubts and objections expressed even during the Consistory."[19] Of these doubts and objections, there was only one first-hand account that was ever published, that of Cardinal Biffi.

In 1995, Cardinal Biffi published a book, *Christus Hodie*, in which he explained that his major concern with the pope's proposed millennial

---

[15] *La Stampa*, November 2, 1993, quoted in Accattoli, *When a Pope Asks Forgiveness*, 53.

[16] George Weigel, *Witness to Hope: The Biography of Pope John Paul II* (New York: HarperCollins, 1999), 741. Additionally, in an e-mail correspondence with George Weigel dated September 19, 2012, he states that "it is probably safe to assume that the content of the memo was about the same as *Tertio Millennio Adveniente*."

[17] Accattoli, *When a Pope Asks Forgiveness*, 55.

[18] Ibid., 58.

[19] Ibid., 58–59.

statement was that "the element of repentance applies to the individual person, but Pope John Paul calls for a community dimension in the examination of conscience."[20] Yet in this communal examination, Pope John Paul draws on the ancient concept of human solidarity that is, that humanity, created in the image and likeness of God, shares in a common bond. Accattoli characterizes Cardinal Biffi's concerns this way:

> Cardinal Biffi treats exclusively of the risks involved in the initiative: the scandal to the simple faithful, the possible confusion about sin in the Church, the need to prove the errors by an objective investigation, the difficulty of avoiding anachronistic statements, and failure to accompany the admission of faults with the assertion that they have not prevented the Church from producing the fruits of sanctity. Strictly speaking, Cardinal Biffi was simply advising prudence in the manner of conducting and concluding the examination proposed by the Pope. He does not say explicitly whether the examination of conscience should be made or not. But the tone of his critique is such that it would be better not to do it, although the Cardinal certainly would not publicly say as much.[21]

Although Pope John Paul II was confronted with direct objections during closed sessions with the Curia, such as those from Cardinal Biffi, as well as indirect ones, he did not retreat from the main tenet of his millennial program: repentance of the Church for its faults, as outlined in the memorandum he had issued to the cardinals in the spring of 1994.

This type of collegiality and dialogue around theological issues would not have been possible at the beginning of the twentieth century. Though the pope didn't act on the advice of the cardinals, which will be discussed below, the idea of a pope being willing to listen to such objections in an open forum was new. Formerly, the use of the neoscholastic method left little room for dialogue. John Paul II, though he heard and understood the objections of the cardinals to his plan, did not agree with them and decided to go forward. This type of dialogue signals that the atmosphere in which theology was being done had undergone a major change by the close of the twentieth century.

---

[20] Giacomo Biffi, *Christus Hodie* (Bologna: EDB, 1995), 23–24.
[21] Accattoli, *When a Pope Asks Forgiveness*, 66.

Having looked at the preparation and consultation in which the pope engaged prior to the dissemination of his millennial program, we will now turn to the discussion of *Tertio Millennio Adveniente*, John Paul II's apostolic letter in which he explains in detail the Church's celebration of the millennium.

## *Tertio Millennio Adveniente*

On November 14, 1994, Pope John Paul II gave his first general, public response to the issues and concerns raised by the cardinals about his millennial program in his apostolic letter *Tertio Millennio Adveniente*. In paragraphs 10 and 16 of this document, the pope draws on the fact that the Church existing in time and in history is on a pilgrimage which will last until the Parousia. The coming of God in the Parousia is an event that the Church anxiously awaits and prepares for by trying to "create conditions to ensure that the power of salvation may be shared by all" (TMA 16). The pope sees the celebration of the Year 2000 in the context of rejoicing in our salvation.

The pope then suggests that the Second Vatican Council was a preparation for this Jubilee because it focused on the mystery of Christ and his Church and the need for the Church, after the disturbing experiences of the First and Second World Wars, to be open to the world (TMA 17). John Paul notes that the impact of the world wars on the Church brought about a focus for Vatican II that was qualitatively different from previous councils. It is reasonable to assume that the preconciliar theologians, especially Mersch, de Lubac, and Congar, were influential in the council's shift of focus. The two world wars had a profound impact on Mersch, de Lubac, and Congar in particular and affected their theology. This is evidenced by both Mersch's and de Lubac's concern for the entire human race being called to become part of the Mystical Body of Christ. It can also be seen in Congar's concern for the Church to find ways to unite divided Christendom. All of these concerns had their foundation in the theologians' experience of living during those world wars. Their theology and the experience of the bishops who had lived through those times influenced the fathers at Vatican II. The documents of Vatican II, in turn, were the foundation for John Paul II's call for the Church to acknowledge its own role in contributing to the world's sins and failings. At the same time, the Church was also the means for the world's conversion and purification.

*Tertio Millennio Adveniente* continues, highlighting:

> that *the Council drew much from the experiences and reflections of*
> *the immediate past*, especially from the intellectual legacy left by
> Pius XII. In the history of the Church, the "old" and the "new" are
> always closely interwoven. The "new" grows out of the "old," and
> the "old" finds a fuller expression in the "new." (TMA 18)

The pope concludes by noting that all of the twentieth-century popes
have "made a significant contribution to the *preparation of that new*
*springtime of Christian life* which will be revealed by the Great Jubilee,
if Christians are docile to the action of the Holy Spirit" (TMA 18). The
pneumatological aspect of John Paul II's millennial program must be
highlighted. John Paul continues to emphasize the importance of the
Holy Spirit's role in assisting the Church to heed the various calls in the
documents of Vatican II to renew the life of the Church. John Paul's words
accentuate a tone of openness and inclusivity of all Christians in the Great
Jubilee celebration.

John Paul II emphasizes that the call for renewal comes from the
Church's desire to be faithful to Jesus Christ. It is out of faithfulness that
the Church questioned her identity and discovered anew the depth of
her mystery as the Body and the Bride of Christ. Vatican II's focus on
the universal call to holiness, reform of the liturgy, and promotion of the
vocation of the laity, religious, priests, deacons, and bishops was part of
the process of Church renewal. The pope ends paragraph 19 noting the
extensiveness of Vatican II's articulation of the need for Christian unity
as well as for dialogue with non-Christian religions.

Highlighting the new moment in the life of the Church after Vatican
II, John Paul notes the striking genre[22] and tone of the council docu-
ments which were presented in the language of the gospel, the Sermon on
the Mount, and the Beatitudes (TMA 20). John Paul then challenges the
Church to enter the new millennium by applying the teachings of Vatican
II as faithfully as possible to the life of every individual and of the whole
Church (TMA 20).

---

[22] John Paul II's highlighting genre and tone is in the same vein as what Ormond
Rush does in his book, *Still Interpreting Vatican II: Some Hermeneutical Principles*
(New York: Paulist Press, 2004).

The pope clearly connects his millennial program to the documents of Vatican II and the ongoing tradition of the Church. Simultaneously, he directs attention to the council's call for reform and renewal of the Church. Because the council's teachings were so broad and comprehensive, John Paul realizes that the best preparation for the new millennium can be found in the documents of Vatican II, and it is with them in mind that he unfolds his millennial program for the Church. Using the conciliar documents as the grounding for the call for the Church to examine, acknowledge, and repent for the sins and failings of "her sons and daughters," the pope could now move with his millennial program of repentance and forgiveness.

In paragraph 33, John Paul put forth the most controversial part of his plan for the celebration of this Jubilee:

> The Church should become more fully conscious of the sinfulness of her children, recalling all those times in history when they departed from the spirit of Christ and his Gospel and, instead of offering to the world the witness of a life inspired by the values of faith, indulged in ways of thinking and acting which were truly *forms of counter-witness and scandal* (TMA 33).

Focusing on the Jubilee itself, he invites the Church to enter the Holy Door with

> a clear awareness of what has happened to her during the last ten centuries. She cannot cross the threshold of the new millennium without encouraging her children to purify themselves, through repentance, of past errors and instances of infidelity, inconsistency, and slowness to act. Acknowledging the weaknesses of the past is an act of honesty and courage that helps us to strengthen our faith, which in turn alerts us to face today's temptations and challenges and prepares us to meet them. (TMA 33)

The acknowledgment of the sins and weaknesses of the past that John Paul enumerated in *Tertio Millennio Adveniente* is tied to themes that the fathers of the council discussed in their documents, as well as the list mentioned earlier in this chapter that von Balthasar had enumerated in his theological reflections. Dennis Doyle observes that the pope closely follows the lead of Vatican II when he discusses the poor historical record of the Church on matters of tolerance and respect for religious freedom, but he also emphasizes the need for "a serious examination of conscience above all on the part of the church of today" (TMA 36). Doyle also suggests that John Paul's "document is a renewed effort in openness to the modern world, including a stress on social justice, the option for the poor, religious freedom, and interreligious dialogue."[23]

Doyle aptly makes the case that John Paul's calling the Church to repentance in *Tertio Millennio Adveniente* is in many ways a natural follow-up to the calls to renewal that are present in the documents of Vatican II. The pope's emphasis on the documents of Vatican II, particularly the need for ecumenical and interreligious dialogue, tolerance, and respect for religious freedom seems to echo the voice of Yves Congar. These issues, particularly the issue of Christian unity, were very close to Congar's heart and were very much a part of his theological work, beginning with his first work, *Divided Christendom*. The sinfulness of the divisions and disunity of Christendom were certainly at the fore of the documents of Vatican II and now were becoming an integral part of the millennial program that the pope was promoting in *Tertio Millennio Adveniente*.

The reception of the latest ecumenical council is certainly part of the mission of the Church; examination of conscience and forgiveness of sins are also very much in keeping with the nature and mission of the Church. When John Paul II's vision of the reception of Vatican II included a communal examination of conscience, however, some people were very concerned about the theological ramifications of such a step. The pope's answer to this legitimate concern is found in *Tertio Millennio Adveniente* 33: "although she is holy because of her incorporation into Christ, the Church does not tire of doing penance: before God and man *she always acknowledges as her own her sinful sons and daughters*."

Subsequent to the promulgation of *Tertio Millennio Adveniente*, in 1995 several commissions were established to oversee the Jubilee preparations. One commission of critical import to our study is the Historical Theological Commission which was headed by Fr. Georges Cottier. The title of this commission bespeaks the questions that John Paul II's millennial

---

[23] Dennis M. Doyle, *Communion Ecclesiology: Vision and Versions* (Maryknoll, NY: Orbis Books, 2000), 81–82.

program of repentance raised and still need to be answered more fully. How do history and theology interface? Official Church documents deny that the Church is an agent of sin; yet John Paul was proposing the Church do penance for a past not necessarily its own but that of its members. Questions such as which histories and which memories needed pardoning began to arise.[24] Though various commissions and symposia were held, i.e., in 1997 the symposium "The Roots of Anti-Judaism in the Christian Environment," and in 1998 a symposium on the Inquisition, differences about the sagacity of this program of repentance continued to abound. The most public differences were aired by Biffi and Cottier. Though they both agreed on the Church's holiness in Christ and on sin as a personal reality, the underlying concern was how this "papal request for pardon" would affect the Church's credibility. Biffi's view was that it would harm the faith of the ordinary Catholic and "might teach Christians that principles such as peace and solidarity are derived from consensus rather than following Christ."[25] Cottier, on the other hand, argued that the Church's credibility would be enhanced by its acknowledgment of the sin and scandal already present; additionally, it would provide an example of how to form and examine conscience by reflecting on the past.[26] Jeremy Bergen, in his analysis of these two positions, explains that the basic theological difference is that Biffi sees sin as external to the Church and Cottier sees it as both internal and external.

Because the content of *Tertio Millennio Adveniente* had nevertheless created such uneasiness, the International Theological Commission (ITC) responded with the document *Memory and Reconciliation: The Church and the Faults of the Past* (December 1999). That document helps deepen the understanding of the context, interpretation, and reception of *Tertio Millennio Adveniente*.

---

[24] Bergen, *Ecclesial Repentance*, 118.
[25] Ibid., 122.
[26] Ibid.

## Memory and Reconciliation:
## The Church and the Faults of the Past[27]

In the introduction to this carefully crafted document, the members of the International Theological Commission state that the purpose of the text is "to clarify the presuppositions that ground repentance for past faults." Clearly, the unprecedented move by the pope to ask for an examination of conscience for faults in the Church's past and to ask for forgiveness in a liturgical ceremony was raising many questions and concerns in theological circles. The ITC presents the theological foundations that would legitimate this bold move by the pope. Bernard Prusak notes that the purpose of the ITC's document was "to give counsel about the way in which the church should proceed in asking for forgiveness."[28]

The ITC begins this task by "proposing a set of questions in order 'to clarify the presuppositions that ground repentance for past faults': Why should it be done? Who should do it? What is the goal and how should this be determined, by correctly combining historical and theological judgment? Who will be addressed? What are the moral implications? And what are the possible effects on the life of the church and on society?"[29] Having laid out its agenda, the ITC starts its discussion by referring to the teachings of Vatican II:

> From a theological point of view, Vatican II distinguishes between the indefectible fidelity of the Church and the weaknesses of her members, clergy or laity, yesterday and today, (12) and therefore, between the Bride of Christ "with neither blemish nor wrinkle . . . holy and immaculate" (cf. Eph 5:27), and her children, pardoned

---

[27] In an e-mail of September 19, 2012, Tom Norris, member of the ITC at the time it was asked to take up this topic, notes that at the beginning Cardinal Ratzinger proposed this topic to the ITC quinquennium in 1998 at the request of John Paul II, with the expectation that a study would be completed in time for the Holy Year. John Paul mentioned the ITC document in a homily given on the first Sunday of Lent, 2000. He refers his hearers to this document for an explanation of why/how he is able to "ask forgiveness" on behalf of the Church.

[28] Bernard M. G. Prusak, "Theological Considerations—Hermenuetical, Ecclesiological, Eschatological Regarding Memory and Reconciliation the Church and the Faults of the Past," *Horizons* (Spring 2005): 137.

[29] Ibid., 138, citing *Origins* 29 (March 16, 2000): 627.

sinners, called to permanent *metanoia*, to renewal in the Holy Spirit. "The Church, embracing sinners in her bosom, is at the same time holy and always in need of purification and incessantly pursues the path of penance and renewal." (MR 1.2)[30]

The ITC chooses to define "Church" using the image of the Bride of Christ from Paul's letter to the Ephesians. By this choice, the ITC is able to uphold the indefectible holiness of the Church while simultaneously acknowledging the ongoing call to its members for conversion from weakness and sinfulness. Understanding this ongoing call of purification is "one of the unfinished aspects of *Lumen Gentium*."[31] The ITC points out the importance of not holding the living responsible for the faults of those now deceased. To exemplify this, the members of the ITC turn to two decrees from Vatican II, *Nostra Aetate* and *Unitatis Redintegratio*:

> The Council also elaborated some criteria of discernment regarding the guilt or responsibility of persons now living for faults of the past. In effect, the Council recalled in two different contexts the non-imputability to those now living of past faults committed by members of their religious communities:
>
> - "What was committed during the passion (of Christ) cannot be imputed either indiscriminately to all Jews then living nor to the Jews of our time."
> - "Large communities became separated from full communion with the Catholic Church—at times not without the fault of men on both sides. However, one cannot charge with the sin of separation those who now are born into these communities and who in these are instructed in the faith of Christ, and the Catholic Church embraces them with fraternal respect and love."[32] (MR 1.2)

[30] Herwi Rikhof, "The Holiness of the Church," in Marcel Poorthuis and Joshua Schwartz, *A Holy People: Jewish and Christian Perspectives on Religious Communal Identity* (Boston: Brill, 2006), 322, points out that an important feature of this ITC document is that it can be seen as a part of the reception process for understanding and applying the theology of *Lumen Gentium* to the Church.

[31] Ibid., 328.

[32] International Theological Commission, "Memory and Reconciliation: The Church and the Faults of the Past," December 1999, http://www.vatican.va/roman _curia/congregations/cfaith/cti_documents/rc_con_cfaith_doc_20000307_memory

The commission considers it of utmost importance to emphasize that these sins are in the past and the responsibility for them lies there. With that in mind, the ITC points out that the examination of conscience for past faults that John Paul is asking the Church to make is rooted in the documents of Vatican II; the ITC also tries to avoid any implication that either John Paul II's millennial documents or Vatican II's documents admit that the Church in itself is sinful. Rather, the ITC underscores the fact that sin exists in the Church in and through her sons and daughters as well as the fact that the present members in no way bear culpability for those sins of past members.

The ITC's concern that the Church does not assume guilt for past mistakes is not unfounded. Since the Church is a living society spanning the centuries, it is difficult to define past faults, because doing so requires appropriate historical judgment. Prusak suggests that one of the ways the ITC is able to embrace the idea of the Church's asking for forgiveness for faults from a prior historical era is through emphasizing that "the Church is in history, but at the same time transcends it. It is only 'with the eyes of faith' that one can see her in her visible reality and at the same time in her spiritual reality as bearer of divine life."[33] The ITC wants to affirm the holiness of the Church and to help the ordinary person who reads about the pope's plea for forgiveness understand the mystery of the Church's existence as in time and yet beyond time.

Another key question the ITC raises about apologizing for faults in the past is: How can today's moral conscience be assigned "guilt" for historical phenomena like the Crusades or the Inquisition? The answer, which must keep in tension the indefectible holiness of the Church while acknowledging the sinfulness of her sons and daughters, can be found in a clearer understanding of the theological foundations of the Church. The commission suggests a theological lens for maintaining the tension between the holiness of the Church because of its association with Christ and the sinfulness of the Church because of its being composed of sinful and weak members.

---

-reconc-itc_en.html, citing Lumen Gentium (8), Nostra Aetate (4) and Unitatis Redintegratio (3).

[33] Prusak, "Theological Considerations," 145–46, citing MR, pars. 3.1-2.

> The Church is holy because, sanctified by Christ who has acquired her by giving himself up to death for her, she is maintained in holiness by the Holy Spirit who pervades her unceasingly. . . . One can distinguish, however, the *holiness of the Church* from *holiness in the Church*. The former—founded on the missions of the Son and Spirit—guarantees the continuity of the mission of the People of God until the end of time and stimulates and aids the believers in pursuing subjective personal holiness. (MR 3.2)

In this paragraph, the authors of *Memory and Reconciliation* assert that the Church, because of its christological foundation, cannot assume the responsibility of the sins of its members. As Jeremy Bergen points out, "Sin is in the church in its members, but this is not the sin of the church. Except that it becomes the responsibility of the church for the sake of confession and forgiveness."[34] The ITC explains this nuanced concept of sin in the following manner:

> Without obscuring this holiness, we must acknowledge that due to the presence of sin there is a need for continual renewal and for constant conversion in the People of God. . . . The Church therefore, "although she is holy because of her incorporation into Christ . . . does not tire of doing penance: Before God and man, she always acknowledges as her own her sinful sons and daughters" of both yesterday and today. (MR 3.3)

The commission draws on the image of the Church as Mother to further explain "the conviction that the Church can make herself responsible for the sin of her children by virtue of the solidarity that exists among them through time and space because of their incorporation into Christ and the work of the Holy Spirit." And "the Church, as a true Mother, cannot but be wounded by the sin of her children of yesterday and today, continuing to love them always, to the point of making herself responsible in all times for the burden created by their sins" (MR 34).

Prusak notes that this image of the Church as Mother is not the most helpful as it "portrays mother Church as an unimpeachable tower of holiness and perfection, differentiated from the 'sinful children' who live

---

[34] Bergen, *Ecclesial Repentance*, 127.

within the bosom of that mother." He suggests that a better image would have been the Church as community. As Prusak points out, Church as community is more inclusive and allows for the coming together of both the holy and sinful, rather than separating the holiness of Mother Church from the sinfulness of her children. The ITC's image seems to foster division rather than reconciliation and unity.[35]

In section 5, the ITC sets out the ethical criteria involved in apologizing and seeking forgiveness. On the level of morality, responsibility can be either objective or subjective:

> Objective responsibility refers to the moral value of the act in itself, insofar as it is good or evil, and thus refers to the imputability of the action. Subjective responsibility concerns the effective perception by individual conscience of the goodness or evil of the act performed. Subjective responsibility ceases with the death of the one who performed the act; it is not transmitted through generation; the descendants do not inherit (subjective) responsibility for the acts of their ancestors. In this sense, asking for forgiveness presupposes a contemporaneity between those who are hurt by an action and those who committed it. The only responsibility capable of continuing in history can be the objective kind, to which one may freely adhere subjectively or not. Thus, the evil done often outlives the one who did it through the consequences of behaviors that can become a heavy burden on the consciences and memories of the descendants. (MR 5.1)

The point of differentiating between these two types of responsibilities is to try to ensure that the current generation does not personally bear responsibility for the sins of their forebears. The role of the current generation in relation to the sins of their forebears is to objectively look at evils of the past, call them such, make a firm purpose of amendment, and thereby, learn from them.

> In such a context, one can speak of a *solidarity* that unites the past and the present in a relationship of reciprocity. In certain situations, the burden that weighs on conscience can be so heavy as to constitute a kind of moral and religious memory of the evil done, which

[35] Prusak, "Theological Considerations," 144.

is by its nature a *common memory*. This common memory gives eloquent testimony to the solidarity objectively existing between those who committed the evil in the past and their heirs in the present. It is then that it becomes possible to speak of an *objective common responsibility*. Liberation from the weight of this responsibility comes above all through imploring God's forgiveness for the wrongs of the past, and then, where appropriate, through the "purification of memory" culminating in a mutual pardoning of sins and offenses in the present. (MR 5.1)

Since the sins of the past often have ramifications in the current age, the ITC explains the need for an ongoing conversion from these sins:

Purifying the memory means eliminating from personal and collective conscience all forms of resentment or violence left by the inheritance of the past, on the basis of a new and rigorous historical-theological judgment, which becomes the foundation for a renewed moral way of acting. (MR 5.1)

Thus the ITC concludes that it is only in light of this objective common responsibility,[36] this unity we hold as human beings, that John Paul can call the Church at the turn of the millennium to a communal examination of conscience and ask forgiveness for sins of the past.

Clearly, the ITC is not in complete disagreement with the pope's millennial program. It is obvious, however, that the ITC wants the communal examination of conscience and the asking of pardon for sins of the past to be received in the correct theological, historical, and ethical context. Though the ITC addresses the need for close attention to the context in which past sins were committed and calls for careful work to be done to

---

[36] See p. 133 of Christopher M. Bellitto's article "Teaching the Church's Mistakes: Historical Hermeneutics in Memory and Reconciliation; The Church and the Faults of the Past," *Horizons* 32, no. 1 (2005). Bellitto takes exception to the ITC's explanation that the sins of the members of the Body of Christ do not taint the Church in any way. Bellitto's point is that the only way to encounter the Church is through its sons and daughters and thereby believes the matter is more complicated than the ITC admits. One could, however, also note that the ITC was aware of the complications and therefore deemed their document necessary.

determine which actions, by which actors, are in need of pardon,[37] there still remain unanswered questions of interpreting this millennial program as historians and theologians have different emphasis in the work of their respective disciplines. Some of these questions involve determining the proper subject of the study (individual Christians or the Church), and how historians are to "reconcile MR's insistence that judgments proper to the present not [be] applied to the past." *Memory and Reconciliation*'s focus is on the "distinction that bishops' authority can be exercised erroneously while the magisterial charism does not admit of fault."[38] Though these aforementioned questions necessitate theological interpretations, the simultaneous need for historical interpretation cannot go unaddressed.

These questions underscore that the ITC's major concern was that this bold move on the part of the pope would be misinterpreted and become a source of scandal to those weak in faith. The pope believed that "because of her responsibility to Truth, the Church cannot cross the threshold of the new millennium without encouraging her children to purify themselves, through repentance, of past errors and instances of infidelity, inconsistency and slowness to act. Acknowledging the weaknesses of the past is an act of honesty and courage" (TMA 33). John Paul proceeded with his plan to have the Church cross the threshold of the third millennium in a spirit of penance and reconciliation. The ITC's explanations articulated in its document set forth a myriad of qualifications about the conditions under which the pope can call the Church to ask for forgiveness for sins of the past. Many questions, however, remain to this day.

As we shall explore in the conclusion, perhaps John Paul II and the ITC would have been better served if they had chosen an image other than that of Mother Church[39] from which to ask for forgiveness. The Fathers of Vatican II offered many images of the Church in *Lumen Gentium*. Though

---

[37] Ibid., 131.

[38] Bergen, *Ecclesial Repentance*, 131–32.

[39] On p. 157 Ephraim Radner in *A Brutal Unity: The Spiritual Politics of the Christian Church* (Waco, TX: Baylor University Press, 2012) makes the case for the use of the Mother image by explaining that the Mother is the *casta meretrix*, not in the sense of a chronological succession of first whore then chaste, first Israel then Gentile Church; rather, the Church is the whore taken by the Lord and in her "takenness" lies her ecclesiality. It must be noted, however, that the Mother image that the ITC and John Paul use

no one image can ever capture fully the mystery of the Church, perhaps using one that accentuated the membership, such as "pilgrim Church," would have presented a better vantage point from which to discuss the sinfulness of the Church and the need for repentance.

## The Papal Day of Pardon: March 12, 2000

Shortly after the release of the ITC's document, John Paul II, on the first Sunday of Lent, March 12, 2000, completed what he intended to do when he wrote *Tertio Millennio Adveniente*, namely, to celebrate the Eucharist with the cardinals and to ask forgiveness from the Lord for the sins, past and present, of the sons and daughters of the Church.[40] In a document released prior to this "Day of Pardon," the Vatican News Service attempts to explain the meaning of the celebration. The wording in that document is significant as it sets the tone that will be continued throughout the liturgy. The upcoming papal statement seeking forgiveness is to be seen as a moment of conversion for the Church's sons and daughters. Throughout this document it is evident that "Christians, as pilgrims . . . remain sinners, frail, weak, and subject to the temptations of Satan . . . despite their incorporation into the Body of Christ"; yet the Church remains ever holy. The upcoming liturgy is referred to as "a service to truth: the Church is not afraid to confront the sins of Christians when she becomes conscious of their errors." It is also made very clear that this day of pardon is for all the people of God as there is a solidarity in sin that exists among all: the bearers of the Petrine ministry, bishops, priests, religious, and lay faithful.

During the liturgy on the day of pardon, there are two moments when repentance and forgiveness become most prominent: the homily and the universal prayer in which there is confession of sins and asking for forgiveness. During the homily, the pope invites all "to make a profound examination of conscience." His call to repentance is as follows:

---

emanates from Ephesians, which would be from what Radner refers to as a chronological succession of the image.

[40] John Paul II, "Day of Pardon," March 12, 2000, http://www.vatican.va/news_services /liturgy/documents/ns_lit_doc_20000312_presentation-day-pardon_en.html.

One of the characteristic elements of the Great Jubilee is what I described as the "purification of memory" (Bull *Incarnationis mysterium*, n. 11). As the Successor of Peter, I asked that "in this year of mercy the Church, strong in holiness which she receives from her Lord, should kneel before God and implore forgiveness for the past and present sins of her sons and daughters." (ibid.) Today, the First Sunday of Lent, seemed to me the right occasion for the Church, gathered spiritually round the Successor of Peter, to implore divine forgiveness of all believers. *Let us forgive and ask forgiveness*!

After calling the Church to this extraordinary moment of forgiveness, the pope acknowledged the work of the International Theological Commission and its concerns when he stated:

It [*Memory and Reconciliation: The Church and the Faults of the Past*] is very useful for correctly understanding and carrying out the authentic request for pardon, based on the *objective responsibility* which Christians share as members of the Mystical Body, and which spurs today's faithful to recognize, along with their own sins, the sins of yesterday's Christians, in the light of careful historical and theological discernment.

He then goes on to make history by publicly asking for forgiveness for "the infidelities to the Gospel committed by some of our brethren." At this point, using the principle of "both/and," the pope enumerates some of the most egregious sins committed *by* Christians and *against* Christians. He notes the sinfulness of the disunity and division among Christians, the failure of Christians to take responsibility for the evils of today, e.g., religious indifference, violations of the right to life, disregard for the poor, and ethical relativism. He then turns to sins committed against Christians, such as persecution for their faith, oppression, and other hardships. It is evident that the pope is expanding the repentance of the Church to include all humanity's sins against humanity and not merely those of Christians. The use of such a technique can be seen to make this papal act more inclusive, that is, including all humanity,[41] or to seemingly temper the idea of the Church's need for such repentance.

---

[41] One should note the inherent difficulties in the use of this technique, namely, the pope can call all humanity to repentance, but he cannot apologize on behalf of all humanity. He can only ask forgiveness on behalf of the Church and its members.

After the papal homily which set the context for the confession of sins and asking for forgiveness, the pope and members of the Curia prayed for pardon from God for seven distinct areas of faults and failings not only of the sons and daughters of the Church but also of all humanity. The seven areas include the general acts of disobedience by members of the Church, the sins committed by leaders of the Church "in the name of faith and morals," the scandal of the disunity that exists among Christians, the horrific crimes committed against the people of Israel, the sins that emanate from disrespect of cultures and religions, the sins of discrimination and exclusion—particularly when it disregards the dignity of women and the diversity of humanity—and the sins that ensue from neglect of the right to life and quality life. Some of these areas of faults and failings were expected, for example, an acknowledgment of the sinfulness of the division among Christians and particularly in the aftermath of the Holocaust, the crimes committed against the people of Israel; others were somewhat surprising, for example, sins committed by Church leaders in the name of faith and morals and the admission that "the equality of your sons and daughters has not been acknowledged." After each category of sin was enunciated, the pope had a period of prayer and then responded by asking God's forgiveness on behalf of those who had sinned. At the end of the litany, the pope embraced the crucifix as a sign of penance. Though the grammar of the pope's prayer of forgiveness tried to "create a rhetorical distance between himself and sinners in the church (he prayed for 'them,' 'those' and 'their' sin),"[42] the confession of sin and asking for forgiveness in some of the areas of faults and failings raised unrealistic hopes that the Church might change its teaching with regard to the ministerial role of women in the Church and with regard to its moral stances.

In contrast to the typical modes of communication in previous eras of the Church, technological advances in communications meant that the areas and acts in need of forgiveness articulated by the pope and the Curia were received immediately by the worldwide community. The reactions from both secular and religious sections of the world were numerous and varied. To these reactions we will now turn, looking first at responses from the secular press.

---

[42] Bergen, *Ecclesial Repentance*, 135–36.

## Reactions to Pope John Paul II's Decision to Ask for Forgiveness: Some Perspectives from the Secular Press

The reactions to the decision by the pope to publicly ask for forgiveness for "the infidelities to the Gospel committed by some of our brethren" were manifold. The opinions and critiques of this decision were covered by both secular and theological media outlets. Clearly, John Paul's decision to celebrate the third millennium since Christ's birth in this manner was ushering in a new historical moment in the Church.

Secular news sources such as CNN and the *New York Times* were quick to make comments on this "unprecedented move" by the pope. The title given the transcript of CNN's Sunday morning news show that aired on March 12, 2000, just hours after the statement asking for forgiveness was made, was "Pope John Paul II Makes Unprecedented Apology for Sins of Catholic Church." The title alone gives an indication of the controversy that was erupting. Jim Bittermann, the CNN correspondent, reported that "even before the ceremonies in St. Peter's, some were saying modern Catholics have nothing to confess for the actions of those in the past and others were saying the pope's mea culpa does not go far enough and is not specific enough."[43] He also noted that "it [the apology] is a reminder the Roman Catholic Church may be theologically infallible, but it is still populated by sinners."[44]

The *New York Times* reported of the event that "the pope's act of repentance, delivered as part of the liturgy of Sunday Mass in St. Peter's Basilica, was a courageous and historic declaration that many of his own cardinals and bishops opposed."[45] This article notes that the statement "was offered on behalf of the church's 'sons and daughters,' but not the church itself, which is considered holy. Nor did John Paul directly address the sensitive issue of whether past popes, cardinals and clergy—not just parishioners—also erred."[46] The reporter for the *Times* obviously was

---

[43] CNN Transcript, "Sunday Morning News: Pope John Paul II Makes Unprecedented Apology for Sins of Catholic Church—March 12, 2000," http://transcripts.cnn.com/TRANSCRIPTS/0003/12/sm.06.html.

[44] Ibid.

[45] "The Pope's Apology," *New York Times*, March 14, 2000, A22.

[46] Ibid.

unaware that by virtue of the sacrament of baptism, the clergy, bishops, and cardinals share in the same sonship as the parishioners (the laity). Richard Neuhaus says of this remark from the *Times*, "that is, of course, patent, nonsense. Bishops, cardinals, and popes are also 'children of the Church' who have sinned. Why, do the editors suppose, does the Pope go to confession every week?"[47]

Neuhaus's comment on the report of the pope's apology in the *Times* affirmed some of the concerns that Mary Ann Glendon had raised in November 1997 in an opinion piece published in *First Things* titled, "Contrition in the Age of Spin Control." In this brief article, Glendon questions, "So why should anyone be nervous about a program of purification aimed at healing historical resentments and evangelizing contemporary men and women? My own uneasiness has nothing to do with what the Pope has said, and everything to do with the way in which the expressions of regret he calls for may be manipulated by spin doctors who are no friends of the Church; indeed by persons for whom no apology will ever be enough until Catholics apologize themselves into nonexistence."[48]

Glendon was concerned "that most people hear of official expressions of regret as filtered through the news media."[49] This concern was not unfounded considering the questions raised by the coverage given by the secular press to this statement of repentance. A major part of the problem is that the secular press does not operate out of a theological mindset; its business is about selling news. In order to sell news, the more controversial it is, the more it sells. Therefore, CNN's coverage, which stated that the Church is "theologically infallible," needed to be explained in much more detail rather than just being glibly inserted. The *Times'* coverage had the appearance of trying to divide the Church by stating that "many of his own cardinals and bishops opposed" the apology and by raising the question as to whether the sinners in the Church included cardinals, bishops, and clergy or just the parishioners.

---

[47] Richard John Neuhaus, "Forgive Us Our Trespasses . . . ," *First Things* no. 104 (June/July 2000): 81–83.

[48] Mary Ann Glendon, "Contrition in the Age of Spin Control," *First Things* no. 77 (November 1, 1997): 10.

[49] Ibid.

Another important apprehension about this apology that Glendon noted was that "the faithful begin to wonder: 'If the Church was wrong about so many things in the past, maybe she's wrong about what she's teaching now.' This is another reason why public acknowledgments of past errors have given rise to anxiety in some quarters of the Church."[50] These mixed reactions from secular media outlets to the papal statement of repentance highlight that there is still more work to do in explaining to ordinary people in the pews how the Church as a historical institution can acknowledge that it has sinned through the actions, not just of its individual children, but of its leaders acting in the name of and on behalf of the Church. It is to this and other theological issues that the papal statement seeking pardon brought to the fore that we will now turn, as we consider some perspectives from theologians on this issue.

## Some Perspectives from Theologians

In this section I will consider the perspectives of eight contemporary theologians: Francis Sullivan, Bradford Hinze, Richard McBrien, Richard Neuhaus, Elizabeth Johnson, Bruno Forte, Antonio Sicari, and Joseph Komonchak. These theologians were selected because they offer a broad spectrum as well as propose a variety of theological issues at state in John Paul's decision to make such a statement of repentance for the sins and faults of the past. Additionally, their mixed reactions speak not only of theological disagreement about the papal statement but also of the confusion that it raised. The vast array of reactions, I contend, connotes that there is still more work to do on the theological understanding of under what circumstances the Church can be referred to as being sinful.

## Francis Sullivan, SJ

Francis Sullivan wrote an essay, "Do the Sins of Its Members Affect the Holiness of the Church?" for the collection *Essays on the Church and Ecumenism in Honour of Michael A. Fahey, SJ*, which was published in 2006. In this essay, Sullivan clearly frames the basic theological issue raised

---

[50] Ibid., 11.

by the pope's millennial statement seeking forgiveness for the Church when he writes:

> There can be no doubt that all Catholic theologians are agreed on these basic propositions: that the Church is unfailingly holy, and that it includes persons guilty of grave sin among its members. They also agree that all of its members who have attained the use of reason are sinners in the sense that they commit "the daily sins which are called venial," and that it is only by a special privilege such as the Blessed Virgin Mary enjoyed, that members of the Church could be free of venial sins throughout their whole lives. On the other hand, Catholic theologians have given different answers to the question whether the sins of its members affect the holiness of the Church, and if so, in what way. One can also express this question by asking whether the holiness of the Church is lessened in proportion to the prevalence of sin among her members, and whether the Church can be described as both holy and sinful, being composed of both holy and sinful members.[51]

Sullivan's answer to the question that he proposes attempts to pull together the ITC's commentary issued on the papal statement of repentance and on the content of the papal statement. Sullivan notes that while John Paul II can admit that "the sins of her sons and daughters have 'sullied' and 'disfigured' the face of the Church," the "theologians of the ITC are not willing to allow sin in the Church to have any effects on the holiness of the Church."[52] Sullivan answers this stance of the ITC by suggesting that perhaps John Paul II's use of the image of the Church as Mother may not have been the preferred image to use in making a statement seeking forgiveness. Sullivan explains that "the maternal solidarity with which she takes upon herself the sins of her children is rather a manifestation of her holiness."[53] Sullivan continues by stating that he would have preferred if

---

[51] Francis Sullivan, "Do the Sins of Its Members Affect the Holiness of the Church?" in *In God's Hands: Essays on the Church and Ecumenism in Honour of Michael A. Fahey, SJ,* ed. Michael S. Attridge and Jaroslav Z. Skira, Bibliotheca Ephemeridum Theologicarum Lovaniensium 199 (Leuven: Leuven University Press, 2006), 253.

[52] Ibid., 266.

[53] Ibid., 266–67.

"Vatican II's notion of the Church as the 'pilgrim people of God'"[54] had been invoked. He further notes:

> As a "people," it is, as Vatican II says, a "human institution, always in need of reform, always in need of purification." It is a people led by human leaders, who are fallible in every decision they make except when they solemnly define a doctrine of faith or morals. As a people on a pilgrimage, while it has a divine guarantee of arriving at the Kingdom of God at the end of its journey, it inevitably takes many a wrong path along the way. And just as it is the holiness of the saints that has always moved them to confess themselves sinners in need of God's pardon, it is in no way a denial of its God-given holiness that the pilgrim people of God should confess its faults and ask forgiveness of those whom it has offended along the way.[55]

Sullivan's insight that the image of the Church as the pilgrim people of God is more capable of holding in tension the holiness and sinfulness of the Church is significant because it connotes a Church on the way and thereby, a Church that doesn't deny either its holiness or its sinfulness.

Though Sullivan does briefly note the collective nature of sin when one refers to the Church not as individual people but as an institution, to discuss this issue further we will turn to some thoughts by Bradford Hinze.[56]

### Bradford Hinze

Bradford Hinze considers how the collective nature of the Church interfaces with such an apologetic statement. He begins by raising the question of whether it is the Church collectively or individuals in the Church who have sinned. According to Hinze, how one answers this question

---

[54] Ibid., 267.

[55] Ibid., 267–68.

[56] Bradford Hinze's writing on the subject of social sin is included in this study because it deals directly with the apologetic statement of John Paul II. In the conclusion, the question of using the language of social sin will be raised as an area for further study. Margaret Pfeil's article on this subject, "Doctrinal Implications of Magisterial Use of the Language of Social Sin," *Louvain Studies* 27, no. 2 (2002): 132–52, will be considered at that point. See pp. 199ff. of the conclusion.

makes a major difference, as the onus for making amends either falls to the Church collectively or the sinful members of the Church. Hinze argues:

> If the sinfulness of the Church is solely a matter of the sins of individuals, then it is the individuals who must change. But if the sinfulness of the Church is a matter of collective, institutional responsibility, do not the Church's doctrines and practices need to be changed in order for the penitential process to be complete? In other words, are there instances when ecclesial repentance can and should serve as a catalyst for doctrinal change? This is a hard question to ask. It makes many people feel uncomfortable.[57]

Hinze puts forth two proposals in order to grapple with this question. First, he states that "there is the need to develop more fully and more self-consciously a dialogical understanding of revelation and the Church."[58] In this proposal, Hinze is calling for a dialogue that "finds its deepest inspiration in the communicative life of the Trinitarian communion of persons and in the interpersonal and social constitution of the human person made in the *imago Trinitatis*."[59] He further explains that there are two approaches to dialogue, one that

> emphasizes obedience to a divinely authorized hierarchical authority and the official doctrinal articulations of this authority and the other that stresses the divinely inspired process of mutual learning and teaching about the fullness of Christian beliefs and practices that takes place among bishops, theologians, and the faithful through dialogue, formal doctrinal statements, and the diversity of receptions. The first contends that communion is arrived at through obedience, whereas the second fosters communion through dialogue.[60]

Furthermore, communion arrived at through obedience focuses more on the individual's response, whereas communion arrived at through dialogue focuses more on the collective response of the community.

---

[57] Bradford E. Hinze, "Ecclesial Repentance and the Demands of Dialogue," *Theological Studies* 61, no. 2 (June 1, 2000): 208.

[58] Ibid., 209.

[59] Ibid.

[60] Ibid., 213–14.

Hinze's contention is that the pope's statement, which includes the social sins of the past, opens the question of "recognizing that the Church collective is sinful."[61] If this is the case, according to Hinze, then Rahner's push during Vatican II for the fathers of the council to speak about the sinful Church has some legitimacy. Hinze writes:

> Rahner invokes the distinction between the objective holiness of the Church's institution and doctrines and the subjective holiness of Church members in order to explain that the members are recognized as both holy and sinful by the council, and by inference, "the Church must be 'subjectively' at once 'holy' and 'sinful.'" Herein lies the basis for speaking about the sinful Church for Rahner.[62]

Having recalled Rahner's belief that the council fathers needed to "speak about the sinful Church," Hinze concludes his article by "pondering an ambiguity in the Church's official position—affirming the need for ecclesial repentance and yet denying corporate responsibility."[63]

Hinze calls for a new paradigm in which "in the light of the developing doctrine of social sin, and what it implies about collective responsibility and accountability, we are now being called upon to reconsider this ancient doctrine so that the *communio sanctorum* can also be recognized, in humility and with no malice implied, as a *communio peccatorum*."[64] Hinze also notes that assuming collective responsibility and accountability will necessitate an openness to "instances where reforming tradition can be the most appropriate act of penance. This openness need not unleash uncontrollable doctrinal relativism, but is the only fitting response to the work of the Triune God who purifies and redeems."[65]

[61] Ibid., 227.

[62] Ibid., 229 citing Karl Rahner, "The Sinful Church in the Decrees of Vatican II," in *Theological Investigations* 6 (Baltimore, MD: Helicon Press, 1969).

[63] Ibid., 232.

[64] Ibid., 232–33, citing the International Theological Commission, "Memory and Reconciliation" (4.2) has acknowledged the substance of what is suggested here. A doctrine of *communio peccatorum* in light of the doctrine of social sin offers an important dimension to the transactions between the living and the dead as insightfully developed in Elizabeth Johnson, *Friends of God and Prophets: A Feminist Reading of the Communion of Saints* (New York: Continuum, 1998).

[65] Ibid., 235.

To understand what is at stake in the questions raised by Hinze's call to an openness to reforming tradition, we will turn to three articles in *Commonweal* in which three theologians, Richard Mc Brien, Richard Neuhaus, and Elizabeth Johnson, shared their thoughts on this question in light of Pope John Paul's millennial statement seeking pardon.

### Richard McBrien, Richard J. Neuhaus, and Elizabeth Johnson

As the Church was making its final preparations for the millennial celebration, *Commonweal* magazine editors asked three noted theologians to share their perspectives on the Church's proposal of expressing sorrow for sins at the turn of the millennium through the lens of these questions:

> Can the church confess error? Will it ever do so? Wouldn't an admission of error—in the church's past defense of slavery or in its official teachings about Judaism, for example—enhance, rather than damage, the church's credibility? Aren't the tortuous efforts to explain away dramatic reversals in church teaching—like the effort to reconcile current teaching and pre–Vatican II understandings about religious liberty—a cause of intellectual scandal as well as moral evasiveness? Isn't it fallacious to fear that admitting error would immediately call "everything" the church teaches into doubt?[66]

Richard McBrien answers these questions by first pointing out the importance of defining what is meant by the term "church." He makes the assumption "that we are speaking of the Catholic church and not the worldwide Body of Christ."[67] If this is the case, he explains the following:

1. The church *can* confess error.
2. While the Roman magisterium has been reluctant (to say the least) to admit error, the hierarchical magisterium more broadly understood has already begun to do so.
3. We have a model for the hierarchical magisterium's admission of error in the statements of the German and French bishops on the Holocaust.[68]

---

[66] The Editors, "Mea Culpa Mea Maxima Culpa: Can the Church Admit Error?" *Commonweal* 126 (November 19, 1999): 12.

[67] Ibid.

[68] Ibid.

With regard to the first point, McBrien notes that "the church can confess error with regard to a particular teaching or disciplinary decree if none of these pertains to the deposit of faith, that is, if the charism of infallibility has not been engaged in their original promulgation."[69] With regards to points two and three, McBrien makes the distinction between the Roman magisterium whose "tendency is to blame sin and error on individual members of the church and not on the church itself"[70] and the hierarchical magisterium outside of Rome, most notably that of France and Germany which "have explicitly acknowledged the sinfulness of their own churches in their failure to speak out against, and even in their active complicity with, the Nazi perpetrators of the Holocaust."[71] Using this model of recognizing the sinfulness of the collective Church as exemplified by the French and German bishops, McBrien believes, will "enhance rather than diminish the church's global credibility and, therefore, its capacity for even more illuminating and compelling teaching in the future."[72]

McBrien's argument highlights the need for the hierarchical magisterium of the Church to move from blaming individuals for errors and sins to an acceptance of collective responsibility for errors and sins.

Richard Neuhaus discusses these questions from a different vantage point—one that differs from McBrien's but is critically important. Neuhaus explains that underneath the question, "can the church confess error?" the real "subject at hand is the development of doctrine."[73] He writes:

> We should not, as is frequently done, pit change against development. Of course there is change. That is undeniable. The question is whether it is the change of discontinuity, correcting an error, or the change of continuity, developing the truth. The evidence is at times ambiguous. The question cannot in all cases be definitively adjudicated by historical study or hermeneutical reflection alone. Faith, which engages both will and disposition, is involved in whether one does or does not think with the church (*sentire cum*

---

[69] Ibid.

[70] Ibid., 14.

[71] Ibid.

[72] Ibid., 16.

[73] Richard John Neuhaus, "'Sentire Cum Ecclesia': Rome, Si, California, No," *Commonweal* 126 (November 19, 1999): 17.

*ecclesia*) and thereby discern the promised guidance of the Spirit in the development of doctrine.[74]

Neuhaus's concern is that unless there is a clear understanding that doctrine develops and grows, then when there is a development in doctrine, the question becomes one of whether the Church has erred: "Has the church taught as true that which we now recognize as false? That way of putting the question raises the stakes by posing the question of whether the Catholic Church is what she claims to be."[75] This type of misinterpretation was exactly the concern of many who were uncertain about John Paul's millennial program and day of pardon.

Unlike McBrien, who was looking at the question of who is responsible for the sin and error of the Church—individuals or the collective Church—Neuhaus saw in the question of sin and error in the Church an underlying concern about how doctrine develops. Neuhaus takes the question of who sinned or erred and who is going to make amends to another level, namely, the questions surrounding the nature of the error and/or sin and how it impacts the development of doctrine. Though it may be construed that Neuhaus is sidestepping the issue of sin and error's existence in the Church, I believe that Neuhaus's concern about the effect of the papal statement of repentance on the question of the development of doctrine or its discontinuity is well founded. Like the ITC, Neuhaus raises the question of whether acknowledging sin and error in the Church should be seen through the lens of development of doctrine or should be seen as the admission of discontinuity within the tradition. This question, though a by-product of the statement of repentance, must be taken into consideration, as it has a significant impact on how one views the Church and its teaching authority within history.

We will now turn to the perspective that Elizabeth Johnson brings to these questions. Elizabeth Johnson begins discussing the questions posed by comparing the Galileo case to what she perceives as a modern-day error in the Church, the "failure to grasp the prejudice against women as a structural sin that pervades the history of 'the whole church,' not just

[74] Ibid., 17–18.
[75] Ibid., 16.

many of its members."[76] Johnson notes with respect to the Galileo trial, "Church leaders clung to traditional religious and cultural assumptions despite new evidence to the contrary."[77] She then explains that "the gospel vision of a community of discipleship of equals is as compelling to persons converted from sexism as the centrality of the sun was to Galileo—neither men nor the earth can claim to be the center of the system."[78] By comparison, Johnson writes that as the Church eventually had to admit its mistakes with Galileo, one day it will have to admit its errors in its treatment of women in the Church. While Johnson is writing from a feminist perspective, her comments actually transcend that context to reflect on the larger question of how the Church deals with acknowledging error historically and today. Her view can be seen as a *via media* between Neuhaus and McBrien. Johnson, like McBrien, is looking at sin and error in the Church from the perspective of how to make amends for the sins and errors committed by the Church as a collective entity against individuals, in this case Galileo or women. At the same time, she, like Neuhaus, is concerned with how doctrine develops—doctrine that she believes needs to be changed or reformed.

Though the questions given by *Commonweal* to each theologian were the same, each theologian offered a unique perspective on what it means for the Church to admit error as well as what consequences would follow such an admission of error. Clearly, the life and mission of the Church with its history, tradition, and dogma need to be taken into account as any theologian grapples with such questions. What could be seen as a bit disconcerting in this article is that the questions being asked by the editors of *Commonweal* presuppose that the pope's decision to ask for forgiveness on behalf of the Church's sons and daughters for sins of the past is one and the same thing as the Church's admission of error. I contend that sin and admission of error are not necessarily the same thing. One can be mistaken and not have sinned. So, though at times there can be a connection between inerrancy and impeccability, the real question that remains

---

[76] Elizabeth A. Johnson, "Galileo's Daughters: What Error Looks Like Today," *Commonweal* 126 (November 19, 1999): 19.

[77] Ibid., 20.

[78] Ibid.

is whether the sinlessness of the Church as a whole and the sinfulness of her individual members is the same or different from the inerrancy of the Church as a whole and the stupidity or errors of her individual members. In order to begin to look at this question more deeply, we will turn to the perspective of Bruno Forte on the subject of what, if any, difference there is between seeking forgiveness for sin and an admission of error.

### Bruno Forte

Bruno Forte, in his article "The Church Confronts the Faults of the Past,"[79] observes that John Paul's decision to ask for forgiveness provoked contradictory reactions within the Church not because of its effects but because of the question of its legitimacy. Forte writes, "The real question has to do with establishing the legitimacy and authenticity of the actions under consideration, and not with ascertaining their effect upon worldly history."[80]

Forte underscores that the eschatological aspect of the Church is one of the reasons why this statement of repentance was so hard to understand. He writes that the Church identifies itself

> with all of its members past and present. This identification flows directly from the Church's awareness of having been established and kept in being by a gift from on high thanks to the mission of the Son and of the Spirit whom he has sent. It is the Spirit who generates and fosters ecclesial community through the Word of God, the sacramental economy, and the witness of charity. Moreover, the deepest self-awareness of the Church includes the conviction that she is not just a community of the elect, but embraces in her bosom both sinners and saints. This embrace is not limited to the present, but extends to the past, thus binding all together in the unity of the mystery that constitutes the Church herself.[81]

In this, Forte highlights the divine aspect of the Church. The Church is unlike any other institution because it is born of the Spirit and continues

---

[79] Bruno Forte, "The Church Confronts the Faults of the Past," *Communio* 27, no. 4 (December 1, 2000): 678.

[80] Ibid., 679.

[81] Ibid., 681, citing *Lumen Gentium* 8.

to exist in and through the Spirit. In the Spirit, no one is lost. All of its members—past, present, and future, saint and sinner—are caught up in the eternal now. Because of this "in time and yet beyond time" aspect of the Church, worldly history does not dictate how the Church and its leaders should act. Rather, obedience to the truth is what should govern the Church and its leaders' actions.

Because there have been moments in the long history of the Church when, by its leaders' actions, the Church has not be governed by truth, it seems to Forte that "recognition of past sins is an act of prophetic freedom that escapes the calculus of immediate results and comes, with the force of a necessity, from obedience to God and to the demands of his truth."[82] For Forte, the misunderstandings which result from the pope's making such a prophetic move as to recognize sins of the past need to be merely taken in stride because the Church is in this world but not of it. In other words, he is saying that one cannot and should not judge the Church only by worldly standards. Because the eternal Church exists in temporal history, the Church cannot and should not become paralyzed by misunderstandings and judgments. At all times, however, the Church can and must do all in its power to operate out of truth in charity and love. In order to understand further the ways in which the secular world misunderstood the Church's statement asking for pardon, we will now turn to the reflection of Antonio Maria Sicari on the Church's repentance.

### *Antonio Maria Sicari, OCD*

Antonio Sicari, in an article titled "The 'Purification of Memory': The 'Narrow Gate' of the Jubilee," points out the symbolic importance of John Paul II's desire to have the "Holy Door of this millennial Jubilee . . . wider than those of the past." Sicari is very cognizant of the "understandable perplexities" that surround this bold move of the pope. He notes that such perplexities include the concern about "crude reconstructions of history, whose sole purpose is to discredit the Church," the concern that "some would put a manipulative 'spin' on these 'acts of repentance,'" and

---

[82] Ibid., 687.

the concern that the Church could lose its authority "at least among the more 'lukewarm.'"[83]

Many of Sicari's concerns have already been raised by other commentators in this study. He builds on those concerns, however, when he writes:

> There is still one more perplexity. It is the most intricate one of all. If it were only a question of apologizing today for past sins that were always recognized as sinful, at least in their inmost nature, then the objections would not be so weighty. But what are we to say about events that we consider sins today, but at the time the Church itself and even some saints, thought were just, legitimate, and in some cases, meritorious? Does this not suggest that the Church is apologizing not only for her children's sins, but also for her way of being and interpreting her own mission in the world, at least at certain times and with respect to certain serious issues?[84]

Sicari's reply to the risk that the apology could be interpreted as an apology not only for the Church's sins but also for the Church's very way of being in the world highlights the Church's understanding of the Christian virtue of hope.

> The Holy Spirit pours out in us the theological virtue we call hope. Hope does not destroy our memories or the sad legacies of our past. Rather, it plunges them all in the certainty of a Love stronger than any evil. "Repentance" for wrong that we have done and "pardon" for wrong we have suffered is thus not merely psychological activity or moral effort, but a victory of love in us. What is true of the individual soul and for the history of every individual human being can and must be true for the Church as a whole.[85]

Sicari, like Forte, notes that the Church's existence, born of the Spirit, may be in the world but is not of the world. The Church must do what is right despite how the world might interpret it. Therefore, the Church must admit that in the past, errors in judgment were made and sins committed.

---

[83] Antonio M. Sicari, "'The Purification of Memory': The 'Narrow Gate' of the Jubilee," *Communio* 27, no. 4 (December 1, 2000): 634.

[84] Ibid., 637.

[85] Ibid., 638.

Sicari writes, "we need to underscore the fact that the pope is not asking the Church to prostrate herself before the world, or before some historical tribunal, but to 'kneel before God' in order to implore his pardon."[86] He notes that the ability of the Church to "ask forgiveness even for ancient sins and errors" highlights "that bond that, in the Mystical Body, unites us to one another."[87] It is this bond that unites us to all that has gone before us and all that will come after us that makes this "purification of memory" a sign of hope that in Christ and in his Church nothing and no one is ever lost.

To further expand on the understanding of hope as crucial to this conversation, Joseph Komonchak explores from a historical perspective how hope has become rekindled in the Church because the Church is now willing to admit and seek forgiveness for its sins.

## Joseph A. Komonchak

In "Preparing for the New Millennium," Joseph Komonchak writes about how apologetics enter into the pope's millennial call for forgiveness. Komonchak points out that there are two important apologetical approaches from two different historical periods which the Church has employed so that it has been able to claim its innate holiness while being composed of sinners. He writes,

> First, especially in post-Reformation polemics, the four attributes of the Church stated in the Creed were turned into "marks" of the Church which, it was thought, could be objectively "demonstrated," biblically and historically to characterize only the Roman Catholic Church. . . .The second, not entirely unrelated, dimension is the experience of the Church over the last several centuries that led to what was called "the siege mentality." In response Catholic apologetics often took the form either of trying to explain (or explain away) the alleged crimes by historical circumstances or of refusing to accept the scale of values often taken for granted by "modernity."[88]

---

[86] Ibid., 639.

[87] Ibid.

[88] Joseph Komonchak, "Preparing for the New Millennium," *Logos* 1, no. 2 (Summer 1997): 40–41.

The move by the Roman Catholic Church after the Reformation to take ownership of the four attributes of the Church as stated in the Creed—one, holy, catholic, and apostolic—immediately sets the Catholic Church as superior over any other Christian denomination. Furthermore, as Komonchak points out, the refusal of the Church to be engaged with the modern world during the late nineteenth and early twentieth centuries gave the impression to the world that the Church was abstracted from history.[89] This abstraction from history left little room for an understanding of the development of doctrine and the need for reform and renewal in the Church.

This defensive, apologetical attitude began to change, however, when Pope John XXIII called for the Second Vatican Council. Komonchak notes that because of the open attitude that John XXIII fostered in convoking Vatican II, theologians such as Congar were able to raise the question of reform in the Church, while Rahner was able to raise the question of the existence of sin in the Church. Prior to Vatican II, such issues were either squelched or elicited a defensive, apologetic response from Church leaders.

Although Vatican II made progress in breaking down this defensive, apologetic attitude, Komonchak notes that it has not disappeared, and he cites the cardinals', especially Cardinal Biffi's, negative reaction and severe misgivings about the pope's idea of such a millennial apology, to substantiate this claim. Komonchak explains from where such misgivings and concerns spring when he writes,

> The underlying theological question is, of course, the relation between what is called the Church and the concrete believers who constitute it in history. It is possible to derive from the Scriptures and the tradition a notion of the Church to which it is very difficult to ascribe error, failings, and sin. How can one say that the Mystical Body, of which Christ is the Head, or the *koinonia* of the Holy Spirit, is responsible for such evils? Must they not be attributed instead to various members of the Church, even its highest authorities? Surely the Church *qua* Church, cannot be held responsible! In addition, is not sin always the act of individuals in their own personal individuality? Can a collective body be thought capable of sin?[90]

---

[89] Ibid.
[90] Ibid., 46–47.

Komonchak, like Hinze, highlights the collective aspect of the Church: namely, that it is composed of a group of individuals that at times act as one. Understanding how this collective aspect of the Church operates is important. We are one Body in Christ. Therefore, as de Lubac explained in *Catholicism*, what happens to one affects the whole Body. Komonchak, drawing on the writing of Karl Rahner, points out that "to deny that the Church as a collective body is capable of sin raises the question of whether the Church as a collective body can be capable of virtue."[91]

Komonchak suggests that the underlying problem is coming to terms with "what, or perhaps better, *who* are the Church?"[92] All too often there seems to be either "an hypostasization or reification of the Church."[93] Again Komonchak references Rahner who "describes the problem in this way: 'The Church—against the tendency to be found in St. Augustine—is somehow, without its being noticed, "hypostasized," she becomes almost like an independently existent "entity," which stands as teacher and guide *over against* the people of God; she does not appear to be this people of God itself (even though structured hierarchically) in its actual state of pilgrimage.'"[94] If what Rahner writes is the case, then the Church becomes removed from the people because of its holiness and their sinfulness.

This sharp division in the Church is not and should not be the case. Rather, as Komonchak states, "the mystery proper consists in God's holy presence in the imperfect community."[95] Komonchak identifies the basic premise underneath all of John Paul II's millennial plans as calling all the faithful to a recommitment to Christ and the Gospel in their local churches. Only through such a global recommitment by individuals in their individual churches will the impact of the millennial statement of repentance by John Paul on behalf of the entire Church begin to achieve its full significance, that is, helping all people to "discern in light of the Gospel what is good and evil in their local situations, sustaining the good and trying to reverse the evil."[96]

[91] Ibid., 47.
[92] Ibid.
[93] Ibid., 49.
[94] Ibid., 49 citing Karl Rahner, "The Sinful Church," 277.
[95] Ibid., 50.
[96] Ibid., 55.

Komonchak raises a significant theological question regarding John Paul II's statement, "who are the Church?" Does one's use of the word "church" come from understanding it as the Mystical Body of Christ or as the people of God? Does one's definition of church presuppose the Church as a collective entity or a community of individuals? The way one answers these questions lays the theological foundation for how one will view sin and error in the Church. Additionally, the answers to these questions will be the basis for which one strives to find an intersection between the indefectibility and inerrancy of the Church as the Mystical Body of Christ and the sinfulness and folly of the Church as the people of God.

In the commentary conclusion that now follows, I will argue that John Paul's unprecedented statement seeking forgiveness for the faults and sins of the Church raised important, lingering questions from discussions at Vatican II about the nature and mission of a Church that is both holy and sinful.

## Analysis of the Reactions

The millennial statement of repentance by John Paul II did not go unnoticed by either the secular or theological media outlets. Indeed, at times, the concerns raised by the ITC about the potential for misunderstanding and misinterpretation of such a bold move by the pope proved not to have been unfounded. The secular press, as was to be expected, reported the event with little understanding of the theological underpinnings of what the Church believes. The diverse reactions and concerns of both secular reporters and theologians to the papal statement of repentance underscore the need for further work in disseminating a clear presentation of the renewed self-understanding of the Church as indefectibly holy while being composed of members who can and do sin that was articulated by the council fathers in the documents of Vatican II.

On the other hand, the theological questions and concerns that emanated from this statement of repentance and day of pardon were and are important facets of the life and mission of the Church. Francis Sullivan's reflection, which suggested that a better image of the Church out of which to make such a statement would have been the pilgrim Church rather than Mother Church, has much merit. Sullivan sees that image as more able to hold both the holiness and sinfulness of the Church in tension without giving sway to one over the other as the Church makes its pilgrimage. Bruno Forte, who writes about the eschatological aspect of the Church, that is, how the Church is both in time and eternal, would also seem to endorse Sullivan's suggestion to embrace the image of pilgrim Church instead of Mother Church when trying to understand the need for and importance of John Paul II's desire to seek forgiveness for the Church's sins. Antonio Sicari, who emphasizes that this statement is about the Church and its relationship with God, not the world *per se*, assists in understanding why there was so much controversy about it. He clearly points out that there are times when the secular world will just not be able to understand a Church that does not claim this world as a lasting city. Again, this idea would seem in a tangential way to support Sullivan's proposal of an image of a Church on pilgrimage to best situate the need for admitting error and sin.

In their *Commonweal* reflections, Bradford Hinze, Richard McBrien, Richard Neuhaus, and Elizabeth Johnson write about what this "apology" means for understanding doctrine and tradition and the development of each of these as the Church moves through history.

Hinze and McBrien would rather have seen the pope emphasize the collective guilt of the Church than that of individuals in his statement. Hinze finds this move desirable because he would like to see the Church dialogue more as a collective whole when it comes to discerning the reform of the tradition. McBrien notes his concern that the Roman hierarchy is more willing to blame individuals for sin than the collective Church. McBrien would like to see the collective Church assume responsibility for the sinfulness of its body.

Neuhaus and Johnson are on opposite sides with regard to the development of doctrine. Neuhaus argues that development of doctrine is often mistakenly juxtaposed with change in doctrine. Neuhaus insists that doctrine does not change but develops and grows within tradition. He makes it clear that faith and an understanding thereof must be the place from which any developments originate. Johnson sees the development of doctrine from the vantage point of the Church admitting error. She compares the Galileo case with the current treatment of women in the Church. She believes that the tradition and doctrine about the role of women in the Church will eventually change.

Although each of the aforementioned theologians offers a different lens from which to view the need to seek forgiveness, their concerns do point out the need for a clear defining of terms. If one is referring to the Church as a collective entity, one must consider the fact that this collective entity is also composed of individuals, and vice versa. With regard to doctrine, one must examine each instance on its own terms and in its own context to decide whether the point of departure is development or change. Depending on one's choice, one will either see a need for admission of error or grow in an understanding of the development of doctrine. Either way, it is critical to define one's terms and foundation.

Finally, the reflections of Joseph Komonchak raise the important point of how the Church has received questions about its sinfulness and its need to reform in the past and how such questions could be received now in light of the millennial plans of John Paul II. Komonchak sees that a defensive, apologetic attitude does not help the Church. Rather, he believes that the Church must own its sinfulness on all levels and try to recommit to living its life in light of the call of the Gospel.

Komonchak also brings to the fore the question that unites all of the concerns that these theologians raised with regard to the millennial statement of repentance of John Paul II, namely, who is the Church? This question is critical and can be seen to be operative in the issues being discussed in regard to the statement. Is the statement being made by Mother Church or for a pilgrim Church? How does the statement affect the eschatological understanding of a Church in time and beyond time? And how does a secular world relate to such a mysterious entity? Is the statement being made on behalf of the collective Church or is it being made only for those sins and errors of individuals? How does such an apologetic statement affect the Church's claim to inerrancy in doctrine if it seems to include admissions of error because Church teachings from the past have developed? Does the statement admit error in doctrine or explain that doctrine grows and develops? All of these questions can be gathered under the one question that Komonchak raises, "Who is the Church?" Underneath this question, I believe, is a critical plea for theologians and for the Church itself as it moves into the twenty-first century to define its terms and realize that, depending on the various images one uses to describe the Church, there can clearly be differing views and opinions on issues and concerns. All too often, the word "Church" is used without a clear indication of which image and definition is under consideration and without acknowledging that with the use of a different image, different concerns will be at stake. For example, what definitions of "Church" were operative in John Paul II's statement of repentance and documents leading up to it? We will deal with this question in the next section.

## *Next Steps:* Novo Millennio Ineunte

Although this millennial statement of repentance and day of pardon were but brief moments in the life of the Church, they had a significant impact as was evident by the myriad responses to them, both secular and theological. John Paul II's millennial statement seeking forgiveness and day of pardon were, indeed, new moments in the life of the Church. The foundation for this millennial apologetic program was prepared by the documents of Vatican II, which renewed the Church's self-understanding through retrieval of the biblical, scriptural, and patristic sources. The council was assisted in doing this by the previous work of theologians such as Mersch, de Lubac, Congar, and Rahner. Journet's theological insights also helped to move forward the need to rework the neoscholastic categories using *ressourcement* materials. Finally, John Paul II's affinity for the theology of Hans Urs von Balthasar also played a significant part in his acknowledgment that sin did indeed exist in the Church. Von Balthasar's theology also provided a framework from which John Paul II was able to proceed with his plan to apologize on behalf of the sons and daughter of the Church for the sins of the past as the third millennium approached.

In *Novo Millennio Ineunte*, John Paul II lays out his pastoral priorities for the third millennium and notes that they are rooted in the documents of Vatican II:

> What a treasure there is, dear brothers and sisters, in the guidelines offered to us by the Second Vatican Council! For this reason I asked the Church, as a way of preparing for the Great Jubilee, to *examine herself on the reception given to the Council*. Has this been done? The Congress held here in the Vatican was such a moment of reflection, and I hope that similar efforts have been made in various ways in all the particular Churches. With the passing of the years, *the Council documents have lost nothing of their value or brilliance*. They need to be read correctly, to be widely known and taken to heart as

important and normative texts of the Magisterium, within the Church's Tradition. Now that the Jubilee has ended, I feel more than ever in duty bound to point to the Council as *the great grace bestowed on the Church in the twentieth century:* there we find a sure compass by which to take our bearings in the century now beginning.

The pope also speaks of the celebration of the two thousand-year anniversary of the birth of Jesus as "a new stage of the Church's journey," as he believes that during this anniversary year, "The Church became more than ever a pilgrim people, led by him who is 'the great shepherd of the sheep' (Heb 13:20)." And he ties both the emphasis on the documents of Vatican II and this new moment in the life of the Church together when he states,

> From the beginning of my Pontificate, my thoughts had been on this Holy Year 2000 as an important appointment. I thought of its celebration as a providential opportunity during which the Church, thirty-five years after the Second Vatican Ecumenical Council, would examine how far she had renewed herself, in order to be able to take up her evangelizing mission with fresh enthusiasm. (NMI 2)

Clearly, John Paul II's millennial program was firmly rooted in the teachings of Vatican II. John Paul continues to emphasize the pivotal gesture of this Jubilee when he writes,

> To purify our vision for the contemplation of the mystery, this Jubilee Year has been strongly marked by the *request for forgiveness.* This is true not only for individuals, who have examined their own lives in order to ask for mercy and gain the special gift of the indulgence, but for the entire Church, which has decided to recall the infidelities of so many of her children in the course of history, infidelities which have cast a shadow over her countenance as the Bride of Christ. For a long time we had been preparing ourselves for this examination of conscience, aware that the Church, embracing sinners in her bosom, "is at once holy and always in need of being purified."[4] Study congresses helped us to identify those aspects in which, during the course of the first two millennia, the Gospel spirit did not always shine forth. How could we forget *the moving Liturgy of 12 March 2000* in Saint Peter's Basilica, at which, looking upon our Crucified Lord, I asked forgiveness in the name of the Church for the sins of

all her children? This "purification of memory" has strengthened
our steps for the journey towards the future and has made us more
humble and vigilant in our acceptance of the Gospel. (NMI 6)

Here John Paul indicates that his seeking forgiveness was not only on
behalf of individuals but also on behalf of all members of the Church. By
saying this, the pope makes a connection between the sins of individuals
in the Church and the collective Church. This connection is significant
because it brings together what has been seen as two distinct understandings of who the Church is. He implies that the Church is both individuals
and a collective simultaneously. By doing so, the pope is able to identify
those areas of the Church in which individuals or the collective body did
not allow the Gospel spirit to shine forth during the course of the first two
millennia, and call the Church, both collectively and as individual members, to repentance. He then is able to urge the entire Church in paragraph
29 of *Novo Millennio Ineunte* to "start afresh from Christ."

Like the *ressourcement* theologians who retrieved the writings of the
early Fathers of the Church and gave theology a new start near the beginning of the twentieth century, John Paul II explains what is needed for the
beginning of the twenty-first century:

It is not therefore a matter of inventing a "new programme." The
programme already exists: it is the plan found in the Gospel and in
the living Tradition, it is the same as ever. Ultimately, it has its centre
in Christ himself, who is to be known, loved and imitated, so that
in him we may live the life of the Trinity, and with him transform
history until its fulfilment in the heavenly Jerusalem. This is a programme which does not change with shifts of times and cultures,
even though it takes account of time and culture for the sake of
true dialogue and effective communication. This programme for
all times is our programme for the Third Millennium. (NMI 29)

The pope then articulates his pastoral priorities moving forward from the
Jubilee celebration, namely, a revisiting of *Lumen Gentium*'s universal call
to holiness and the primary role of grace in the Christian life. John Paul
believes that attention to these priorities will build up the Church as a
sacrament of love for the whole human race and assist in fostering growth
in the unity of the Mystical Body of Christ, the Church.

## Conclusion

The millennial program of John Paul II, particularly his insistence that the Jubilee Year be an occasion for apologizing for the historic faults and failings of the Church since the birth of Christ, as well as his calling the Church to renew its commitment to the self-understanding articulated in *Lumen Gentium*, were significant moments in the life of the Church. The millennial statement of repentance and the day of pardon allowed for the Church to begin to see itself as the early Fathers did, sinful in its members, individually and collectively, but moving forward and striving for holiness each step of the way. John Paul's emphasis on grace and the universal call to holiness helps the Church embrace its pilgrim nature as taught at Vatican II and not be paralyzed by its sinfulness. I contend that by reflecting on past faults and failings and moving forward with an emphasis on the primary role of grace in the individual and collective life of the Church, John Paul II's millennial program was effective in making the Church more credible in the world.[97] Further, I suggest that, in the face of the abuse crisis erupting in the Church over the past decade, John Paul's ability to humbly ask for pardon and forgiveness can serve as an important marker demonstrating the Church's self-awareness: although divine in its life in and of Christ, the Church acknowledges that it is still subject to the weakness, sinfulness, and frailty of the humans who compose it.

In John Paul II's millennial program, it is possible to see the fruits of Vatican II's renewed understanding of the holiness and sinfulness of the Church, for which it owed much to the *ressourcement* theologians examined in this study. With the exception of Rahner's work, however, John Paul II's millennial program, in which he seeks pardon and forgiveness, went beyond what these theologians envisioned. Now the question is, where do we go from here? To that forward-looking question, we will now turn.

---

[97] Bergen, in *Ecclesial Repentance* (p. 222), writes about the significance of a repenting Church for the twenty-first century as it speaks to one of the key features of postmodernity that all perspectives including the holiness of the Church are limited. Thereby, the discussion of a sinful Church opens up space for the Church to give testimony to its nature and source of holiness, Christ.

# Conclusion

At the beginning of this study, I drew on the apostolic letter of Pope John Paul II, *Tertio Millennio Adveniente*, to raise two questions: (1) How can sinners be part of the body of Christ? (2) Does the membership of sinners in the Church affect its holiness?

This study argues that the writings of six preconciliar theologians, Emile Mersch, Henri de Lubac, Hans Urs von Balthasar, Yves Congar, Charles Journet, and Karl Rahner, laid the groundwork for the discussion that ensued at Vatican II about how the Church remains indefectibly holy while being composed of people who sin.

Influenced by those discussions, the fathers of the council acknowledged that the holy Church is always in need of purification and constantly follows the path of penance and renewal (LG 1 and 8). This way of understanding the holiness and sinfulness of the Church can be seen as an important retrieval of the early Fathers and as foundational for John Paul II's public acknowledgment of the sins of the sons and daughters of the Church at the beginning of the twenty-first century. The bold proclamation of the Church's need for purification by the council fathers at Vatican II that was further highlighted by John Paul II's millennial statement of repentance would not have been possible without the renewed understanding of the Church's nature and mission that the council fathers at Vatican II articulated. This renewed self-understanding included an acknowledgment that the Church, though indefectibly holy, walks in history and is composed of members who can and do sin.

This renewal of the Church's self-understanding began to take root in the early twentieth century. Retrieval of the scriptural and patristic sources regarding the Church as indefectibly holy while being composed of members who can and do sin was instrumental in laying the groundwork for this shift in the Church's self-understanding.

In order for this renewal to take place the Church had begun to re-appropriate its own historical self-understanding. Theologians such as Emile Mersch, whose writings focused on the Church as the Mystical Body of Christ, a living organism that has grown and developed since its inception, and de Lubac, whose use of paradox as a way for the Church to hold in tension its holiness and sinfulness, its temporality and eternal nature, its visibility and invisibility, assisted greatly in the Church's ability to understand how it can operate both in time and beyond time.

Retrieval of the early Fathers' understanding of the Church as sacrament was key in expanding the Church's perspective and helping it to embrace the world anew. Rediscovering the significance of the Fathers' writings on our supernatural dignity as resting upon our common human dignity also advanced the movement of the Church to engage and minister to the world in a more deliberate manner.

As the preconciliar theologians began to rediscover the deep awareness in Scripture and in the writings of the Fathers that humanity encounters God in and through the Church that walks in history, there was a need for a renewed understanding of how it is possible for sin to exist in the Church. One of the clearest examples of this sinfulness was made by Yves Congar in his first work, *Divided Christendom*. Congar believed that there was no greater scandal in the Church than the sinfulness of the disunity and divisions in Christianity.

Although the idea of the Church as sinful in its members was not new, it was viewed with suspicion, as it was a major shift from the neoscholastic method of doing theology that had become *the* approved method in the Church. Differences in approach to the Church's holiness and sinfulness are exemplified by Charles Journet's efforts, on the one hand, to rework neoscholastic categories and attribute the Church's growth in holiness to the work of the Holy Spirit, and, on the other hand, Karl Rahner's insistence on the need to accept the reality of the Church's sinfulness. The emphasis of each of these theologians reflects the struggle around how one speaks of the Church as indefectibly holy while admitting that its members are sinners who are striving to grow in holiness.

Although Journet's theology may have created an opening for some bishops at the council to consider the *ressourcement* method of theology, by the end of the twentieth century, John Paul II's plans for the celebration of the millennium, influenced by von Balthasar's theology, were leaning more in the direction of Rahner's approach than Journet's. Despite the fact that Rahner's theological reflection on the "Church of Sinners" was never fully embraced by the council, his position can be seen as the beginning of a conversation which continues to be very important in regard to the situation of the sexual abuse of minors by some ordained members that exploded in the Church at the turn of the twenty-first century.

John Paul II's apostolic letters *Novo Millennio Ineunte* and *Tertio Millennio Adveniente*, and the papal day of pardon seeking forgiveness for the sins of the Church on March 12, 2000, marked a further development in and appropriation of a renewed theology of the Church as holy and sinful. This study has argued that John Paul II's millennial program of pardon was the fruit of a century of theological reflection on the nature and mission of the Church that began with *ressourcement* theology and was advanced by the convocation of Vatican II and its subsequent documents, particularly *Lumen Gentium*.

The new understanding of the nature and mission of the Church that was articulated in *Lumen Gentium* enabled John Paul to usher in a new moment in the life of the Church. This new moment took place in a liturgical context on "March 12, 2000 in Saint Peter's Basilica, at which, looking upon our Crucified Lord, I asked forgiveness in the name of the Church for the sins of all her children" (NMI 6). As the new millennium approached, the pope had seen the need to "identify those aspects in which during the course of the first two millennia, the Gospel spirit did not always shine forth" (NMI 6) and to ask for forgiveness for them.

The pope had read the signs of the times and knew that the beginning of the third millennium was the appropriate time to call the Church to "start afresh from Christ" (NMI 29). Like the *ressourcement* theologians who retrieved the writings of the Fathers of the Church to give theology a new start at the beginning of the twentieth century, John Paul II gave the Church a new start at the beginning of the twenty-first century. He did not invent a new program, but, as he said, "the programme already exists: it is the plan found in the Gospel and in the living Tradition, it is the same as ever" (NMI 29). Nevertheless, the pope did something never done before. At a public liturgical ceremony, he acknowledged and sought forgiveness for the sins of the sons and daughters of the Church over the last ten centuries. Although he did not explicitly state, as perhaps some would have wanted, that the Church was sinful, he did acknowledge that sin existed in the action and inaction of the sons and daughters of the Church down through the centuries. Even this admission caused unease among some theologians and members of the hierarchy for fear of misinterpretation.

# Further Theological Considerations

The fear that John Paul II's millennial statement seeking forgiveness for the sins of the sons and daughters of the Church might be misinterpreted, I contend, sets an important agenda for the twenty-first century, namely, to further reflect on and develop its response to questions about the extent to which we can speak not only of a Church of sinners but also of a sinful Church. I believe that the question, "what, or perhaps better, *who* are the Church?"[1] that Joseph Komonchak raised in regard to preparing for the new millennium is the place from which to begin to address how we speak of sin, sinners, and the Church. This is important because certain definitions of the Church do not lend themselves to the discussion of the sinfulness of the Church.

Along with the critical need to define one's terms, it is essential to keep the principle of both/and in mind as one discusses the issue of the holiness and sinfulness of the Church. From Mersch's retrieval of the biblical and patristic sources that expound on the Church as the Mystical Body of Christ and as the Bride of Christ, it is clear that the Church is indefectibly holy. As Congar notes, however, from his dismay at the divisions and disunity among Christian denominations, the Church as the people of God is on pilgrimage, is on the way, and therefore, can and does sin. Acknowledging that the Church, while on the way, sins, does not negate its holiness. The problem arises when one holds that discussing the sinfulness of the Church or the Church's repenting and asking forgiveness for its sins

---

[1] Joseph Komonchak, "Preparing for the New Millennium," *Logos* 1, no. 2 (Summer 1997): 40–41.

means that the Church isn't holy. The Church's holiness and sinfulness can and must be held together. The question remains, how?

I think that continuing to draw on the various writings of the theologians discussed in chapter 1 can help map out an answer that strikes a balance between the images of the Church offered by Mersch and Congar. One way to start to bring these two images together is through the use of de Lubac's lens of paradox. One needs to acknowledge that if one overemphasizes the image of the Church as the people of God on pilgrimage, the result can leave the Church mired in its sins, weaknesses, and failings. On the other hand, if one overemphasizes the image of the Church as the Mystical Body of Christ and the Bride of Christ, the result can be a Church whose credibility is hampered when faced with its history of participating in and, thereby, being complicit in the sins that divided Christendom, spread anti-Semitism, fought crusades against Moslems, and in our own day seemingly ignored the well-being of children by allowing the clerical abuse of children to continue unaddressed, covered-up, and denied. So, needing to keep these images in balance is crucial. Recognizing that the Church is both in history and beyond history is a key factor, in my opinion, in the search for a way to answer the question that Komonchak raises, "what, or perhaps better, *who* are the Church?" The "who" part of Komonchak's question is easily answered: the Church is all of its members, lay, religious, priests, hierarchy; the "who" of the Church with their faults, failings, and sins as well as their striving for holiness compose the membership of the Church. The "what" part of Komonchak's question can be seen to reference the Church as an institution, as a whole body: the Church as an institution with its sacramental structure is a leaven for holiness in the world. The Church as an institution, however, has at times failed to live as its intrinsic holiness requires. It is important to remember these various aspects of the Church, namely, composed of individuals and yet a corporate body, as well as to realize that both aspects are on the way moving to the kingdom of God where "the church [will be] in all her glory, having no spot or wrinkle or any such thing; but that she will be holy and blameless" (Eph 5:27).

Komochak's noting that the Church as an institution has failed to live as its holiness should necessitate leads us to the question that Bradford Hinze raised concerning John Paul II's day of pardon: namely, was he asking forgiveness for the sins of individuals in the Church or for the sins of the Church collectively? Margaret Pfeil, in an article written in 2002, addresses this question by exploring the doctrinal implications of the use of the language of social sin. Pfeil begins by stating that the council fathers purposefully did not use the language of social sin in writing documents of Vatican II "lest the centrality of personal agency in formal sin be undermined."[2] She notes, however, that the language of social sin began to emerge after Vatican II with the conference of Latin American bishops at Medellín, Colombia, in 1968. There, the bishops first spoke of "sinful situations" and "institutionalized violence."[3] In 1979, Pfeil recalls that John Paul II in Puebla, Mexico, invokes Mary as the refuge who "enables us to overcome the multiple 'structures of sin' in which our personal, family, and social life is wrapped."[4] John Paul II's use of the phrase, "structures of sin" made way for a new theological category, the reality of social sin. This category was given a foundation in John Paul II's subsequent apostolic *exhortation, "Reconciliatio et paenitentia."* Pfeil notes that in this document, John Paul gives three acceptable meanings of social sin: every sin that has social repercussions is a social sin; a direct attack on one's neighbor can be considered a social sin; and sin in relationships between and among human classes, nations, or groups of nations is indicative of social sin. In this same discussion, John Paul II warns against invoking social sin as a way to water down personal sin.[5] Pfeil explains that in *"Reconciliatio et paenitentia"* and successive documents, John Paul II never undercuts the centrality of personal agency and moral responsibility for sin. Though John Paul began using the language of social sin around 1979, in his millennial program, he does not ask for forgiveness of the institutional or structural

[2] Margaret Pfeil, "Doctrinal Implications of Magisterial Use of the Language of Social Sin," *Louvain Studies* 27, no. 2 (2002): 134, citing Antonio de Castro Mayer's written intervention on chaps. 5–8, "Schema on the Liturgy," in *Acta Synodalia Sacrosancti Concilii Oecumenici Vaticani II*, vol. 1, par. 2 (Vatican: Polyglot Press, 1970), 695, and Bishop Zauner, "Relatio," in *Acta Synodalia Sacrosancti Concilii Oecumenici Vaticani II*, vol. 2, par. 3 (Vatican: Polyglot Press, 1972), 275.

[3] Ibid., 135.

[4] Ibid., 137, citing John Paul II, "Responsible for One Another," Address at the Basilica of Our Lady of Zapopán, Guadalajara, January 30, 1979), *L'Osservatore Romano*, February 19, 1979), 3.

[5] Ibid., 140.

failings of the Church, but rather for the sins of the sons and daughters of the Church. As Pfeil points out, the magisterial invocation of the language of social sin is in a slow process of developing, as there is a need to keep in tension "personal responsibility for sin and the unconscious, indeliberate activity involved in the creation and maintenance of sinful systems, institutions, and structures."[6] In light of the clerical abuse scandals, there is an evident and urgent need for further research and study of the use of the language of social sin to be done so that the Church can take responsibility for institutional faults and failings without ever losing its inherent holiness.

Another direction for development is found in von Balthasar's brief essay which describes the Church as a *casta meretrix*. In this work, von Balthasar unpacks the importance of the word "covenant" as he traces, as Congar also did, the Church's history through both the Old and New Testaments. He points out that throughout history, God has reached out to his people who are sinful, unfaithful, and idolatrous and has offered them a covenant of life and love. Covenant is an image that is not often used to describe the Church, but it is one that could have much merit to help probe the question of to what extent the Church is sinful and a Church of sinners. This image puts the question in a wider context. The word "covenant" suggests an agreement that is in history. Its use in Scripture frequently describes how God, the initiator of the covenant, reaches out to his sinful, weak, and unfaithful people to bring them back to fidelity to him.

Coupling the idea of Church as in a covenantal relationship with God with Rahner's insight that the Church is the sacrament of Christ for the world might help provide a renewed understanding for the twenty-first century as to "who the Church is." The Church is definitely called to holiness and to bring that holiness to the world. For Rahner, it is in and through the Church that Christ is embodied in history. Rahner's image of the Church as sacrament for the world, like von Balthasar's image of the Church as in a covenantal relationship, is expansive—in history and yet calling humanity beyond its infidelities, weaknesses, and failures to sacramentality, to holiness.

---

[6] Ibid., 152.

Finally, Journet's emphasis on the Spirit as the formal cause of the Church should not be overlooked. This insight may have assisted the council fathers in moving beyond neoscholastic categories, and I think that it could help us in the twenty-first century to move beyond the polarization that occurs when one emphasizes the holiness of the Church over and against the sinfulness of the Church and vice versa.

How can the various insights of these preconciliar theologians, along with the developments made by the council fathers and Pope John Paul II, be woven together to address the question of to what extent can we speak not only of a Church of sinners but also of a sinful Church? I would suggest again that the lens of paradox is necessary. I also think that using the words "covenant" and "sacrament" as descriptions of the Church is extremely helpful in trying to articulate this paradox of sin and holiness of the Church for the twenty-first century. A stronger emphasis on the role of the Spirit is also key, as the dynamism of the Spirit suggests an ability to move from sin to holiness. Finally, I believe that when speaking of the holiness of the Church, it would be most advantageous to use the adjective "eschatological." To speak of the eschatological holiness of the Church embodies the paradox of being in and beyond this world and highlights that the Church's holiness too is a work in progress. Continuing to unpack these terms and insights is of utmost importance as the Church, its leaders, and its members strive to understand to what extent it is holy and sinful.

Another agenda item for the twenty-first century suggested by John Paul II's millennial program of repentance is finding a way to admit error without eroding the teaching office and authority of the Church. How can the Church assert its holiness in light of the sinfulness and errors of its members? How integral to understanding the nature and mission of the Church is its claim to holiness? These questions arising from John Paul II's millennial program of repentance are, I believe, critical to address as they have been a source of polarization and misunderstanding in the Church. Although they have not been the subject of discussion lately, they remain in the background of current disagreements about the Church's nature and mission. Clearly, concerns about John Paul II's seeking forgiveness for sins of the Church were not unfounded and can be seen to have emanated from the unaddressed problem of the use of terms without articulating the distinct definition operative.

As the twenty-first century continues to unfold, however, it is clear that the mystery of the Church that the council fathers articulated in *Lumen Gentium* demands more careful attention. John Paul II understood that this mystery was large enough to encompass holiness and sinfulness, truthfulness and error. He was unafraid to "transform history" by his courageous acknowledgment that sin and error exist in the Church. He knew that without admitting sin and error, there appeared to be no need for grace and no need to grow in holiness. Though John Paul did not address the sinfulness of the Church as a whole, as an institution, this could be a logical next step in the developing understanding of the holiness and sinfulness of the Church. One place to start is to acknowledge that admitting the presence of social sin in the Church does not in any way negate the holiness of the Church and its continual call to conversion and renewal.

John Paul II's millennial program seeking forgiveness and pardon had unwittingly been a preparation for the Church's need to repent in recent times of the grievous sin of the clerical abuse of minors. Although the Church is not there yet, we need to continue to find ways to be courageous in admitting our faults and sins. The Church must find the language to be able to admit sinfulness and error and yet continue to profess its eschatological holiness. The Church needs to learn that admitting sin and error is not problematic, but denying it is. Admitting sin and error opens up the space to allow God's healing grace to enter. We need to find ways as a Church not just to say, but to live, what is proclaimed at the Easter Vigil when the Exsultet is sung, "O truly necessary sin of Adam, destroyed completely by the Death of Christ! O happy fault that earned so great, so glorious a Redeemer!" We do not need to defend ourselves; we just need to ask for forgiveness for the ways in which we as a Church have sinned and continue to sin, both collectively and individually. Only when the Church and its leaders can, in humility, embrace more fully its sinfulness and its errors while not negating its call to holiness will the Church mirror Christ, the *Lumen Gentium*, the light of the nations.

# Bibliography

Abbott, Walter M., ed. *The Documents of Vatican II*. New York: Guild Press, 1966.

Accattoli, Luigi. *When a Pope Asks Forgiveness: The Mea Culpa's of Pope John Paul II*. Translated by Jordan Aumann. Boston, MA: Pauline Books & Media, 1998.

Alberigo, Giuseppe. *A Brief History of Vatican II*. Maryknoll, NY: Orbis Books, 2006.

Alberigo, Giuseppe, and Joseph A. Komonchak, eds. *The History of Vatican II*, Volume 3, *The Mature Council, Second Period and Intercession, September 1963–September 1964*. Maryknoll, NY: Orbis Books, 2000.

———. *The History of Vatican II*, Volume 3, *Church as Communion, Third Period and Intercession, September 1964–September 1965*. Maryknoll, NY: Orbis Books, 1995.

Anderson, C. Colt. "Bonaventure and the Sin of the Church." *Theological Studies* 63, no. 4 (2002): 667.

Anderson, Floyd, ed. *Council Daybook: Vatican II, Session 3*. Washington, DC: National Catholic Welfare Conference, 1965.

———. *Council Daybook, Vatican II, Session 4: Sept. 14 to Dec. 8, 1965*. Washington, DC: National Catholic Welfare Conference, 1966.

Anon. "A Vision for the Millennium." *Tablet* 253, January 2, 1999.

———. "John Paul's World View on the Threshold of the New Millennium." *Tablet* 254, January 15, 2000.

———. "The Pope's Apology." *New York Times*, March 14, 2000.

Arraj, Jim. *Mind Aflame: The Theological Vision of One of the World's Great Theologians; Emile Mersch*. Chiloquin: Inner Growth Books, 1994.

Attridge, Michael S. and Jaroslav Z. Skira, eds. *In God's Hands: Essays on the Church and Ecumenism in Honour of Michael A. Fahey, SJ*. Leuven: Leuven University Press, 2006.

Auricchio, John. *The Future of Theology*. Staten Island, NY: Alba House, 1970.

Ayres, Lewis. "The Soul and the Reading of Scripture: A Note on Henri de Lubac." *Scottish Journal of Theology* 61, no. 2 (January 1, 2008): 173–90.

Badcock, Gary D. *The House Where God Lives: Renewing the Doctrine of the Church for Today*. Grand Rapids, MI: William B. Eerdmans Publishing Company, 2009.

Baker, Kenneth. *Fundamentals of Catholicism*. San Francisco: Ignatius Press, 1982.

——. *Fundamentals of Catholicism*, Volume 1, *Creed, Commandments*. San Francisco: Ignatius Press, 1982.

——. *Fundamentals of Catholicism*, Volume 2: *God, Trinity, Creation, Christ, Mary*. San Francisco: Ignatius Press, 1983.

——. *Fundamentals of Catholicism*, Volume 3: *Grace, the Church, the Sacraments, Eschatology*. San Francisco: Ignatius Press, 1983.

Balthasar, Hans Urs von. *Church and World*. New York: Herder & Herder, 1967.

——. "*Casta Meretrix*." In *Explorations in Theology: Spouse of the Word*. Translated by John Saward. San Francisco: Ignatius Press, 1991.

——. *The Office of Peter and the Structure of the Church*. Translated by Andrée Emery. San Francisco: Ignatius Press, 2007.

——. *The Theology of Henri de Lubac: An Overview*. San Francisco: Ignatius Press, 1991.

Baschab, Charles Reinhard. *A Manual of Neo-Scholastic Philosophy*. St. Louis: B. Herder Book Company, 1923.

Beeck, Frans Jozef van. *Catholic Identity After Vatican II: Three Types of Faith in the One Church*. Chicago: Loyola Press, 1985.

Bellitto, Christopher M. "Teaching the Church's Mistakes: Historical Hermeneutics in Memory and Reconciliation: The Church and the Faults of the Past." *Horizons* 32, no. 1 (2005): 123–35.

Bellord, James. *Meditations on Christian Dogma*, 3rd ed. Callan: Convent of Mercy, 1906.

Benedict XVI. "Christmas Address of His Holiness Benedict XVI to the Roman Curia," http://w2.vatican.va/content/benedict-xvi/en/speeches/2005/december/documents/hf_ben_xvi_spe_20051222_roman-curia.html.

Benson, Robert Hugh. *Christ in the Church*. New York: Sheed & Ward, 1941.

Bergen, Jeremy M. *Ecclesial Repentance: The Churches Confront Their Sinful Pasts*. New York: T. & T. Clark International, 2011.

Bernardi, Peter J. "A Passion for Unity." *America* 192, no. 12 (April 4, 2005): 8–11.

——. *Paradoxes of Catholicism*. New York: Longmans, 1913.

Biffi, Giacomo. *Casta Meretrix: The Chaste Whore*. Translated by Richard J. S. Brown. London: The Saint Austen Press, 2001.

——. *Christus Hodie*. Bologna: EDB, 1995.

Boersma, Hans. *Nouvelle Théologie and Sacramental Ontology: A Return to Mystery*. Oxford: Oxford University Press, 2009.

——. "The Eucharist Makes the Church." *Crux* 44, no. 4 (December 1, 2008): 2–11.

Boguslawski, Steven and Robert Fastiggi, eds. *Called to Holiness and Communion: Vatican II on the Church.* Scranton, PA: University of Scranton Press, 2009.

Boissard, Guy. *Charles Journet (1891–1975): Biographie.* Paris: Salvator, 2008.

Boney, William J. and Lawrence, Molumby, eds. *The New Day: Catholic Theologians of the Renewal.* Richmond, VA: John Knox Press, 1968.

Bouyer, Louis. *Church of God: Body of Christ and Temple of the Spirit.* Chicago: Franciscan Herald Press, 1982.

Butler, Basil Christopher. *The Theology of Vatican II.* Rev. and enlarged ed. Westminster, MD: Christian Classics, 1981.

Cardman, Francine. *The Encyclopedia of Christianity*, Volume 1 A–D, s.v. "Cyprian of Carthage." Grand Rapids, MI: William B. Eerdmans Publishing Company, 1991.

*Catechism of the Catholic Church*, 2nd ed. Vatican City: Libreria Editrice Vaticana, 2000.

Cavanaugh, William T. *Migrations of the Holy: God, State, and the Political Meaning of the Church.* Grand Rapids, MI: William B. Eerdmans Publishing Company, 2011.

Cayre, Fulbert. *Manual of Patrology and History of Theology.* Paris: Society of St. John the Evangelist, Desclée & Company, 1936.

Chadwick, Henry. *The Early Church.* New York: Penguin, 1993.

Chantraine, Georges. "Beyond Modernity and Postmodernity: The Thought of Henri de Lubac." *Communio* 17 (June 1, 1990): 207–19.

————. *Henri de Lubac.* Etudes Lubaciennes 6. Paris: Éditions du Cerf, 2007.

Chapman, Mark E. "De Lubac's Catholicism through Lutheran Eyes: Appreciation, Application, Convergence." *One in Christ* 29, no. 4 (January 1, 1993): 286–301.

Clifford, Catherine E., and Richard R. Gaillardetz. *Keys to the Council: Unlocking the Teaching of Vatican II.* Collegeville, MN: Liturgical Press, 2012.

CNN Transcript. "Sunday Morning News: Pope John Paul II Makes Unprecedented Apology for Sins of Catholic Church." March 12, 2000. http://transcripts.cnn.com/TRANSCRIPTS/0003/12/sm.06.html.

*Compendium, Catechism of the Catholic Church.* Washington, DC: United States Conference of Catholic Bishops, 2006.

Congar, Yves. *The Mystery of the Church: Studies by Yves Congar.* Translated by A. V. Littledale. Baltimore: Helicon Press, 1960.

————. *Divided Christendom: A Catholic Study of the Problem of Reunion.* Translated by M. A. Bousfield. 1st English ed. London: The Centenary Press, 1939.

————. *I Believe In The Holy Spirit.* Translated by David Smith. New York: Herder & Herder, 1997.

————. *L'église: Une, Sainte, Catholique et Apostolique.* Paris: Editions du Cerf, 1970.

————. *My Journal of the Council*. Translated by Mary John Ronayne and Mary Cecily Boulding. English translation editor Denis Minns. Collegeville, MN: Liturgical Press, 2012.

————. *The Meaning of Tradition*. Translated by A. N. Woodrow. San Francisco: Ignatius Press, 2004.

————. "The Need for Patience." *Continuum* 2, no. 4 (December 1, 1965): 684–93.

————. *Tradition and Traditions: An Historical and a Theological Essay*. London: Burns & Oates, 1966.

————. *True and False Reform in the Church*. Translated with an Introduction by Paul Philibert. Collegeville, MN: Liturgical Press, 2011.

Connolly, James M. *The Voices of France*. New York: Macmillan, 1961.

D'Ambrosio, Marcellino. "Henri De Lubac and the Recovery of the Traditional Hermeneutic." PhD dissertation, Catholic University of America, 1991.

————. "Ressourcement Theology, Aggiornamento, and the Hermeneutics of Tradition." *Communio* 18 (December 1, 1991): 530–55.

Del Colle, Ralph. *Christ and the Spirit: Spirit-Christology in Trinitarian Perspective*. New York: Oxford University Press, 1994.

Dieterich, Henry. "Steering the Church Toward Holiness." *National Catholic Register* 60, June 17, 1984.

Doyle, Dennis M. *Communion Ecclesiology: Vision and Versions*. Maryknoll, NY: Orbis Books, 2000.

————. "Henri de Lubac and the Roots of Communion Ecclesiology." *Theological Studies* 60, no. 2 (June 1, 1999): 209–27.

————. "Journet, Congar, and the Roots of Communion Ecclesiology." *Theological Studies* 58, no. 3 (September, 1997): 461–79.

Dulles, Avery. *A Church to Believe In*. New York: Crossroad Publishing Company, 1982.

————. "After Our Likeness: The Church as the Image of the Trinity." *First Things*, no. 87 (November 1, 1998): 50–52.

————. "A Half Century of Ecclesiology." *Theological Studies* 50, no. 3 (1989): 419–42.

————. *A History of Apologetics*. 2nd ed. San Francisco: Ignatius Press, 2005.

————. *Church and Society: The Laurence J. McGinley Lectures, 1988–2007*. New York: Fordham University Press, 2008.

————. "Henri de Lubac: In Appreciation." *America* 165, no. 8 (September 28, 1991): 180–82.

————. *Magisterium: Teacher and Guardian of the Faith*. Naples, FL: Sapientia Press of Ave Maria University, 2007.

————. "Mere Apologetics." *First Things*, no. 154 (June–July 2005): 15–20.

————. "Should the Church Repent?" *First Things*, no. 88 (December 1, 1998): 36–41.

————. *The Assurance of Things Hoped For: A Theology of Christian Faith*. New York: Oxford University Press, 1997.

————. *The Catholicity of the Church*. New York: Oxford University Press, 1987.

————. "The Church as 'One, Holy, Catholic, and Apostolic.'" *One in Christ* 35, no. 1 (January 1, 1999): 12–26.

————. *The New World of Faith*. Huntington, IN: Our Sunday Visitor, 2000.

————. *The Resilient Church*. New York: Doubleday and Company, 1977.

————. "True and False Reform." *First Things*, no. 135 (August–September 2003): 14–19.

————. "Asking Forgiveness." *America* 182, no. 10 (March 25, 2000): 3.

Dych, William V., *Karl Rahner*. New York: Continuum Press, 2000.

Evans, G. R., ed. *The First Christian Theologians: An Introduction to Theology in the Early Church*. Malden, MA: Wiley-Blackwell, 2004.

Faggioli, Massimo. *Vatican II: The Battle for Meaning*. Mahwah, NJ: Paulist Press, 2012.

Fiorenza, Francis Schüssler, and John P. Galvin, eds. *Systematic Theology: Roman Catholic Perspectives*. Minneapolis, MN: Augsburg Fortress Publishers, 2000.

Flannery, Austin, ed. *Vatican Council II: The Basic Sixteen Documents; Constitutions, Decrees, Declarations*. Collegeville, MN: Liturgical Press, 2014.

————. *Vatican Council II: The Conciliar and Postconciliar Documents*. Collegeville, MN: Liturgical Press, 2014.

Flynn, Gabriel, and Paul D. Murray, eds. *Ressourcement: A Movement for Renewal in Twentieth-Century Catholic Theology*. Oxford: Oxford University Press, 2012.

Flynn, Gabriel, ed. *Yves Congar: Theologian of the Church*. Grand Rapids, MI: William B. Eerdmans Publishing Company, 2006.

————. *Yves Congar's Vision of the Church in a World of Unbelief*. Burlington, VT: Ashgate Publishing, 2004.

Ford, David, ed. *The Modern Theologians: An Introduction to Christian Theology in the Twentieth Century*. 2nd ed. Malden, MA: Wiley-Blackwell, 1997.

————. *The Modern Theologians: An Introduction to Christian Theology Since 1918*. 3rd ed. Malden, MA: Wiley Blackwell, 2005.

Forte, Bruno. "The Church Confronts the Faults of the Past." *Communio* 27, no. 4 (December 1, 2000): 676–87.

————. *The Church, Icon of the Trinity: A Brief Study*. Boston, MA: St. Paul Books & Media, 1991.

Gaillardetz, Richard R. *The Church in the Making: Lumen Gentium, Christus Dominus, Orientalium Ecclesiarum*. New York: Paulist Press, 2006.

Gibbons, James. *The Faith of Our Fathers: Being a Plain Exposition and Vindication of the Church Founded by Our Lord Jesus Christ*, 110th ed. New York: P. J. Kennedy, 1917.

Glendon, Mary Ann. "Contrition in the Age of Spin Control." *First Things*, no. 77 (November 1, 1997): 10–12.

Greiner, Maximilian. "Henri de Lubac." *Communio* 22, no. 2 (January 1, 1993): 99–163.

Grumett, David. *De Lubac: A Guide for the Perplexed*. London: T. & T. Clark, 2007.

Gunton Colin E. *The Cambridge Companion to Christian Doctrine*. Cambridge, UK: Cambridge University Press, 1997.

Haggerty, Janet. *The Centrality of Paradox in the Work of Henri de Lubac, SJ*. New York: Fordham University Press, 1987.

Hahn, Scott. *Covenant and Communion: The Biblical Theology of Pope Benedict XVI*. Grand Rapids, MI: Brazos Press, 2009.

Hahnenberg, Edward P. *Ministries: A Relational Approach*. New York: Crossroad Publishing Company, 2003.

Haight, Roger. *Christian Community in History: Ecclesial Existence*. New York: Continuum, 2008.

———. *Christian Community in History: Volume 1; Historical Ecclesiology*. New York: Continuum, 2004.

———. *Christian Community in History: Volume 2: Comparative Ecclesiology*. New York: Continuum, 2005.

———. Personal Communication. "Ecclesiology From Above and Ecclesiology from Below." October 7, 2010.

———. *Experience and Language of Grace*. Mahwah, NJ: Paulist Press, 1979.

Hamer, Jerome. *The Church Is a Communion*. Translated by Ronald Matthews. New York: Sheed & Ward, 1964.

Hartley, Thomas J. A. *Thomistic Revival and the Modernist Era*. Toronto: Institute of Christian Thought, University of St. Michael's College, 1971.

Hebblethwaite, Margaret and Peter Hebblethwaite. *John XXIII: Pope of the Century*, 2nd ed. New York: Continuum, 2000.

Heim, Maximilian Heinrich. *Joseph Ratzinger: Life in the Church and Living Theology; Fundamentals of Ecclesiology*. San Francisco: Ignatius Press, 2007.

Henn, William. "Yves Congar and *Lumen Gentium*." *Gregorianum* 86, no. 3 (2005): 563–92.

Himes, Michael J. *Ongoing Incarnation*. New York: Crossroad Publishing Company, 1997.

Hines, Mary and Declan Marmion, eds. *The Cambridge Companion to Karl Rahner*. Cambridge, UK: Cambridge University Press, 2005.

Hinze, Bradford E. "Ecclesial Repentance and the Demands of Dialogue." *Theological Studies* 61, no. 2 (June 1, 2000): 207–38.

International Theological Commission. "Memory and Reconciliation: The Church and the Faults of the Past." December, 1999. http://www.vatican.va/roman_curia/congregations/cfaith/cti_documents/rc_con_cfaith_doc_20000307_memory-reconc-itc_en.html.

John XXIII. "Allocutio in Sollemni SS. Concilii Inauguratione." Speech given October 11, 1962. http://w2.vatican.va/content/john-xxiii/la/speeches/1962/documents/hf_j-xxiii_spe_19621011_opening-council.html.

———. *Pope John XXIII: Essential Writings; Selected with an Introduction by Jean Maalouf*. Maryknoll, NY: Orbis Books, 2008.

John Paul II. "Blessing and Final Prayer." Vatican Basilica, March 12, 2000. http://www.vatican.va/news_services/liturgy/documents/ns_lit_doc_20000312_bened-day-pardon_it.html.

———. *Celebrate 2000!: A Three Year Reader; Reflections on Jesus, the Holy Spirit, and the Father*. Ann Arbor, MI: Charis, 1996.

———. "Day of Pardon," Vatican Basilica, March 12, 2000. http://www.vatican.va/news_services/liturgy/documents/ns_lit_doc_20000312_presentation-day-pardon_en.html.

———. "Homily of the Holy Father, Day of Pardon, Sunday, March 12, 2000." http://w2.vatican.va/content/john-paul-ii/en/homilies/2000/documents/hf_jp-ii_hom_20000312_pardon.html.

———. "*Incarnationis Mysterium*, Bull of Indiction of the Great Jubilee of the Year 2000." http://www.vatican.va/jubilee_2000/docs/documents/hf_jp-ii_doc_30111998_bolla-jubilee_en.html.

———. *Novo Millennio Ineunte*. Apostolic Letter dated January 6, 2001. http://w2.vatican.va/content/john-paul-ii/en/apost_letters/2001/documents/hf_jp-ii_apl_20010106_novo-millennio-ineunte.html.

———. "Prayer of John Paul II for the First Year of Preparation (1997) for the Great Jubilee of the Year 2000." http://www.vatican.va/jubilee_2000/docs/documents/ju_documents_24-feb-1997_prayer_en.html.

———. "Prayer of John Paul II for the Second Year (1998) of Preparation for the Great Jubilee of the Year 2000: Come, Spirit of Love and Peace." http://www.vatican.va/jubilee_2000/docs/documents/ju_doc_22121997_prayer_en.html.

———. "Prayer of John Paul II for the third year (1999) of preparation for the Great Jubilee of the Year 2000." http://www.vatican.va/jubilee_2000/docs/documents/ju_doc_01061999_prayer_en.html.

———. *Tertio Millennio Adveniente*. Apostolic Letter dated November 10, 1994. http://w2.vatican.va/content/john-paul-ii/en/apost_letters/1994/documents/hf_jp-ii_apl_19941110_tertio-millennio-adveniente.html.

———. "Universal Prayer: Confession of Sins and Asking for Forgiveness." Vatican Basilica, March 12, 2000. http://www.vatican.va/news_services/liturgy/documents/ns_lit_doc_20000312_prayer-day-pardon_en.html.

———. *Ut Unum Sint:* Encyclical Letter of the Holy Father John Paul II on Commitment to Ecumenism. United Kingdom: Catholic Truth Society, 1995.

Johnson, Elizabeth A. "Galileo's Daughters: What Error Looks Like Today." *Commonweal* 126 (November 19, 1999): 18–20.

Journet, Charles. *The Church of the Word Incarnate: An Essay in Speculative Theology.* Translated by A. H. C. Downes. London: Sheed and Ward, 1955.

———. *The Theology of the Church.* Translated by Victor Szczurek. San Francisco: Ignatius Press, 2004.

Kärkkäinen, Veli-Matti. *An Introduction to Ecclesiology: Ecumenical, Historical, and Global Perspectives.* Downers Grove, IL: InterVarsity Press, 2002.

Kerr, Fergus. *Twentieth-Century Catholic Theologians.* Malden, MA: Blackwell Publishing, 2007.

Kloppenburg, Bonaventure. *The Ecclesiology of Vatican II.* Translated by Matthew J. O'Connell. Chicago: Franciscan Herald Press, 1974.

Komonchak, Joseph A. "Theology and Culture at Mid-Century: The Example of Henri de Lubac." *Theological Studies* 50 (1990): 579–602.

———. "Preparing for the New Millennium." *Logos: A Journal of Catholic Thought and Culture* 1, no. 2 (Summer 1997): 34 –55.

———. *Who are the Church?* Milwaukee, WI: Marquette University Press, 2008.

Körner, Bernhard, and Adrian Walker. "Henri Lubac and Fundamental Theology." *Communio* 23 (December 1, 1996): 710–24.

Kreeft, Peter. *Catholic Christianity: A Complete Catechism of Catholic Beliefs Based on the Catechism of the Catholic Church.* San Francisco: Ignatius Press, 2001.

Kress, Robert. *The Church: Communion, Sacrament, Communication.* Mahwah, NJ: Paulist Press, 1985.

———. "Whether the Holy Church, Which Is Also the Church of Sinners, Is a Sinful Church?" STD dissertation, Pontificia Studiorum Universitas a S. Thoma Aq. in Urbe, 1968.

Lakeland, Paul. *Yves Congar: Spiritual Writings.* Maryknoll, NY: Orbis Books, 2010.

Lamb, Matthew L., and Matthew Levering. *Vatican II: Renewal within Tradition.* New York: Oxford University Press, 2008.

Lennan, Richard, ed. *An Introduction to Catholic Theology.* Mahwah, NJ: Paulist Press, 1998.

———. *Ecclesiology of Karl Rahner.* Oxford: Clarendon Press, 2002.

———. "Faith in Context: Rahner on the Possibility of Belief." *Philosophy & Theology* 17, no. 1 (January 1, 2005): 233–58.

Leo XIII. *Aeterni Patris.* Encyclical of Pope Leo XIII on the Restoration of Christian Philosophy. http://w2.vatican.va/content/leo-xiii/en/encyclicals/documents/hf_l-xiii_enc_04081879_aeterni-patris.html.

Livingston, James C. *Modern Christian Thought.* 2nd ed. Minneapolis, MN: Fortress Press, 2006.

Lubac, Henri de. *At the Service of the Church: Henri de Lubac Reflects on the Circumstances That Occasioned His Writings.* Translated by Anne Elizabeth Englund. San Francisco: Ignatius Press, 1993.

———. "Catholicism." *Communio* 15 (June 1, 1988): 234–48.

———. *Catholicism: Christ and the Common Destiny of Man.* Translated by Lancelot C. Sheppard and Elizabeth Englund. San Francisco: Ignatius Press, 1988.

———. *Corpus Mysticum: The Eucharist and the Church in the Middle Ages: Historical Survey.* Translated by Gemma Simmonds with Richard Price and Christopher Stephens. Edited by Laurence Paul Hemming and Susan Frank Parsons. London: SCM Press, 2006.

———. *More Paradoxes.* Translated by Anne Englund Nash. San Francisco: Ignatius Press, 2002.

———. *Paradoxes of Faith.* Translated by Ernest Beaumont. San Francisco: Ignatius Press, 1987.

———. *The Church: Paradox and Mystery.* Translated by James R. Dunne. Staten Island, NY: Alba House, 1969.

———. *The Motherhood of the Church: Followed by Particular Churches in the Universal Church.* Translated by Sergia Englund. San Francisco: Ignatius Press, 1982.

———. *The Mystery of the Supernatural.* Translated by Rosemary Sheed. New York: Crossroad Publishing, 1998.

———. *Theological Fragments.* Translated by Rebecca Howell Balinski. San Francisco: Ignatius Press, 1989.

———. *The Splendor of the Church.* Translated by Michael Mason. San Francisco: Ignatius Press, 1986.

———. "Witness of Christ in the Church: Hans Urs von Balthasar." *Communio* 2 (Fall 1975): 228–49.

MacLoughlin, James. *Catholic Faith in Outline: A Summary of Instruction; A Guide for Preacher and Teacher.* Westminster, MD: Newman Press, 1956.

Malanowski, Gregory E. "The Christocentrism of Emile Mersch and Its Implications for a Theology of Church." STD dissertation, Catholic University of America, 1988.

Mannion, Gerard. *Ecclesiology and Postmodernity: Questions for the Church in Our Time.* Collegeville, MN: Liturgical Press, 2007.

————. ed. *The Vision of John Paul II: Assessing His Thought and Influence.* Collegeville, MN: Liturgical Press, 2008.

Mattei, Roberto de. *Il Concilio Vaticano II. Una Storia Mai Scritta.* Bavaria: Lindau, 2010.

McBrien, Richard P. "A Repenting Church: France & Germany Show the Way." *Commonweal* 126 (November 19, 1999): 12.

————. *Catholicism, Volume I.* Minneapolis, MN: Winston Press, 1980.

————. *Catholicism, Volume II.* Minneapolis, MN: Winston Press, 1980.

McCool, Gerald A. *Catholic Theology in the Nineteenth Century: The Quest for a Unitary Method.* New York: Fordham University Press, 1977.

————. *The Neo-Thomists.* Milwaukee, WI: Marquette University Press, 1994.

McGrath, Alister E. *Historical Theology: An Introduction to the History of Christian Thought.* Malden, MA: Blackwell, 1998.

————. *The Blackwell Encyclopedia of Modern Christian Thought.* Malden, MA: Blackwell, 1995.

McGoldrick, P. "Sin and the Holy Church." *Irish Theological Quarterly* 32, no. 1 (1965): 3–27.

McPartlan, Paul. "Catholic Perspectives on Sacramentality." *Studia Liturgica* 38, no. 2 (January 1, 2008): 219–41.

————. "Eucharistic Ecclesiology." *One in Christ* 22, no. 4 (January 1, 1986): 314–31.

————. *Sacrament of Salvation: An Introduction to Eucharistic Ecclesiology.* Edinburgh: T. & T. Clark, 1995.

————. "The Eucharist, the Church, and Evangelization: The Influence of Henri de Lubac." *Communio* 23 (December 1, 1996): 776–85.

————. *The Eucharist Makes the Church.* Edinburgh: T. & T. Clark, 1993.

————. "The Idea of the Church: Abbot Butler and Vatican II." *Downside Review* 121, no. 422 (January 1, 2003): 39–52.

————. "You Will Be Changed into Me": Unity and Limits in du Lubac's Thought." *One in Christ* 30, no. 1 (January 1, 1994): 50–60.

Mersch, Emile. *The Theology of the Mystical Body.* Translated by Cyril Vollert. St. Louis: Herder, 1951.

————. *The Whole Christ: The Historical Development of the Doctrine of the Mystical Body in Scripture and Tradition.* Translated by John R. Kelly. Milwaukee, WI: Bruce Publishing Company, 1938.

Mettepenningen, Jürgen. *Nouvelle Theologie—New Theology: Inheritor of Modernism, Precursor of Vatican II.* Edinburgh: T. & T. Clark International, 2010.

Milbank, John. "The Suspended Middle: Henri de Lubac and the Debate Concerning the Supernatural." In *Modern Catholic Thinkers: An Anthology.* New York: Harper, 1960.

Miller, Michael J., and Rudolf Voderholzer. *Meet Henri de Lubac*. San Francisco: Ignatius Press, 2007.

Mongrain, Kevin. *The Systematic Thought of Hans Urs von Balthasar: An Irenaean Retrieval*. New York: Crossroad Publishing Company, 2002.

Morerod, Charles. "A Roman Catholic Point of View about the Limits of the Church: The Article of Professor Phidas and the Roman Catholic Point of View." *Greek Orthodox Theological Review* 42, nos. 3–4 (Fall–Winter 1997): 343–49.

Mortimer, Alfred G. *Catholic Faith and Practice*. New York: Longmans, Green, and Company, 1897.

Moulins-Beaufort, Eric de, and David Christopher Schindler. "The Spiritual Man in the Thought of Henri de Lubac." *Communio* 25 (June 1, 1998): 287–302.

Murphy, Francesca A. "De Lubac, Ratzinger, and von Balthasar: A Communal Adventure in Ecclesiology." In *Ecumenism Today: The Universal Church in the 2lst Century*, edited by Francesca A. Murphy and Christopher Asprey, 45–80. Burlington, VT: Ashgate Publishing, 2008.

Myers, Edward. *The Mystical Body of Christ*. The Treasury of the Faith Series: 19. New York: Macmillan, 1931.

Neufeld, Karl H. "In the Service of the Council: Bishops and Theologians at the Second Vatican Council (for Cardinal Henri de Lubac on his 90th Birthday)." In *Vatican II: Assessment and Perspectives Twenty Five Years After (1962–1987), Volume 1*, edited by René Latourelle, 74–105. Mahwah, NJ: Paulist Press, 1988.

Neuhaus, Richard John. "Forgive Us Our Trespasses . . . ," *First Things* 104 (June/July 2000): 81–81.

———. "Sentire cum Ecclesia: Rome, si, California, no." *Commonweal* 126 (November 19, 1999): 16–18.

Nichols, Aidan. *A Spirituality for the Twenty-First Century*. Huntington, IN: Our Sunday Visitor, 2003.

———. *Catholic Thought Since the Enlightenment: A Survey*. 1st ed. Pretoria: University of South Africa, 1998.

———. *Divine Fruitfulness: A Guide through Balthasar's Theology Beyond the Trilogy*. Introduction to Hans Urs von Balthasar. Washington, DC: Catholic University of America Press, 2007.

———. *From Newman to Congar: The Idea of Doctrinal Development from the Victorians to the Second Vatican Council*. Edinburgh: T. & T. Clark, 1990.

———. *The Shape of Catholic Theology: An Introduction to Its Sources, Principles, and History*. Collegeville, MN: Liturgical Press, 1991.

———. *Thought of Pope Benedict XVI: An Introduction to the Theology of Joseph Ratzinger*. New York: Burns & Oates, 2007.

———. *Yves Congar*. Wilton, CT: Morehouse Publishing, 1989.

Nutt, Roger W. "Sacerdotal Character and the "*Munera Christi*": Reflections on the Theology of Charles Journet." *Gregorianum* 90, no. 2 (2009): 237–53.

O'Callaghan, Paul. "The Holiness of the Church in *Lumen Gentium.*" *The Thomist* 52 (October 1988): 673–701.

O'Donnell, John. *Hans Urs von Balthasar.* New York: Continuum International Publishing Group, 1991.

O'Donovan, Leo J. "A Changing Ecclesiology in a Changing Church: A Symposium on Development in the Ecclesiology of Karl Rahner." *Theological Studies* 38, no. 4 (December 1, 1977): 736–62.

O'Malley, John. *A History of the Popes: From Peter to the Present.* Lanham, MD: Sheed & Ward, 2009.

―――. *Four Cultures of the West.* Cambridge, MA: Harvard University Press, 2004.

―――. "The Millennium and the Papalization of Catholicism." *America* 182, no. 12 (April 8, 2000): 8.

―――. *What Happened at Vatican II.* Cambridge, MA: Harvard University Press, 2010.

O'Meara, Thomas. "The Teaching Office of Bishops in the Ecclesiology of Charles Journet." *Jurist* 49, no. 1 (1989): 23–47.

Pambrun, James R. "The Presence of God: A Note on the Apologetics of Henri de Lubac and Teilhard de Chardin." *Église et théologie* 10, no. 3 (October 1, 1979): 343–68.

Paul VI. *Ecclesiam Suam: The Paths of the Church.* Mahwah, NJ: Paulist Press, 1964.

―――. *Evangelii Nuntiandi.* Apostolic Exhortation on Evangelization in the Modern World. Washington, DC: United States Catholic Conference, 1976.

Pekarske, Daniel T. *Abstracts of Karl Rahner's Theological Investigations 1–23.* Milwaukee, WI: Marquette University Press, 2003.

Pfeil, Margaret. "Doctrinal Implications of Magisterial Use of the Language of Social Sin." *Louvain Studies* 27, no. 2 (2002): 132–52.

Pius X. *Pascendi Dominici Gregis.* Encyclical on the Doctrines of the Modernists, September 8, 1907. http://w2.vatican.va/content/pius-x/en/encyclicals /documents/hf_p-x_enc_19070908_pascendi-dominici-gregis.html.

Pius XII. *Mystici Corporis.* Encyclical Letter on the Mystical Body of Christ. New York: American Press, 1962.

Poorthuis, Marcel, and Joshua Schwartz. *A Holy People: Jewish and Christian Perspectives on Religious Communal Identity.* Boston: Brill, 2006.

Prusak, Bernard P. "Theological Considerations—Hermeneutical, Ecclesiological, Eschatological Regarding *Memory and Reconciliation: The Church and the Faults of the Past.*" *Horizons* 32, no. 1 (2005): 136–51.

Radner, Ephraim. *A Brutal Unity: The Spiritual Politics of the Christian Church*. Waco, TX: Baylor University Press, 2012.

Rahner, Karl. *Foundations of Christian Faith: An Introduction to the Idea of Christianity*. New York: Crossroad Publishing Company, 1982.

————. *The Church and the Sacraments*. New York: Herder and Herder, 1963.

————. *Theological Investigations*. Vol. 2, *Personal and Sacramental Piety*. Translated by Karl H. Kruger. Baltimore, MD: Helicon Press, 1963.

————. *Theological Investigations*. Vol. 5, *Later Writings*. Translated by Karl H. Kruger. New York: The Crossroad Publishing Company, 1970.

————. *Theological Investigations*. Vol. 6, *Concerning Vatican Council II*. Translated by Boniface Kruger. Baltimore, MD: Helicon Press, 1969.

Ratzinger, Joseph. *A New Song for the Lord: Faith in Christ and Liturgy Today*. Translated by Martha M. Matesich. New York: Crossroad Publishing Company, 1996.

————. *Called to Communion: Understanding the Church Today*. Translated by Adrian Walker. San Francisco: Ignatius Press, 1996.

————. *Introduction to Christianity*. Translated by J. R. Foster. San Francisco: Ignatius Press, 2004.

————. *Pilgrim Fellowship of Faith: The Church as Communion*. Edited by Stephan Otto Horn and Vinzenz Pfnür. Translated by Henry Taylor. San Francisco: Ignatius Press, 2005.

————. *Principles of Catholic Theology: Building Stones for a Fundamental Theology*. Translated by Mary Frances McCarthy. San Francisco: Ignatius Press, 1987.

————. "Responses to Some Questions Regarding Certain Aspects of the Doctrine on the Church." June 29, 2007. http://www.vatican.va/roman _curia/congregations/cfaith/documents/rc_con_cfaith_doc_20070629 _responsa-quaestiones_en.html.

————. *Theological Highlights of Vatican II*. Mahwah, NJ: Paulist Press, 1966.

————. *The Meaning of Christian Brotherhood*. Translated by W. A. Glen-Doepel. San Francisco: Ignatius Press, 1993.

————. *The Nature and Mission of Theology: Essays to Orient Theology in Today's Debates*. Translated by Adrian Walker. San Francisco: Ignatius Press, 1995.

Rausch, Thomas P. *Pope Benedict XVI: An Introduction to His Theological Vision*. Mahwah, NJ: Paulist Press, 2009.

————. *Towards a Truly Catholic Church: An Ecclesiology for the Third Millennium*. Collegeville, MN: Liturgical Press, 2005.

Reardon, Bernard M. G. *Liberal Protestantism*. Stanford, CA: Stanford University Press, 1968.

————. *Religious Thought in the Nineteenth Century: Illustrated from Writers of the Period.* 1st ed. London: Cambridge University Press, 1966.

————. *Roman Catholic Modernism.* Stanford, CA: Stanford University Press, 1970.

Reinisch, Leonhard, ed. *Theologians of Our Time: Karl Barth [and Others].* Notre Dame, IN: University of Notre Dame Press, 1964.

Reno, Russell R. "Theology after the Revolution." *First Things* no. 173 (May 1, 2007): 15–21.

Rowland, Tracey. *Ratzinger's Faith: The Theology of Pope Benedict XVI.* New York: Oxford University Press, 2008.

Ruddy, Christopher. *The Local Church: Tillard and the Future of Catholic Ecclesiology.* New York: Crossroad Publishing Company, 2006.

Rush, Ormond. *Still Interpreting Vatican II: Some Hermeneutical Principles.* Mahwah, NJ: Paulist Press, 2004.

Russo, Antonio. *Henri De Lubac.* Cinisello Balsamo: San Paolo, 1994.

Rynne, Xavier. *Vatican Council II.* Maryknoll, NY: Orbis Books, 1999.

Sanks, T. Howland. *Authority in the Church: A Study in Changing Paradigms.* Missoula, MT: Scholars' Press, 1974.

Schillebeeckx, Edward, ed. *The Church and Mankind: Dogma,* Volume 1, *Concilium.* Glen Rock, NJ: Paulist Press, 1965.

Schindler, David L. *Hans Urs von Balthasar: His Life and Work.* San Francisco: Ignatius Press, 1991.

————. "Reorienting the Church on the Eve of the Millennium: John Paul II's New Evangelization." *Communio* 24 (1997): 728–79.

————. "The Centenary of the Birth of Henri de Lubac." *Communio* 23 (December 1, 1996): 710–805.

————. "The Theology of Henri de Lubac, Communio at Twenty Years." *Communio* 19 (Fall 1992): 332–509.

Schultenover, David. *A View from Rome: On the Eve of the Modernist Crisis.* New York: Fordham University Press, 1993.

Schoof, Ted Mark. *A Survey of Catholic Theology, 1800–1970.* Mahwah, NJ: Paulist Press, 1970.

Scott, Martin J. "The Holiness of the Catholic Church." *Christ to the World* 51, no. 4 (July 2006): 302–11.

Shelley, Thomas J. "A Somber Anniversary: a Century Ago, a Promising American Theological Journal Fell Victim to the Modernist Crisis." *America* 198, no. 11 (March 31, 2008): 14–16.

Sicari, Antonio M. "'Communio' in Henri de Lubac." *Communio* 19 (Fall 1992): 450–64.

————. """The Purification of Memory: The Narrow Gate of the Jubilee." *Communio* 27, no. 4 (December 1, 2000): 634–42.

Siniscalchi, Glenn B. "Vatican II on Holiness: An Ecumenical Apologetics." *Ecumenical Trends* 37, no. 10 (November 2008): 10–12.

Smart, Ninian, John Clayton, Patrick Sherry, and Steven T. Katz, eds. *Nineteenth-Century Religious Thought in the West*. New York: Cambridge University Press, 1988.

Smith, George D., ed. *The Teaching of the Catholic Church: A Summary of Catholic Doctrine*. New York: Macmillan, 1948.

Stacpoole, Alberic, ed. *Vatican Two Revisited: By Those Who Were There*. San Francisco: Harper San Francisco, 1986.

Steinfels, Peter. "Beliefs." *New York Times*, April 3, 1999.

Sullivan, Francis A. *Creative Fidelity: Weighing and Interpreting Documents of the Magisterium*. New York: Paulist Press, 1997.

————. Personal Communication. "Charles Journet." July 16, 2010.

————. Personal Communication. "Neo-Scholasticism." August 13, 2010.

————. *The Church We Believe In: One, Holy, Catholic, and Apostolic*. Mahwah, NJ: Paulist Press, 1988.

————. "The Meaning of "*subsistit in*" as Explained by the Congregation for the Doctrine of the Faith." *Theological Studies* 69, no. 1 (March 2008): 116–24.

————. "The Papal Apology." *America* 182, no. 12 (April 8, 2000): 17.

Sullivan, Maureen. *The Road to Vatican II: Key Changes in Theology*. Mahwah, NJ: Paulist Press, 2007.

Talar, Charles. *New Catholic Encyclopedia: Supplement 2010*. 3rd ed., s.v. "Modernism." Farmington Hills, MI: Gale Publishing, 2010.

Tanquerey, Adolphe. *A Manual of Dogmatic Theology*. Translated by John J. Burns. New York: Desclee Company, 1959.

Tavard, George H. *The Pilgrim Church*. New York: Herder and Herder, 1967.

*The Church and Mankind: Dogma*, Volume 1. *Concilium*. Glen Rock, NJ: Paulist Press, 1965.

Tilliette, Xavier. "Henri de Lubac: The Legacy of a Theologian." *Communio* 19 (Fall 1992): 332–41.

Voderholzer, Rudolf. "Dogma and History: Henri de Lubac and the Retrieval of Historicity as a Key to Theological Renewal." *Communio* 28, no. 4 (December 1, 2001): 648–68.

Vondey, Wolfgang. *Heribert Mühlen: His Theology and Praxis. A New Profile of the Church*. Lanham, MD: University Press of America, 2004.

Vorgrimler, Herbert, ed. *Commentary on the Documents of Vatican II*. New York: Herder and Herder, 1967.

Walsh, Christopher J. "Henri de Lubac and the Ecclesiology of the Postconciliar Church: An Analysis of His Later Writings (1965–1991)." PhD dissertation. Catholic University of America, 1993.

———. "Henri de Lubac in Connecticut: Unpublished Conferences on Renewal in the Postconciliar Period." *Communio* 23 (December 1, 1996): 786–805.

Wang, Lisa. "*Sacramentum Unitatis Ecclesiasticae*: The Eucharistic Ecclesiology of Henri de Lubac." *Anglican Theological Review* 85, no. 1 (December 1, 2003): 143–58.

Weigel, George. *The End and the Beginning: Pope John Paul II—The Victory of Freedom, the Last Years, the Legacy.* New York: Doubleday Religion, 2010.

———. *Witness to Hope: The Biography of Pope John Paul II.* 1st ed. New York: Harper Collins, 1999.

Whitehead, Kenneth D., and William E. May., eds. *After Forty Years: Vatican Council II's Diverse Legacy.* South Bend, IN, St. Augustine Press, 2007.

Whitehead, Kenneth D. *The Renewed Church: The Second Vatican Council's Enduring Teaching about the Church.* Naples, FL: Sapientia Press of Ave Maria University, 2009.

Wicks, Jared. "Further Light on Vatican Council II." *Catholic Historical Review* 95, no. 3 (2009): 546–69.

Williams, A. N. "The Future of the Past: The Contemporary Significance of the Nouvelle Théologie." *International Journal of Systematic Theology* 7, no. 4 (October 1, 2005): 347–61.

Wood, Susan. "Henri de Lubac, SJ (1896–1991): Theologian of the Church." *Theology Today* 62, no. 3 (October 1, 2005): 318–28.

———. *Spiritual Exegesis and the Church in the Theology of Henri de Lubac.* Grand Rapids, MI: William B. Eerdmans Publishing Company, 1998.

———. "The Church as the Social Embodiment of Grace in the Ecclesiology of Henri de Lubac." PhD dissertation. Milwaukee, WI: Marquette University, 1986.

Yetzer, Bernard E. "Holiness and Sin in the Church: An Examination of *Lumen Gentium* and *Unitatis Redingratio* of the Second Vatican Council." STD dissertation. Ann Arbor, MI: UMI, 1991.

Zapelena, Timotheus. *De Ecclesia Christi, Pars Altera Apologetico Dogmatica.* Romae: Apud aedes Universitatis Gregorianae, 1954.

———. *De Ecclesia Christi: Pars Apologetica.* Editio sexta. Romae: Pontificia Universitas Gregoriana, 1955.

———. *De Ecclesia Christi Summarium.* 2nd ed. Romae: Apud aedes Universitatis Gregorianae, 1932.

# Index